Developing Mobile Applications Using SAP NetWeaver® Mobile

SAP PRESS is a joint initiative of SAP and Galileo Press. The know-how offered by SAP specialists combined with the expertise of the publishing house Galileo Press offers the reader expert books in the field. SAP PRESS features first-hand information and expert advice, and provides useful skills for professional decision-making.

SAP PRESS offers a variety of books on technical and business related topics for the SAP user. For further information, please visit our website: *www.sap-press.com*.

Jan Rauscher, Volker Stiehl
The Developer's Guide to the
SAP NetWeaver Composition Environment
2008, approx. 370 pp., hardcover, with DVD
ISBN 978-1-59229-171-7

Eichholz, Lichte, Nüvemann
Mobile Applications in Warehouse and Shipping with SAP WM
SAP PRESS Essentials 29
2007, approx. 130 pp., softcover
ISBN 978-1-59229-126-7

Ganz, Gürtler, Lakner
Maximizing Web Dynpro for Java
2006, 497 pp., hardcover
ISBN 978-1-59229-077-2

Karl Kessler et al.
Java Programming with SAP NetWeaver
2008, 2nd, revised and extended edition
approx 650 pp., hardcover, with DVD
ISBN 978-1-59229-181-6

Thomas Pohl, Ramprasadh Kothandaraman,
Venkat Srinivas Seshasai

Developing Mobile Applications Using SAP NetWeaver® Mobile

Bonn • Boston

ISBN 978-1-59229-141-0

1st edition 2007

Aquisitions Editor Florian Zimniak
Developmental Editor Jutta VanStean
Copy Editor Ruth Saavedra, Saratoga, CA
Cover Design Nadine Kohl
Layout Design Vera Brauner
Production Steffi Ehrentraut
Typesetting Typographie & Computer, Krefeld
Printed and bound in Germany

© 2007 by Galileo Press
SAP PRESS is an imprint of Galileo Press,
Boston, MA, USA
Bonn, Germany

All rights reserved. Neither this publication nor any part of it may be copied or reproduced in any form or by any means or translated into another language, without the prior consent of Galileo Press, Rheinwerkallee 4, 53227 Bonn, Germany.

Galileo Press makes no warranties or representations with respect to the content hereof and specifically disclaims any implied warranties of merchantability or fitness for any particular purpose. Galileo Press assumes no responsibility for any errors that may appear in this publication.

All of the screenshots and graphics reproduced in this book are subject to copyright © SAP AG, Dietmar-Hopp-Allee 16, 69190 Walldorf, Germany.

SAP, the SAP logo, mySAP, mySAP.com, mySAP Business Suite, SAP NetWeaver, SAP R/3, SAP R/2, SAP B2B, SAPtronic, SAPscript, SAP BW, SAP CRM, SAP EarlyWatch, SAP ArchiveLink, SAP GUI, SAP Business Workflow, SAP Business Engineer, SAP Business Navigator, SAP Business Framework, SAP Business Information Warehouse, SAP inter-enterprise solutions, SAP APO, AcceleratedSAP, InterSAP, SAPoffice, SAPfind, SAPfile, SAPtime, SAPmail, SAP-access, SAP-EDI, R/3 Retail, Accelerated HR, Accelerated HiTech, Accelerated Consumer Products, ABAP, ABAP/4, ALE/WEB, BAPI, Business Framework, BW Explorer, Enjoy-SAP, mySAP.com e-business platform, mySAP Enterprise Portals, RIVA, SAPPHIRE, TeamSAP, Webflow and SAP PRESS are registered or unregistered trademarks of SAP AG, Walldorf, Germany.

Research In Motion, the RIM logo, BlackBerry, the BlackBerry logo and SureType are registered with the U.S. Patent and Trademark Office and may be pending or registered in other countries — these and other marks of Research In Motion Limited are used under license.

All other products mentioned in this book are registered or unregistered trademarks of their respective companies.

Contents at a Glance

1	An Introduction to Mobility	19
2	Mobile Technology	37
3	SAP NetWeaver Mobile Challenges and Capabilities	57
4	Data Orchestration Design Time	75
5	Design Time to Build Mobile Applications	135
6	Mobile Application Lifecycle Management	163
7	Design Study of an Occasionally Connected Mobile Application using Mobile Applications for Laptop	193
8	Support of Peripheral Devices	253
9	Tips for a Successful Implementation of Mobile Projects	271
10	Design Study of a Connected Mobile Application Using Mobile Web Dynpro Online	283
11	Developing Mobile Components for PDA	301
	Appendix	307
A	SAP Mobile Application Portfolio	309
B	Glossary	335
C	Bibliography	339
D	The Authors	341

Contents

Preface 15

1 An Introduction to Mobility 19

- 1.1 The Impact of Mobility on the Business World 21
- 1.2 The Mobile Workforce 21
  - 1.2.1 Types of Mobile Workers 22
  - 1.2.2 Mobile Work Styles 22
- 1.3 Different Types of Workers 24
  - 1.3.1 Tacit Workers 24
  - 1.3.2 Transactional Workers 25
  - 1.3.3 Transformational (Physical) Workers 26
- 1.4 Mobility Case Studies 26
  - 1.4.1 Sales Rep 26
  - 1.4.2 Field Service Technician 27
  - 1.4.3 Warehouse Management 28
  - 1.4.4 Homeland Security Agent 28
  - 1.4.5 Insurance Agent 29
  - 1.4.6 Healthcare Employee 29
  - 1.4.7 Plant Production Management 29
- 1.5 Advantages of a Mobile Environment 30
- 1.6 Requirements for a Mobile Platform 31
  - 1.6.1 Device Management 32
  - 1.6.2 Backend Integration 32
  - 1.6.3 Data Distribution 33
  - 1.6.4 Business Data Abstraction 33
  - 1.6.5 Peripheral Support 34
  - 1.6.6 Security 34
  - 1.6.7 Component-Based Architecture 34
  - 1.6.8 Application Extensibility 34
  - 1.6.9 IDE to Design New Mobile Applications 34
- 1.7 Summary 35

2 Mobile Technology 37

- 2.1 Mobile Devices 37
  - 2.1.1 Laptops and Notebooks 37
  - 2.1.2 Tablet PCs 38
  - 2.1.3 PDAs 39

		2.1.4	Smartphones	41
	2.2	Application Development and Runtime Environments for Mobile Devices		42
		2.2.1	Java Technology for Wireless Devices	43
		2.2.2	Microsoft's .NET Compact Framework	47
	2.3	Connectivity		48
		2.3.1	Application Types Based on Network Connection Availability	48
		2.3.2	Network Technologies	50
	2.4	Summary		56

3 SAP NetWeaver Mobile Challenges and Capabilities ... 57

	3.1	SAP NetWeaver Mobile 7.1 Challenges		57
		3.1.1	Numerous Synchronizing Devices and Multiple Sources of Information	58
		3.1.2	Long Synchronization Times	58
		3.1.3	Data Volume To Be Sent to the Devices	59
		3.1.4	Data Consistency	59
		3.1.5	Real-Time User Experience	60
		3.1.6	Frequently Changing Organizational Structure	61
		3.1.7	Manageability of the System Landscape	61
		3.1.8	Model-Driven Application Development	62
	3.2	SAP NetWeaver Mobile 7.1 Capabilities		62
		3.2.1	DOE	64
		3.2.2	SAP NetWeaver Mobile Client Platform	68
		3.2.3	SAP NetWeaver Mobile Administrator	70
	3.3	Summary		72

4 Data Orchestration Design Time ... 75

	4.1	DOE Design Time Conceptual Overview		75
		4.1.1	A Brief Recap of the DOE	75
		4.1.2	Meta Model Overview	77
		4.1.3	Data Object	79
		4.1.4	Backend Integration	82
		4.1.5	Distribution Model	83
		4.1.6	Device Assignment Logic	87
		4.1.7	Subscription Generation Data Object	88

4.2	Modeling Data Objects and Backend Adapters		90
	4.2.1	SWCV	90
	4.2.2	Handling Data Objects	92
	4.2.3	Backend Adapters	101
4.3	Data Distribution Modeling		112
	4.3.1	Data Distribution	112
	4.3.2	RMM	113
	4.3.3	Distribution Model	117
4.4	Summary		134

5 Design Time to Build Mobile Applications 135

5.1	Mobile Applications for Laptop to Build Occasionally Connected Mobile Applications		135
	5.1.1	Integration	136
	5.1.2	Prerequisites for the Client Device	137
	5.1.3	Developing a Mobile Application Using Mobile Applications for Laptop	140
5.2	Mobile Web Dynpro Online		158
	5.2.1	Overview of the Available UI Elements	159
	5.2.2	Specific Considerations for Nokia Series 80 Devices	160
	5.2.3	Specific Considerations for BlackBerry Wireless Handhelds	160
	5.2.4	Specific Considerations for Pocket PCs	161
5.3	Summary		161

6 Mobile Application Lifecycle Management 163

6.1	The Mobile Application Development Process		168
6.2	Initial Setup		174
6.3	Mass Device Administration		177
	6.3.1	Device Class	178
	6.3.2	Device Inventory	179
	6.3.3	Device Configuration	181
6.4	Administration and Monitoring Tools		182
6.5	Third-Party Device Management Integration		187
6.6	Patch Deployment and Upgrade		188
6.7	Lifecycle Management of Mobile Web Dynpro Online Applications		191
6.8	Summary		191

Contents

7 Design Study of an Occasionally Connected Mobile Application using Mobile Applications for Laptop .. 193

- 7.1 Scenario Description 193
- 7.2 Development Process 194
- 7.3 User Interface 195
- 7.4 Defining Data Objects and Distribution Model 197
  - 7.4.1 Creating a Software Component Version 197
  - 7.4.2 Modeling the Data Objects 198
  - 7.4.3 Creating the Employee Data Object 200
  - 7.4.4 Creating the Equipment Data Object 203
  - 7.4.5 Creating the Customer Data Object 206
  - 7.4.6 Creating the ServiceOrder Data Object 209
  - 7.4.7 Creating the WorkCenter Data Object 211
  - 7.4.8 Create the Associations Between the Data Objects 213
  - 7.4.9 Customizing the RMM 215
  - 7.4.10 Define the Distribution Logic 216
  - 7.4.11 Defining the Distribution Model 217
  - 7.4.12 Creating a Distribution Dependency 219
  - 7.4.13 Adding a Rule to the Distribution Model 220
  - 7.4.14 Defining a Data Completeness Group 222
- 7.5 Defining Backend Adapters 222
- 7.6 Configuring SAP NetWeaver Developer Studio 226
- 7.7 Creating Development Components 227
- 7.8 Importing Data Objects from the DOE 229
- 7.9 Defining the Model Classes as Public 230
- 7.10 Defining the Queries 231
- 7.11 Creating the Application 232
- 7.12 Defining Context Binding 233
- 7.13 Defining Supply Functions for the Node Elements 236
- 7.14 Defining the Method for Calling the Query 239
- 7.15 Specifying the Navigation Schema 240
- 7.16 Specifying the Navigation Schema for the Exit Button 242
- 7.17 Customizing the CustomerDetails View 243
- 7.18 Customizing the OrderDetails View 247
- 7.19 Building, Deploying, and Running the Application 250
- 7.20 Summary 251

8 Support of Peripheral Devices ... 253

- 8.1 Peripheral Input/Output Services Infrastructure ... 254
  - 8.1.1 PIOS Architecture ... 254
  - 8.1.2 PIOS Design Time Components ... 255
  - 8.1.3 PIOS Runtime Components ... 256
  - 8.1.4 Driver Selection Tool ... 256
- 8.2 PIOS API Core ... 256
  - 8.2.1 Printer API ... 257
  - 8.2.2 Scanner API ... 260
  - 8.2.3 RFID API ... 266
- 8.3 Summary ... 268

9 Tips for a Successful Implementation of Mobile Projects ... 271

- 9.1 Selecting the Appropriate Devices ... 271
  - 9.1.1 Device Form Factor ... 272
  - 9.1.2 Device Processor and Memory Capacity ... 272
  - 9.1.3 Data Entry Method ... 272
  - 9.1.4 Network Support ... 272
  - 9.1.5 Peripheral Device Support ... 273
  - 9.1.6 Other Considerations ... 274
  - 9.1.7 Conclusion ... 274
- 9.2 Performance and Sizing ... 275
  - 9.2.1 SAP Standard Application Benchmark (SAPS) ... 275
- 9.3 Sizing of Mobile Applications ... 275
  - 9.3.1 Initial Replication ... 276
  - 9.3.2 Delta Synchronization ... 276
  - 9.3.3 Client Sizing ... 277
  - 9.3.4 Network Sizing ... 278
- 9.4 Security ... 278
  - 9.4.1 User Management ... 279
  - 9.4.2 Communication Channel Security ... 280
  - 9.4.3 Single Sign-On ... 280
- 9.5 Summary ... 281

10 Design Study of a Connected Mobile Application Using Mobile Web Dynpro Online ... 283

- 10.1 Scenario Description ... 283
- 10.2 Development Process ... 284

Contents

10.3	Prerequisites	285
10.4	Creating a Web Dynpro Project	286
10.5	Import an Adaptive RFC Model and Generate the Java Proxies	287
10.6	Creating a Custom Controller Context and Binding it to the Model	289
10.7	Mapping Custom Controller Context Elements to View Context Elements	290
10.8	Creating Actions and Declaring Methods	291
10.9	Defining the View Layouts	292
10.10	Implementing the Action Event Handler and the Method of the Custom Controller	294
10.11	Building, Deploying, Configuring, and Running your Application	296
10.12	Summary	298

11 Developing Mobile Components for PDA ... 301

11.1	The Component Concept for Mobile Applications	302
11.2	Relationship Between Mobile Applications for Laptop and Mobile Applications for PDA	304
11.3	Summary	306

Appendix ... 307

A	SAP Mobile Application Portfolio			309
	A.1	Mobile Enterprise Applications		309
	A.2	The Mobile Ecosystem		311
		A.2.1	Wireless Carriers and Service Providers	312
		A.2.2	Device Manufacturer and OS Supplier	313
		A.2.3	IT Department	313
		A.2.4	Mobile Application Supplier	314
	A.3	SAP xApps for Mobile Business		314
		A.3.1	SAP xApp Mobile Time and Travel (SAP xMTT)	316
		A.3.2	SAP xApp Mobile Asset Management (SAP xMAM)	319
		A.3.3	SAP xApp Mobile Asset Management for Utilities (SAP xMAM for Utilities)	323
		A.3.4	SAP xApp Mobile Sales for Handhelds (SAP xMSA)	326

	A.3.5	SAP xApp Mobile Direct Store Delivery (SAP xMDSD) 328
	A.3.6	Cross-Application Components including RFID, Mobile Alert, Electronic Signature Capture, and Geographical Information System (GIS) integration 332
B	Glossary 335
C	Bibliography 339
D	The Authors 341

Index 343

Preface

SAP NetWeaver Mobile 7.1 is the new platform for the development of mobile business applications and is the result of the long-standing experience that SAP has in the area of message-oriented middleware technologies. It leverages the open integration and application platform offered by SAP NetWeaver to integrate business applications on mobile devices. From a design time perspective, it provides an infrastructure that allows mobilizing your existing or new business processes, and from a runtime perspective, it enables users of mobile devices to carry out their tasks without a permanent connection to the backend system. Thus, the users of the mobile client devices such as laptops, tablet PCs, and personal digital assistants (PDAs) can be integrated in the automated business processes with the backend system. This integration makes manual and paper-based processes redundant and results in higher efficiency and more reliable data.

In this book, we want to present some of the highlights and key capabilities of this new platform. It is aimed at readers who want to get familiar with the basic concepts of this platform.

How this Book is Structured

In this section, we will provide you with a brief outline of the topics covered in each chapter:

- In Chapter 1, we will provide a short introduction to the concept of mobile domains and provide some examples of business processes that are candidates for a mobile scenario.
- In Chapter 2, we outline some aspects of mobile technology. We discuss the characteristic properties and types of mobile devices, present the various software standards, and give a short introduction in the mobile network "jungle."
- Chapter 3 focuses on the key capabilities of the data orchestration engine (DOE). It contains all of the requirements to run a mobile

scenario that consists of thousands of mobile devices and shows how those requirements are solved by SAP's mobile platform.

- Chapter 4 describes the design time aspects of the Data Orchestration Engine (DOE). It explains the basic concepts of the Data Orchestration Workbench, such as the modeling of the business entities for mobile application or data objects and the distribution schema based on which data will be distributed to the devices.
- Chapter 5 describes the design time aspects of developing a mobile application that runs on a physical device. This chapter describes the tools contained in the SAP NetWeaver Developer Studio to create a Java-based mobile application.
- Chapter 6 contains an overview of the lifecycle management capabilities of the DOE, such as the development process for mobile applications, the mass device administration, the administrative and monitoring tools, and deployment and upgrade support etc. A good understanding of these capabilities is important to minimize the total cost of ownership of the mobile system landscape.
- Chapter 7 provides a design study of a mobile application and contains a tutorial that enables developers to create a mobile application from scratch.
- In Chapter 8, a framework is presented that allows application developers to access peripheral devices. The support of peripheral devices, such as barcode scanners and mobile printers, is required in many mobile scenarios.
- Chapter 9 deals with the implementation of a mobile project. We want to give some tips and Best Practices to implement a mobile project based on the experience of SAP's support team for mobile applications. They can help you to avoid pitfalls when you introduce a mobile solution in your company.
- Chapter 10 contains a design study of a connected mobile application. Although the focus of this book is occasionally connected mobile applications, we provide a tutorial on how you can build a connected mobile application.
- Chapter 11 is a forward-looking section and provides a short overview of the new design time to create component-based mobile applications for PDAs and how this design time is integrated in the development infrastructure of SAP NetWeaver.

Acknowledgments

This book has been produced with the help of several people who have reviewed the material and offered invaluable suggestions. Their contributions and advice have helped us meet the objectives of this book.

We offer our thanks and special appreciation to the following people for their contributions:

- Florian Zimniak, acquisitions editor, for guiding us through the book development process.
- Jutta VanStean, developmental editor, for playing an important role during the final phase of writing this book. Jutta provided general support to the authors, helped publish the book in the English language, and offered many suggestions for the presentation of the chapters.
- Ruth Saavedra, copy editor, for proofreading the manuscript and preparing it for the typesetter.
- Steffi Ehrentraut, production editor, for managing the production and successful release of the book.
- Marion Blum and Lisa Granville-Dirker, senior information developers, for revising some of the chapters and providing many suggestions for improvements.
- Venkatesh D.K., solution expert, for revising individual chapters and providing invaluable feedback

Walldorf and Bangalore

Thomas Pohl
Ramprasadh Kothandaraman
Venkat Srinivas Seshasai

Mobility is a global trend that allows people to organize themselves in a flexible way. It affects daily life as well as the way people work together.

1   An Introduction to Mobility

In this chapter, we discuss several aspects of mobility, including what the term *mobility* means, how mobility impacts business, typical examples of mobile solutions, and the requirements of a mobile platform. Let us start by looking at the original meaning of the word *mobility*. It comes from the Latin *mobilitas* and means motion, agility, and flexibility, but also changeability or lack of stability. Mobility is an important part of human culture. Depending on the context, there are different types of mobility, as outlined in the following list:

- **Material mobility**

    Material mobility refers to the ability to move persons or goods through or in space. The capabilities to move through or in space have improved tremendously over time. While in the 19th century, people were restricted to moving only around their own neighborhoods, our radius of action has increased over time thanks first to the invention of the railway, which enabled us to surpass natural limitations of mobility, and later on, to the invention of the automobile, which became a symbol of individual freedom. Nowadays, airplanes provide global mobility and allow us to reach almost any place on earth in less than two days, and lately we see an entirely new phenomenon — the space tourism industry offering wealthy individuals trips into orbit.

    To ensure safe movement of people and goods using the aforementioned methods of transportation, we have developed the necessary infrastructure consisting of railway tracks, roads and bridges, and controlled air space. Also, authorities have defined rules to avoid traffic accidents, and planning tools are used to avoid traffic congestion. Furthermore, the selection of the most efficient means of transportation with regard to consumption of

Different types of mobility

energy resources and timely delivery becomes more and more important.

> **An Analogy**
>
> Maybe you know the book *Around the World in Eighty Days* by Jules Verne, published in 1873. The story starts in London, where in the Reform Club, Mr. Fogg gets involved in an argument over an article in the *Daily Telegraph*. With the opening of a new railway section in India, it should be possible now to travel around the world in 80 days. Mr. Fogg is sure that he can do it, and accepts a wager of £20,000, which he will receive if he can complete the trip in time. Together with his servant Passepartout, he leaves London by train in the direction of Egypt. During the adventurous journey, he has to pass several tests, all of which he can solve. Back to London, it seems that he lost his bet by one day, but because he moved to the east and passed the international date line, Mr. Fogg can still reach the club in time, wins his bet, and finds true love.

▶ **Nonmaterial mobility**

Nonmaterial mobility is the ability to have access to all kinds of information regardless of space and time. In today's business world, access to all kinds of data and information across geographical borders is essential. The necessary technologies are already available. The Internet has grown to an extent nobody expected in its early days, making it possible to access public information or to log on to a company's intranet from almost anywhere. For people who work from different physical locations, mobile devices of all types and sizes and for different purposes are available, along with wireless networks and mobile applications. Sending and receiving mail on handheld devices has become standard for many business workers, and the emergence of the Mobile Internet in recent years has completely changed customers' behavior by making information and entertainment services available independent of time and location.

While the high expectations regarding mobile business (mainly the increase of workers' efficiency and reduction of the total cost of ownership (TCO) during the late 1990s e-commerce era, which is also known as the dot.com era) could not be met, mobile business is an overall trend that will continue to influence business and commerce. Over the past few years alone, technology has evolved significantly and can now support business models and application scenarios that are optimized for mobile use. In general, mobility has a clear impact on the business world, as we will outline in the next section.

1.1 The Impact of Mobility on the Business World

It is clear that social trends have a significant impact on the way people work together. For example, globalization has transformed the earth into a global village, which is mainly due to mobility and the related technologies enabling this mobility. Thus, for enterprises, it becomes more and more important to provide employees with an effective infrastructure that deals with the challenges of mobility. There is also a trend toward flexible project teams located in different countries and time zones, and mobile technologies that allow collaboration regardless of where you are provide the infrastructure for decentralized work. The earlier working model that was based on rigid structures at one central location with fixed working times is becoming more and more outdated.

Mobile working models

To stay competitive, enterprises have to optimize their internal processes across the value chain. For example, managers may want to approve their employees' vacation requests or purchase requests quickly. In the government sector, mobile interfaces to backend processes are well suited to optimize administrative processes so that they meet the expectations of citizens, for example, in the areas of civil engineering and emergency services. In the consumer product industry, the direct delivery of goods such as soft drinks, beer, and bottled water to stores can be optimized by mobile devices that keep track of delivery operations. Let us now take an in-depth look at the mobile workforce as it exists in the United States today.

1.2 The Mobile Workforce

According to Gartner [SAP Gartner SAS], more than 69.2 million workers (more than 45%) in the United States are away from their primary work area for more than 20% of the work week, which is what Gartner defines as the threshold to call an employee a mobile worker (see Figure 1.1).

1 An Introduction to Mobility

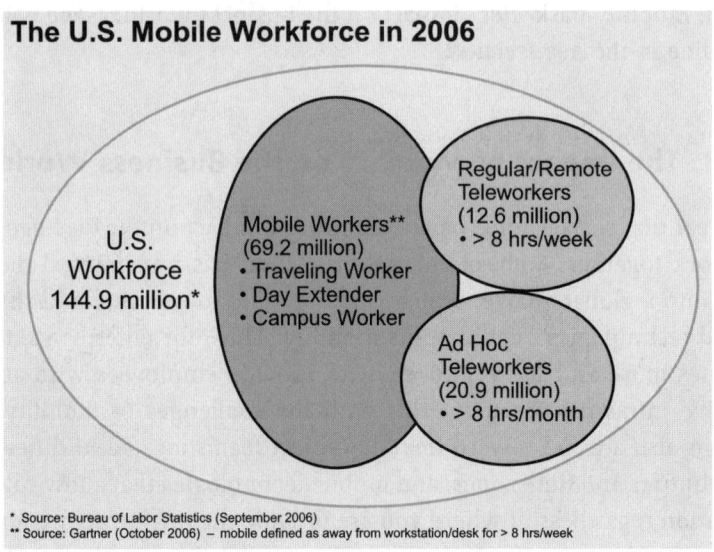

Figure 1.1 The U.S. Mobile Workforce in 2006 (Source: Gartner)

1.2.1 Types of Mobile Workers

Mobile workers by distance traveled

Depending on the distance a worker travels from his office location, Gartner distinguishes between mobile workers and teleworkers. Mobile workers compose about 48% of the U.S. workforce, and teleworkers compose about 23%.

The mobile workers are split into:

- Traveling workers, who travel unlimited distances
- Campus workers, who travel only within a company's facilities
- Day extenders, who mainly work in their office environments and extend their working days by one or two hours offsite to increase their productivity

In contrast to mobile workers, teleworkers work from home.

Each of these types of mobile workers have different work styles, which we will look at next.

1.2.2 Mobile Work Styles

To fulfill their tasks and increase their productivity, different types of mobile workers prefer different work styles. Figure 1.2 provides an overview of the work styles based on an analysis by Gartner. We will look at each of these styles in more detail in this section.

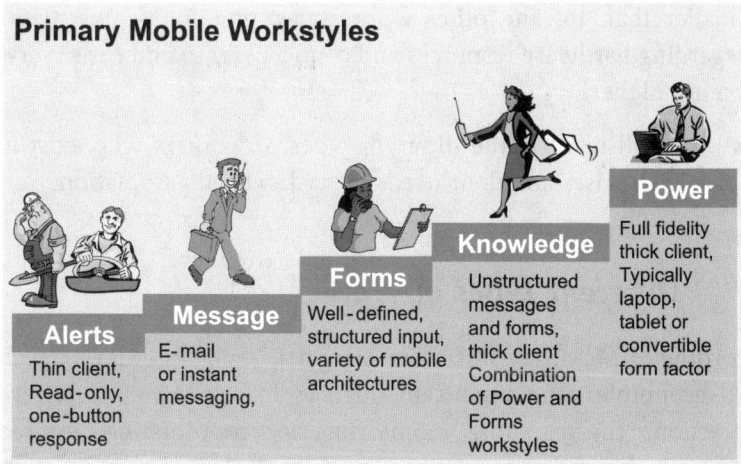

Figure 1.2 Primary Work Styles (Source: Gartner)

- The *alerts* work style primarily occurs in field service where workers are notified of important events or have to acknowledge that they have received certain information. Typically, only a small amount of data is exchanged and this data is mostly read-only. A response can be provided in a simple manner, for instance by pressing a button. Data storage on the device is not required; a browser-based online application can provide the required functionality.
- The *message* work style is based on information exchange via email as provided by devices supporting "always on" functionality and email push support. These workers stay in touch with their colleagues using offline communication.
- The *forms* work style refers to work that requires data entry in a form-based application. Typical examples are sales specialists who want to promote and sell products in the field or field service technicians who perform planned or unplanned plant maintenance. They need unlimited access to their basic data, such as products and service orders even if no (wireless) network is available. The functionality that is available on the mobile frontend must also be available in the backend system.

Work styles

▶ The *knowledge* and *power* work styles are characterized by requiring a large amount of unstructured information, which needs to be prepared for further processing. The degree of automation is smaller than for the other work styles, and the requirements regarding hardware resources and connectivity to enterprise servers are higher.

Next, we will identify the different types of workers who exist in today's enterprises and their needs for task-related automation.

1.3 Different Types of Workers

According to McKinsey [Johnson, Manyika, Yee], "in today's developed economies, the significant nuances in employment concern interactions: the searching, monitoring, and coordinating required to manage the exchange of goods and services .... Currently, jobs that involve participating in interactions rather than extracting raw materials or making finished goods account for more than 80% of all employment in the United States." Depending on the interactions, McKinsey distinguishes between different kinds of workers, including tacit workers, transactional workers, and transformational (physical) workers. We will take a closer look at each of these types of workers and the degree of IT enablement of different activities they require.

1.3.1 Tacit Workers

Access to all kinds of information

Tacit workers include managers, sales people, lawyers, judges, and engineers who mainly deal with non-routine work that requires significant interaction with other employees, customers, and suppliers. The results of their activities are complex decisions, based on knowledge, judgment, experience, and instinct. As you can see in the U.S. employment overview shown in Figure 1.3, tacit workers are the fastest growing segment of the workforce.

Due to the job profile of a tacit worker, productivity cannot be increased by automation or standardization. Instead, to be successful, they are dependent on access to reliable structured or unstructured information as a basis for their decisions. To support the tacit worker with software tools and to increase efficiency, it is necessary to deliver relevant business information on demand and to provide the most appropriate tools to collaborate and interact. Sometimes, tacit workers are referred to as information workers.

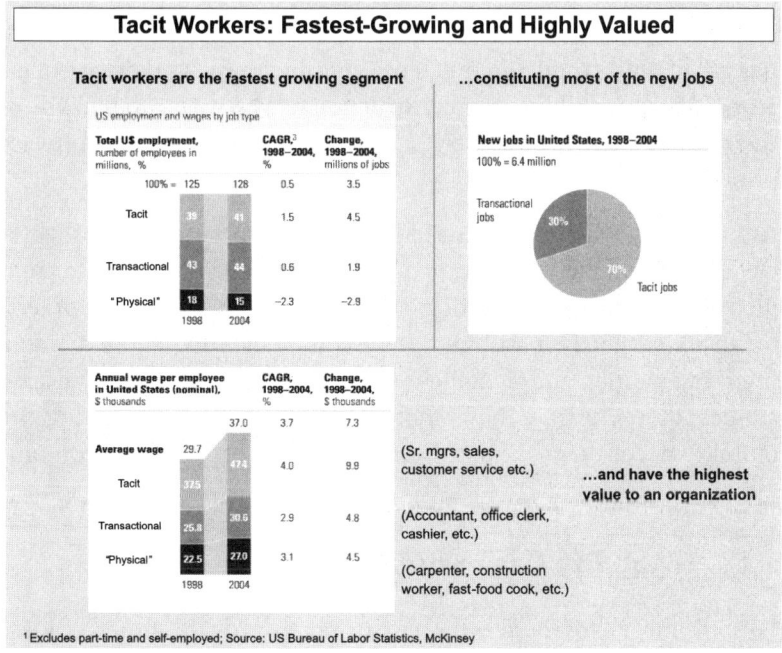

Figure 1.3 Tacit Workers According to a U.S. Employment Survey (Source: McKinsey)

1.3.2 Transactional Workers

Transactional workers mostly perform routine work such as clerical tasks and data processing that is usually carried out in a rule-based manner and thus can be structured and automated. Their job consists of transactional routine work; typical examples include production line operators, utility meter readers, and cashiers. Transactional workers' productivity can be increased by supplying them with appropriate software tools for daily tasks. They mostly deal with structured information that can be provided in a specific format. Service technicians, for instance, require instant access to maintenance orders and information for the business partners they have to visit. Maintenance orders must be assigned to the appropriate technician by the back office.

Structured information provided in a specific format

1.3.3 Transformational (Physical) Workers

Physical work Transformational workers deal with extracting raw materials or turning raw materials into finished goods. While this type of worker was predominant at the turn of 20th century, only 15% of all U.S. employees worked as transformational worker in 2004. Their activities are mainly production related. Typically, these workers are operators of heavy machinery or construction workers. Due to the type of their work, these workers are in general not the focus of software providers.

As you can see from the descriptions of the different types of workers, IT enablement of different activities varies from partial to complete automation of transactional activities. It supports tacit workers, for example, in their daily work by complementing and extending their capabilities and activities. We will now look at several case studies that illustrate how mobile applications can support the mobility needs of workers in a variety of different types of positions.

1.4 Mobility Case Studies

To look more closely at what IT can do to provide more business value, this section will outline several case studies specific to certain job functions, showing how mobile technology can impact business in the year 2010. These case studies show the functionality that a mobile application should offer, ideally, for a variety of functions.

1.4.1 Sales Rep

Mobile sales scenario Our first case study involves the position of sales rep. Ideally, mobile applications provide sales reps access to product and pricing data so they can make their customers attractive offers. Using a mobile application, sales reps can also receive a list of all clients they need to visit before they leave for a trip, and route and visit planning is automated using GPS-enabled navigation software. To avoid duplicate effort and errors, and to update the backend system in real time, orders can be created electronically on the spot using an application that provides the appropriate business logic and services to synchronize the data with the backend system. It also lets sales reps capture signatures electronically. Planning tools help sales reps prioritize tasks and improve communication and interactions with their clients. Time sheet entries are captured automatically. Access to detailed customer relationship management (CRM)-related information is guaranteed. An analytics engine helps forecast sales based on different scenarios. Furthermore, it is possible to search for additional information on demand by sending queries to the company's intranet. To improve in-car productivity, content can be accessed using speech technology. A context-driven user interface (UI) adapts to the user's specific needs, and data push technology automatically keeps the data in sync with the data in the backend system. Thus, the sales scenario can be supported by mobile applications in a very efficient way. The sales rep has direct access to all required information to advise the customer and to create sales orders.

1.4.2 Field Service Technician

The working day of mobility-enabled field service technicians usually starts in the morning when they download lists of work orders. Thus, they no longer need to go to a service depot to pick up printouts. Route and visit planning is provided automatically as well, and the system helps prioritize tasks and communicate with the client. Emergency requests are coordinated centrally in an automated way. Additional information, such as previsit troubleshooting and related drawings, is available on demand, anywhere and anytime. A live video feed showing the damaged equipment can be used to consult with other specialists to quickly solve the problem. Invoicing can be done on the spot, and signature capture is integrated in the application. If spare parts are required, inventory can be looked up, and orders can be created in real time. Utility workers can capture meter readings without manual interaction. Follow-up activities such as timesheet entries are handled automatically, leading to accurate data that can be evaluated by reporting tools. Car fleet management can be improved and costs reduced by better real-time planning and execution. Field service technicians can benefit from a mobile solution to a great extent, because it helps them execute their service orders and update the data in the backend system on time.

Mobile service scenario

1.4.3 Warehouse Management

Warehouse management scenario

Warehouse management is a data-intensive function that focuses on ensuring the integrity of inventory data, streamlining the packing and shipping process and managing the workers' work load. Radio frequency identification (RFID) chips help track goods movements from order to pickup. Exception management is automated, and problems are identified and resolved in real time. Using a mobile device, consignment material can be scanned quickly, forklift operators are alerted, and the appropriate assembly lines are instructed to start assembling the items. Items are automatically assigned storage spaces in the warehouse. Outbound shipping costs are minimized by enabling automatic determination of the most cost-effective shipping method for each order. Signatures are captured electronically for acknowledgement, and the trucking company generates an invoice, which is updated in the warehouse management system. Finally, payment is triggered in the accounting system. Since the inventory and shipping data is up-to-date, customers can be informed about the delivery status. Warehouse management is a scenario that fits very well in a mobile system landscape. Many of the tasks in this scenario can be automated, and external sensors such as RFID chips can ensure accurate and automated data processing.

1.4.4 Homeland Security Agent

Homeland security scenario

Homeland security includes employees of agencies such as the Transportation Security Administration (TSA), Infrastructure Protection, Immigration and Customs Enforcement, and the Coast Guard. In emergency situations, quick responses are crucial. Using a mobile infrastructure, emergency evacuation plans can be carried out more effectively by taking into account the location of existing buildings or the specific constraints of handicapped people. Looking up information on criminal suspects can be done in real time. Security alerts with detailed information can be raised and spread quickly among field agents, and the databases of the Department of Homeland Security can be queried by the application. Cameras can be installed to observe sensitive places, and the application allows viewing and controlling the use of these cameras.

1.4.5 Insurance Agent

The task of insurance agents consists of handling clients' insurance policies, such as life, health, property, and liability insurance. To make the sale in the first place, the agent has to convince the customer to sign a contract to cover his insurance needs. The names of these potential customers have been preselected and downloaded to a mobile device in the morning. During the conversation with the customer, the insurance agent has to provide discounts to meet customer's expectations. In some cases, a manager's approval is required, which can be provided within a short time frame. After the deal is closed, the signed agreements are routed automatically for processing and mailing to the customers.

Mobile insurance scenario

In a different scenario, a customer calls the insurance agent to notify him about an accident. The insurance agent or company representative can enter the information in the system using a mobile device, provide assurance of cost coverage, and assign a field agent who will get in touch with the customer to assess the damage. The agent also files the claim for the customer and receives a live video transmission of the damage for further evaluation. This video can be stored in the backend system for later reference.

1.4.6 Healthcare Employee

In the healthcare sector, the ability to review electronic patient records, obtain test results in real time, access drug formulas, and enter diagnosis-related information during patient visits will increase efficiency. Ward rounds can be tracked by senior physicians who are in different locations, and X-ray or computer tomography photographs can be shared quickly among experts. Information related to patients, including patient master data, admission appointments, and risk factors, can be captured at the point of care, and the nursing staff can quickly retrieve duty roster, medical treatment, and diagnosis information.

Mobile healthcare scenario

1.4.7 Plant Production Management

Our final case study involves plant production management. Plant production managers need to be able to access up-to-the-minute production information, production exceptions, and key performance

Mobile plant production management scenario

indicators such as overall equipment effectiveness, regardless of their location on the plant floor.

As you can see, information workers as well as transactional workers can greatly benefit from mobile solutions. In the next section, we will discuss the advantages of a mobile environment in more detail.

1.5 Advantages of a Mobile Environment

Benefits of mobilizing business processes

The list of scenarios involving mobile applications that create additional business value is almost infinite. Mobility is an overall trend, and by supporting management and employees with the appropriate mobile infrastructure, companies will increase efficiency and productivity. The following advantages of making business processes mobile are common to all scenarios discussed in this chapter:

- **Cost efficiency**
  Costs can be reduced because business processes can be implemented more efficiently.

- **Time efficiency**
  The time required to carry out various tasks can be reduced; time that otherwise would be idle can be used for productive work (for example, waiting periods at the airport).

- **Real-time business**
  Data can be accessed and updated in real time even if the employee is not in the office; follow-up processes such as procurement can be triggered based on more accurate data.

- **Employee satisfaction**
  Mobile solutions enhance the degree of mobility of employees, providing higher flexibility for performing tasks.

- **Customer satisfaction**
  Access to real-time data enables field workers to provide optimal customer service.

- **Master data quality**
  Paper work is minimized; business logic that is implemented in mobile applications ensures data consistency.

Because, as mentioned earlier, the list of potential mobile business scenarios is almost unlimited, SAP cannot ship a separate application for each scenario. However, SAP does offer various mobile applications to cover different business needs, which will be discussed in detail in Appendix A, *SAP Mobile Application Portfolio*. In addition, SAP ships a mobile application platform called SAP NetWeaver Mobile 7.1 that enables software partners and customers to implement their own scenarios, making business processes that have been implemented in the SAP backend system mobile. This, in turn, enables customers to run business processes on mobile devices. A large part of this book will show you how to do this and describe the tools shipped by SAP. For now, however, let's look at the requirements needed for a mobile application platform.

1.6 Requirements for a Mobile Platform

The mobile applications offered by SAP cover a wide range of business processes. Thus, to come up with a holistic end-to-end approach, it is not sufficient to provide a mobile application that runs on a specific mobile device. This is where the mobile platform approach comes into play because all mobile applications will run on the mobile platform SAP NetWeaver Mobile 7.1.

However, before we start describing the capabilities of SAP's mobile platform and the benefits it offers to customers, end users, administrators, and software partners in more detail in Chapter 3, *SAP NetWeaver Mobile Capabilities*, we will first cover several important requirements for the mobile infrastructure. To make a business process mobile, it is important to have the right tools in place to administer the mobile system landscape during operation, to extend the functionality of the mobile application, or even to develop a new mobile application on top of existing components. The requirements we will go over cover the areas of device management, backend integration, data distribution, business data abstraction, peripheral support, security, component-based architecture, application extensibility, and the integrated development environment (IDE) to design new mobile applications.

> **Note**
>
> In Chapter 3, we will see how the SAP NetWeaver Mobile 7.1 platform covers those requirements.

1.6.1 Device Management

Device administration

A mobile landscape can consist of hundreds or thousands of mobile devices, such as laptops, personal digital assistants (PDAs), and so on, depending on the amount of data that must be processed and the constraints defined by the business scenario. Various mobile applications with different versions and consisting of different components, device drivers, and software patches might be deployed to those devices. After the devices have been set up and the appropriate software package has been installed, the devices must receive the initial business data. Each device might require different business data depending on the tasks the device owner is assigned. In many IT departments, system management software is already installed, so some customers require integration capabilities with existing system management applications such as Microsoft System Management Server. Lost or stolen devices must be disabled and replaced by new devices. To minimize user downtime, a device recovery tool is required to set up a new device based on the user's profile. To minimize the security risks imposed by stolen devices, a destroy message should be sent to a device that is marked as stolen in case somebody tries to connect to the server. If there is a problem with the device, the administrator needs additional information contained in trace and log files to quickly identify the cause of the problem. He also needs access to a troubleshooting database that contains all known issues and provides hints on how to solve them.

1.6.2 Backend Integration

Adapter to backend systems

To make a business process mobile, it is mandatory that appropriate backend adapters are available that integrate a mobile application into the backend system landscape. Standard backend are adapters available to connect to an SAP backend system, which support the RFC protocol. Using these backend adapters, backend services can be called to process incoming and outgoing requests from the mobile device. A backend service can be implemented as a BAPI, but standard web services can be called as well. Thus, enterprise services that are available in SAP Enterprise Resource Planning (ERP) 6.0, for instance, are fully integrated, and the open web service standard allows connecting to the backend system from other independent software vendors (ISVs) as well.

The core of the mobile platform is a message-oriented middleware that consolidates data from different sources, calculates the receiver of a message, depending on distribution rules configured by the customer, and puts the message in the right queue. To define the message structure according to the needs of the mobile application, a design time environment is provided by the data orchestration engine (DOE), which also allows modeling dependencies between messages. In many cases, a message containing business partner data should be followed by a message containing the assigned sales orders to ensure semantic integrity.

Mobile devices such as PDAs have limited capabilities to process large data sets, so a data distribution model that can be configured by the customer according to his specific needs is key to the successful implementation of a mobile scenario. To lower the TCO of a mobile solution, the performance and sizing aspect plays an important role in the architecture of the mobile middleware. For example, if 500 mobile service technicians start working in the morning and request their order data from the backend system, there will be a performance bottleneck, which requires special consideration to save the hardware resources of the backend system.

1.6.3 Data Distribution

A very important feature of a mobile solution is the ability to assign the business data to the target device. Sales representatives, for example, expect to get the sales orders that are assigned to their sales centers, and service technicians require service orders assigned to their work places. Along with these orders, other dependent data, such as business partner- or product-related information is also required. A rule-based approach is required to model those dependencies, instead of implementing them in the application's code.

Assignment of data to end users

1.6.4 Business Data Abstraction

In general, large enterprises have many backend systems, and the same business object might be represented differently in each. To give the application an "interface" and to decouple it from a specific backend representation, it is crucial to have the ability to abstract the backend data structure. Furthermore, data mapping is required to translate from device representation to backend representation.

1.6.5 Peripheral Support

In many business scenarios, the device capabilities are complemented by peripheral devices such as barcode scanners, RFID tags, or printers, and drivers are required to access them.

1.6.6 Security

Business data in general are sensitive and need a secure environment for storage on the device and transmission through the air. Logon information, such as passwords, that will be transmitted to backend servers must be protected, and single sign on (SSO) should be an optional feature to make logging in easier.

1.6.7 Component-Based Architecture

Generic services such as data persistency on the device or synchronization services should be available as separate components. Similarly, generic business functionality such as signature capture or order management should be available. UI patterns are required to provide the same look and feel across different platforms.

1.6.8 Application Extensibility

In some cases the mobile standard application has to be tailored to specific customer needs. Additional fields might be necessary, or the UI might have to be adapted. To achieve this requirement, the application's extensibility has to be incorporated in the design. The UI and business logic have to be strictly separated, and the application has to be provided with extension points in order to change existing business logic.

1.6.9 IDE to Design New Mobile Applications

The market for mobile enterprise applications is far from being saturated. To enable customers and partners to implement their own applications, an IDE is required to design and implement new mobile applications for the various application types leveraging SAP's enterprise service-oriented architecture (enterprise SOA) paradigm.

1.7 Summary

In this chapter, we discussed some general aspects of mobility and their impact on the business world. Many business scenarios can be made mobile, and this has many advantages, such as saving costs and increasing the efficiency of the business process. To make this happen, a mobile platform is required to provide all the functions that are required by a mobile infrastructure.

In the next chapter, we present some aspects of mobile technology. We give a short overview of mobile devices and software standards for mobile devices and discuss some basics about wireless networks.

Mobile devices, mobile software platforms, and wireless networks are key technological enablers to mobilize business processes. A good understanding of these technologies is an important prerequisite to implementing a mobile project, and we will discuss them in this chapter.

2 Mobile Technology

In this chapter, we present the technical aspects of mobile applications, such as the devices on which mobile applications can run, the different mobile frameworks and operating systems, and some basics about wireless networks that are required by mobile applications to connect with a backend system.

2.1 Mobile Devices

Mobile applications run on so-called *handheld* devices, which are pocket-sized computing devices that provide display functionality and a real or virtual keyboard for user input. Many types of handheld devices exist, depending on the usage. In this section, we give an overview of the various device types, including laptops and notebooks, tablet PCs, PDAs, and smart phones.

Virtual keyboards

2.1.1 Laptops and Notebooks

Laptops were the first devices that made mobile computing possible. Apart from specific applications such as 3D games that require high-end graphical and computing capabilities, the differences between laptops and desktops with regard to computing power are negligible in most cases. Like desktops, laptops consist of components such as a processor, display, disks, removable storage, RAM, keyboard, input devices, and so on. In general, they are equipped with batteries. Specific processors such as the Intel® Core™, the Intel Pentium® M, and the AMD Athlon™ XP-M are optimized for low power consumption and low heat output to extend the battery life. For marketing reasons, the term *notebook* was coined to promote extra compact, light devices.

Form factor Notebooks and laptops are available in different form factors. The screen size is in a range between 10.4" and 19". On laptops with the classical 4 to 3 format the resolution usually is 1,024 × 768, and on a 16 to 10 screen the resolution is typically 1,920 × 1,200 pixels. The so-called subnotebook is a small, lightweight portable computer with a screen smaller than 12" and a weight of less than 5 lbs.

2.1.2 Tablet PCs

The tablet PC was first introduced by Microsoft and their partners in 2002. It can be operated with an integrated digitizer, provides hardware function buttons, and runs on Windows XP Tablet PC Edition.

Active and passive digitizers Meanwhile there are two types of digitizers: the active and the passive digitizer. The active digitizer is operated by a pen that enables the digitizer to keep track of the pen's specific position when it is near the digitizer. This feature allows the user to hover over the screen providing additional functionality such as displaying tool tips or displaying menu entries without activating them. The passive digitizer consists of a touch screen and can be operated by any stylus or finger. When the user presses the touch screen, the location on the screen is detected and the cursor jumps to this place. Tablet PCs come in different form factors, as outlined in the following list:

- **Convertible**
  The convertible tablet PC consists of a base body with a keyboard attached and a display that is attached to the base at a single joint. The joint allows the user to rotate the screen by 180 degrees and fold it down to the keyboard, providing a writing surface.

- **Slate**
  The slate tablet PC does not have a keyboard. This device is operated only by pen and hardware function buttons to meet the specific needs of mobile usage. It is more compact and weighs less than the convertible. Slate tablet PCs come in different screen sizes ranging from 8.4" to 14.1".

2.1.3 PDAs

PDAs are handheld devices that are capable of hosting a wide range of applications for both business and consumer use. In many cases, they can be seen as an extension of a desktop PC. A sample PDA is shown in Figure 2.1. PDAs have the following characteristics:

- Typically, PDA's are equipped with a personal information management (PIM) software package, which enables them to support functionality such as calendar management, task and contact management, email, and text and spreadsheet processing. Using synchronization software such as Microsoft ActiveSync®, data from the PIM database can be exchanged between the PDA and the desktop PC so that users can access the same information on the PDA and the PC. *PIM*

- Most PDAs from different vendors such as Dell, Fujitsu, Siemens, HP, Symbol, and Toshiba are based on the Microsoft Pocket PC/Windows Mobile® operating system, whereas Palm OS® runs mainly on Palm devices, and some devices such as the Sharp Zaurus™ run on specific Linux distributions such as OPIE.

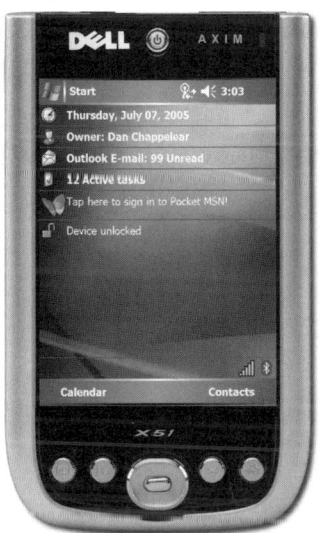

Figure 2.1 A Dell Axim™ X51v PDA

- PDAs can be operated in different ways. A touch screen allows user interaction by tapping the screen with a stylus to activate buttons or menu entries, and a virtual keyboard can be used to enter *Touch screen* text. Some PDAs such as the HP iPAQ hw6915 have full keyboards to facilitate data entry.

- PDAs are equipped with liquid crystal display (LCD) screens like those found on laptops. The screen size and resolution may vary. The most recent devices such as the Dell Axim X51v have a screen size of 3.7" and a resolution of 640 × 480 pixels.
- The memory of a PDA can be RAM- or ROM-based. Data in RAM are lost when the battery goes down, whereas data in ROM are nonvolatile. Lost data is a serious issue, especially in case of business applications. This is why modern operating systems save applications and data to ROM instead of RAM, with the disadvantage of performance degradation.
- To extend the built-in RAM, many PDAs provide extension slots for SD cards. Other optional features included in modern devices are a USB host, a GPS receiver, a microphone, a speaker, and a camera.
- Most PDAs come with a browser that allows accessing the Internet via wireless networks. For communication between PDAs, many of them are equipped with an IrDA infrared port, and they also come with a Bluetooth® connection to communicate with other devices, such as a GPS mouse or a headset.
- For extreme environments and working conditions, there are rugged constructions to withstand rigorous usage (see Figure 2.2).

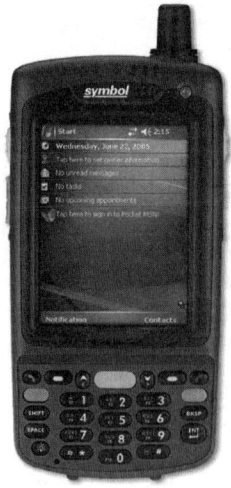

Figure 2.2 Symbol's MC70 Rugged Enterprise Digital Assistant

2.1.4 Smartphones

A smartphone is a handheld device that incorporates the functionalities of a PDA and a mobile phone. When a PDA is equipped with additional phone capabilities, we speak of a *PDA phone*, whereas a mobile phone that comes with data-oriented, PDA-like functionality is a *smartphone* in the original sense. It is difficult to give an exact definition of a smartphone, because most mobile phones come with some kind of data processing capability. In contrast to PDAs, which are used mainly for data-centric applications, smartphones are used primary for voice-centric applications.

Phone capabilities

There are a lot of smartphone vendors and devices. Let us take a look at two examples of smartphones, the Nokia 9300 and the BlackBerry® 8700g.

Nokia 9300

The Nokia 9300 is a smartphone that runs on the operating system Symbian OS™ 7.0 and supports Java™ MIDP 2.0 and Personal Profile. It features two displays with a resolution of 640 × 200 and 128 × 128 pixels, respectively, a QWERTY keyboard, and multimedia functionality. A sample Nokia 9300 is shown in Figure 2.3.

Figure 2.3 Nokia 9300 Smartphone

BlackBerry 8700g

The BlackBerry 8700g is a wireless handheld device that supports push email, mobile telephone, text messaging, web browsing, and other wireless information services. It runs on a proprietary operating system and is equipped with a QWERTY keyboard. A BlackBerry 8700g is shown in Figure 2.4.

> **Note**
>
> Research in Motion (RIM) provides a BlackBerry Java Development Environment to build Java Micro Edition (Java ME) applications for Java-based BlackBerry devices, which is Mobile Information Device Profile (MIDP) compliant.

Figure 2.4 BlackBerry 8700g

2.2 Application Development and Runtime Environments for Mobile Devices

Mobile devices, and their respective markets, are very diverse. Mobile devices have some shortcomings such as limited memory and computing power and differ in important properties, including the following:

- Operating system (Pocket PC, Symbian, Linux, Palm OS)
- Device capabilities (touch screen, phone support, wireless network support)

- Hardware equipment (network adapters, etc.)
- Screen form factors (landscape, portrait)
- Operating mode (stylus based, hardware buttons, keyboard)

Due to the mobile device market fragmentation, it is hard to make the "write once, run everywhere" paradigm a reality. A mobile application that is designed for a specific mobile device doesn't run automatically on a mobile device of a different manufacturer. However, two standardization approaches are available that allow application developers to abstract from specific mobile devices and device manufacturers. They include Java technology for wireless devices, and Microsoft's .NET Compact Framework. Let us look at them in detail.

Write once, run everywhere

2.2.1 Java Technology for Wireless Devices

Sun Microsystems, Inc., the manufacturer of Java technologies, has divided these technologies into three editions, each targeting specific industry requirements:

- **Java 2 Platform, Enterprise Edition (J2EE)**
  This is an industry standard for developing portable and scalable server-side Java applications.
- **Java 2 Platform, Standard Edition (J2SE)**
  This is a platform for developing and deploying Java applications on desktops
- **Java 2 Platform, Micro Edition (J2ME)**
  This is an application platform for mobile devices.

Figure 2.5 provides an overview of these technology stacks and their target markets.

The technology stack for mobile devices is essentially divided into two parts focusing on high-end and low-end devices, respectively. Sun Microsystems, Inc. introduced the concept of *configurations* and *profiles* to deal with the different requirements of mobile devices.

2 | Mobile Technology

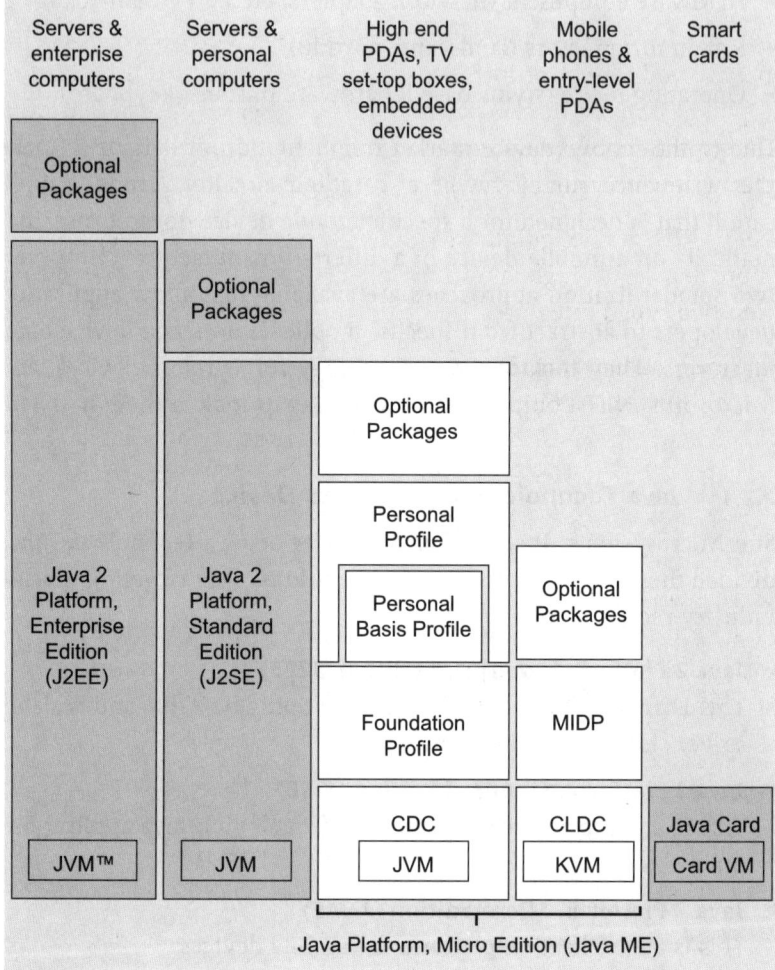

Figure 2.5 The Java Platform (Source: Sun Microsystems, Inc.)

Configurations and Profiles

Basically, configurations define the minimum set of libraries and virtual-machine features that must be available in each implementation of the Java ME environment. However, due to the fragmentation of the market, configurations are not sufficient to cover all requirements from vertical markets that might be very different. Applications for point-of-sales terminals require different features than applications for navigation systems. On the other hand, it is important to support interoperability within a vertical device market.

To address these issues and to expand the features defined in the configuration for specific vertical markets, the concept of *profiles* has been introduced. A profile is a set of standard APIs that is defined on top of a configuration. By combining a configuration with a profile, the application development and runtime environment for a device class can be completed.

Combining configuration and profile

Let us look at configurations and the devices to which they apply in more detail. At a high level, mobile consumer devices can be divided into two broad categories:

- **Small mainstream devices**
  This device class is composed of resource-constraint devices such as mobile phones, pagers, and mainstream personal digital assistants. Those devices have limited capabilities with regard to memory, processor, and graphics.

- **High-end devices**
  This device class is composed of devices such as smartphones, TV set-top boxes, RFID readers, and high-end personal digital assistants. In general, these devices have a 32-bit microprocessor and more memory than the small mainstream devices.

To provide suitable development and runtime environments that meet the requirements of the various devices described earlier, the J2ME platform has been divided into two base configurations:

- The Connected Limited Device Profile (CLDC) for small devices. *CLDC*

- The Connected Device Profile (CDC) for more capable devices. See Figure 2.6 for an illustration of the purpose of CDC devices. There are CDC devices for stationary use as well as mobile use. For instance, CDC is available for certain high-end mobile phones running on Symbian OS and PDAs that run the Windows Mobile OS, but they are also imbedded in Blu-Ray DVD player and set-top boxes. The purpose of CDC devices stretches from industry-specific scenarios such as automation to general deployment scenarios such as game consoles or copiers. *CDC*

2 | Mobile Technology

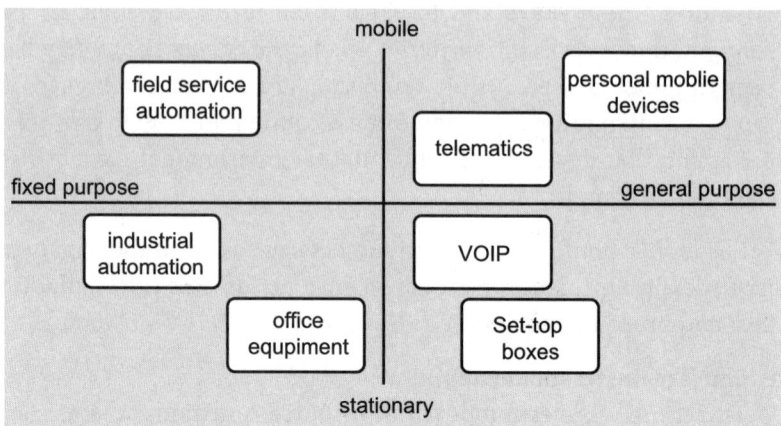

Figure 2.6 Purpose of CDC Devices (Source: Sun Microsystems, Inc.)

According to the Sun specification, the typical target devices for the configurations have the following capabilities:

- **CLDC**
    - 16-bit or 32-bit microprocessor
    - 160KB or more nonvolatile memory for the CLCD library and virtual machine
    - 192KB or more memory in total available for Java platform
    - Low power/battery consumption
    - (Wireless) networking capability

MIDP   CLDC can be expanded by the MIDP. It is suited to support a broad range of cell phones and mainstream PDAs. The current version of MIDP specification is MIDP 2.0. Among others, MIDP addresses the following features:

- Graphical user interfaces optimized for small display size
- Support of data entry using phone keypads
- Function buttons, touch screens, keyboards
- Wireless networking and messaging capabilities

- **CDC**
    - 32-bit microprocessor
    - 2.5MB ROM or more available to the Java application environment

46

- 2MB RAM available to the Java application environment

On top of CDC, three profiles are supported, which are built on each other:

- Foundation Profile
- Personal Basis Profile
- Personal Profile

The most comprehensive profile is the Personal Profile. It provides full support of the Abstract Windows Toolkit (AWT) and applets.

AWT

To further extend the capabilities of a profile, optional packages have been defined. A selection of existing optional packages includes:

- RMI optional package to support distributed application protocols based on a subset of J2SE RMI

  RMI

- Java Database Connectivity (JDBC) optional package to support relational databases based on a subset of JDBC 3.0 API

  JDBC

- Java TV API to control functionality provided by television receivers

- Java Bluetooth and Object Exchange (OBEX) API to support wireless communication via Bluetooth and support OBEX

2.2.2 Microsoft's .NET Compact Framework

The platform for mobile devices offered by Microsoft is called the .NET Compact Framework, which is currently released in version 2.0. Together with Microsoft Visual Studio, it provides a development and runtime environment for mobile devices running on the Pocket PC/Windows Mobile operating system. Basically, the .NET Compact Framework is a subset of the .NET Framework, which is a development and execution environment mainly for desktop PCs. Thus, the basic paradigms of the .NET Framework also apply to the .NET compact framework.

Microsoft Visual Studio

Basically, the .NET Compact Framework consists of two parts, the common language runtime (CLR) and the .NET Compact Framework class library. The CLR is the execution environment for managed code and provides services such as memory management, garbage collection, thread management, and security management.

CLR

2 | Mobile Technology

Managed code The term *managed code* comes from the fact that .NET applications run under the control of CLR. Code that is not controlled by CLR and that has direct access to the underlying operating system services, is called *unmanaged* or *native* code.

In contrast to Win32 programming using native code, applications for .NET are written in managed code (C# or Visual Basic.NET), which supports strong type safety and cannot create memory leaks due to garbage collection. Since the runtime executes instruction list (IL) bytecode generated by the compiler, it does not care about the high-level language that has been used to implement the application; the language can be selected according to the developer's skills.

2.3 Connectivity

Mobile enterprise applications need to be integrated in the enterprise business process and thus require a connection to the enterprise server by using a network, preferably a wireless one. Applications can have specific requirements to the network in terms of the following:

- Network availability
- Network bandwidth and latency
- Network security and reliability

Next, we will discuss the impact of network availability on the application design, followed by a brief overview of wireless network technology.

2.3.1 Application Types Based on Network Connection Availability

Connected and occasionally connected mobile applications Applications can be of two types: *occasionally connected* or *connected*. We will look at both in more detail in this subsection.

Occasionally Connected Applications

In many mobile scenarios, a (wireless) network is not permanently available. For example, a service technician might be working at a remote location or in a building that is shielding wireless networks.

This user needs an application that does not require permanent access to a network. This type of application is called an occasionally connected application.

To enable the user to proceed with his work when a network is not available, an occasionally connected application needs to have the following components:

- UI layer that exposes the business functionality
- Business logic layer to check and process the entries made by the user
- Persistency layer to save the entries made by the user
- Synchronization services to exchange data with a backend system

    The synchronization service starts once the network is available. During the synchronization, data that were changed or created on the device are uploaded to the backend system, and data from the backend system can flow down to the device.

Connected Applications

In contrast to occasionally connected applications, connected applications require permanent network access. In general, connected applications are browser-based applications that are connected to a backend system.

Comparing Occasionally Connected Applications with Connected Applications

Comparing the basic types of applications, it is obvious that the design of occasionally connected applications is more complicated than the design of connected applications. Occasionally connected applications are in general rich clients consisting of a presentation layer, a business logic layer, and a persistence layer and require synchronization services to exchange data between the backend system and the mobile device. In addition, an infrastructure is necessary that allows the administrator to configure which data should go to which devices.

Rich client application

Occasionally connected applications provide a richer set of functionality and can deal with more complex scenarios than their online counterparts. The answer to the question of which application type should be preferred depends on the business scenario. For campus-based workers, who have permanent access to the company's network and who require a simple application where data entry is supported by peripherals such bar code scanners or RFID readers, a connected application is sufficient. For sales representatives, who need to have direct access to a large set of business partners, products, and other business objects to quickly create a new sales order, an occasionally connected application is the better option. The terms *connected application* and *online application* are often used synonymously.

2.3.2 Network Technologies

To exchange data between a mobile device and an enterprise server, a physical connection (a network) is necessary. Networks can be categorized in different ways, including one-to-one and one-to-many.

One-to-Many or One-to-One Communications

Broadcasting　As in human interaction, there are different types of network communication. For example, broadcast networks send out information to multiple receivers (machines) using a single communication channel. Depending on the address field that is contained in the information, only the intended recipients process the information packet, and all other listeners ignore it.

> **Example**
>
> As an analogy, although airport announcements are broadcast to all people located in the broadcast area, only the intended receiver(s) pay attention to announcements such as "Passenger Smith is required to proceed to gate A7" or "Flight number 18 is ready for boarding."

Multicasting　It is also not always necessary to send the information to all machines. In a so-called multicasting scenario, for example, the information is sent to only a group of machines. Each machine can subscribe to any or all groups. Multicasting provides a more efficient infrastructure to send information to recipients as compared to broadcasting. In the airport example given earlier, for example, it is not necessary to broadcast information about departing flights in the arrival terminal. Both broadcasting and multicasting are also considered one-to-many communications.

In contrast to the network types above, in a *point-to-point* or *unicast* network, individual pairs of machines are connected to each other. Depending on the network topology (star, ring, or mesh network), multiple routes through intermediate machines are possible for a packet on its way from the sender to the receiver. As a consequence, algorithms that optimize the packet routes are important for fast data transmission. Point-to-point or unicast communications are also considered one-to-one communications.

<small>Unicasting</small>

Local or Wide Area Networks

Another important factor to consider for network classification is the physical range within which networked machines are located. Based on this range, several network types exist, including the following:

<small>Physical range</small>

- **Personal Area Network (PAN)**
  This network type connects a set of devices that are in the proximity of a single person. The range of such a network is typically a few meters. For instance, a PAN can consist of mouse, printer, and keyboard connected to a computer. A PDA, which is connected via a cradle to a desktop PC to exchange data, can also be a PAN. Wired PANs may use USB or Firewire, whereas wireless PANs may use Bluetooth or IrDA as their underlying network technology. PANs can also be used to connect to a higher-level network and the Internet.

- **Local Area Network (LAN)**
  This network type connects machines in a single building or campus within a range of a few kilometers. They are widely used to connect computers and to share resources such as printers or hard disks in a company. Most current LANs are based on the IEEE 802.3 standard, commonly known as Ethernet, allowing data transmission rates from 10Mbps up to 10Gbps. The machines may be physically connected by a cable such as a category 5 cable (CAT5), which is an unshielded twisted pair cable designed for high signal integrity. The way in which the machines are arranged is called the *network topology*. Two common topologies for a broadcast LAN include a *bus* or a *ring* topology. In a *linear bus*, all

<small>IEEE 802.3</small>

machines are connected to a common transmission medium with exactly two endpoints. All data are transmitted over this medium and can be received by all machines in this network. In a ring, all machines are connected in a circular way, where the first and last machine are connected to each other. All data circulate from one machine to the next in a single direction.

- **Metropolitan Area Network (MAN)**
  This network type covers a larger area than a LAN. Usually it spans several blocks of buildings up to entire cities. An example of a MAN is the cable television networks that are available in many cities. In contrast to a LAN, a MAN is not generally owned by a single organization. Instead, the MAN and its equipment are owned and operated by a consortium of users or by a network provider. Often, a MAN can be used for Internetworking of local networks.

- **Wide Area Network (WAN)**
  This network type spans a broad geographical area, which can be country or a continent. Typically, WANs are used to connect LANs together, for instance enabling employees located in different countries to communicate with each other. *Routers* are used as junctions between networks to transfer data from one network to the other. The largest WAN is the commonly used *Internet*. In general, the owners of the computers (or hosts) are different from the owners of the communication lines. WANs can use packet-switched or circuit-switched connections. For circuit switching, a dedicated connection between the two communication endpoints is set up for their exclusive use for the duration of the communication. In contrast, packet-switching splits the information to be transmitted into small packets, which are routed through the network. This makes it possible to share the communication lines.

Table 2.1 provides an overview of the characteristic properties of the network types that we just discussed. Please note that the transfer rates (bandwidth) are theoretical values. In reality, the transfer rates are in general smaller, and the values for data uplink (sent data) and downlink (received data) might be different. There is also additional overhead caused by the protocol.

Packet switched, circuit switched

	PAN	LAN	MAN	WAN
Bandwidth	Up to 2MB/s	Up to 10 GB/s	Up to 150MB/s	Up to 75MB/s
Area Range	Short (N*1m)	Medium (N*1km)	Medium-long (N*10km)	Long (N*1000km)
Standard	IrDA (IrDA 1.0 up to 115KB/s, Bluetooth (Bluetooth 2.1 up to 2MB/s)	802.11	802.6	GSM (9.6KB/s), GPRS (171.2KB/s), EDGE (200KB/s), UMTS (384KB/s–2MB/s), HSDPA(7.2MB/s), WiMAX (75MB/s), 2.5G–3.5G

Table 2.1 Network Characteristics

Mobile Networks

Due to their importance for mobile devices, we will describe the mobile network standards Global System for Mobile Communications (GSM), General Packet Radio Service (GPRS), Enhanced Data Rates for GSM Evolution (EDGE), Universal Mobile Telecommunications System (UMTS), and High Speed Downlink Packet Access (HSDPA) in more detail, as follows. Mobile network technologies are classified by their generation (G) and are denoted as 2G, 2.5G, 3G, or 3.5G, depending on their capabilities.

- **Global System for Mobile Communications (GSM)**   *Cellular network*
  GSM is the most popular standard in the world for mobile phones. GSM networks operate in different frequency ranges. The 900MHz and 1,800MHz ranges are used in most parts of the world, such as Europe, the Middle East, Africa, and most parts of Asia. The 850- and 1900MHz ranges are used in the United States, Canada, and many other countries in the Americas. The 400MHz range is primarily used in Scandinavia. GSM is a cellular network, that is, made up of a number of cells, which are each served by a base station. When a mobile phone makes a call, it searches for cells in the immediate vicinity. To connect to the GSM network, GSM devices have a detachable smart card, the Subscription Identity Module, commonly known as SIM card. The SIM card contains the user's subscription information and a phonebook. GSM

is a 2G technology standard in the context of mobile phone standards.

- **General Packet Radio Service (GPRS)**
  GPRS is a mobile network standard that is based on GSM. GPRS is a packet-switched protocol, which means multiple users share the same transmission channel. The transmission channel is used only if data are transferred. By always-on operation mode, we mean there is a virtual connection to the transmission channel. In contrast, in the older circuit switched data (CSD) standard, which is included in the GSM standard, a connection establishes a circuit for the exclusive usage of this connection. Therefore, GPRS data transfer is typically charged depending on the transferred data volume and not based on the connection time, as is the case for GSM. GPRS is a 2.5G network technology.

- **Enhanced Data Rates for GSM Evolution (EDGE)**
  EDGE is a mechanism to increase the transfer rates in GSM-based mobile networks by using a more efficient modulation technique. Using EDGE, GPRS becomes EGPRS, providing higher transfer rates than GPRS. EDGE is a 3G network technology.

- **Universal Mobile Telecommunications System (UMTS)**
  UMTS is a 3G mobile network technology standard and is based on Code Division Multiple Access (CDMA) technology. UMTS provides much higher transfer rates than GSM. A UMTS-enabled device can send or receive several data streams at once. For instance, a mobile user can make a call and receive emails simultaneously. Data can be transferred in the Frequency Division Duplex (FDD) or Time Division Duplex (TDD) mode. In the FDD mode, the mobile station and the base station have different frequencies for uplink and downlink data transfer. In TDD, the mobile station and the base station use the same frequency but use different time slots. UMTS is a 3G network technology.

- **High Speed Downlink Packet Access (HSDPA)**
  HSDPA provides a large performance increase compared to the other mobile network standards. This is achieved through techniques that amplify EDGE performance past GPRS on the last mile between basis station and mobile device. HSDPA-enabled mobile devices are equipped with improved receivers and thus provide higher voice quality. HSDPA is a 3.5G network technology.

Margin note: Frequency division duplex, time division duplex

Wireless Networks

A wireless network is a network based on radio waves and is part of the IEEE 802.11 family of wireless networking standards. These standards are published by the Institute of Electrical and Electronics Engineers (IEEE) and include multiple over-the-air modulation techniques. In the 802.11 standard, the usage of the Carrier Sense Multiple Access/Collision Avoidance (CSMA/CA) mechanism is mandatory. It allows multiple network stations to access the same transmission medium simultaneously. The most used standard today is 802.11g, which was released in 2003 and enables a data transfer rate of 54MB/s, using the frequency band of 2.400–2.485 GHz, which is license-free. It supersedes the older 802.11b standard, which enabled transfer rates of only 11MB/s. 802.11n is a new emerging standard for wireless local networks. The maximum data transfer for this standard is planned to be about 600MB/s.

IEEE 802.11

There are two different types of usage for a WLAN: *infrastructure mode* and *ad hoc* mode. In the infrastructure mode, there is a dedicated wireless access point (WAP) that coordinates the different clients. The WAP can provide access to a cable-based Ethernet network. In the ad hoc-mode, there is no dedicated base station. Instead, the connection is set up between the devices directly. In this configuration, also called a mesh network, each device is connected to one or more devices.

Infrastructure mode, ad hoc mode

Worldwide Interoperability for Microwave Access (WiMAX) is another name for the IEEE 802.16 standard. It was positioned as a stationary alternative to Digital Subscriber Line (DSL) or as a mobile alternative to UMTS. Taking data transfer rates and range of coverage of the basis station into account, WiMAX in general is superior to WLAN. A basis station typically covers an area with a radius of 2–3km.

IEEE 802.16

For mobile applications, the availability of a mobile network, such as GPS, GPRS, EDGE, UMTS, or HSDPA, or the availability of a wireless network, such as WLAN or WiMAX, plays an important role. The various networks differ with regard to their availability, their transfer rates, their pricing, and so on. To select the appropriate network, the requirements of the mobile application regarding the data volume that needs to be transferred should be taken into consideration.

2.4 Summary

In this chapter, we discussed several basic facts about mobile technology. Mobile devices are very diverse and come with different screen sizes, data entry capabilities, and storage and computing capabilities. This diversity allows the customer to select the most appropriate device for the specific use case, but the mobile solutions have to support the different runtime environments. The Java ME standard helps classify mobile devices and provides a specification for a framework that takes the different capabilities of mobile devices into account. Thus, applications that are J2ME compliant run on a large set of mobile devices.

To connect to the server, the mobile application needs to access a (preferably wireless) network for data transfer. Many standards are available, and the descriptions of the different available network technologies in this chapter will help you better orient yourself in the "network jungle".

In Chapter 3, we will describe the capabilities of SAP's mobile platform, SAP NetWeaver Mobile 7.1. You will learn how SAP software solves the issues that were outlined in Chapter 1.

This chapter helps readers gain understanding of the SAP NetWeaver Mobile 7.1 platform's key design objectives and capabilities. A good understanding of these issues will help in the understanding of the architecture and tools.

3 SAP NetWeaver Mobile Challenges and Capabilities

A mobile platform that has to support thousands of mobile devices faces many technical challenges. The solution to these challenges requires a specific design and architecture that is tailored to the specific needs of the platform. The main design goal is to lower the total cost of ownership (TCO) of the entire solution by providing an infrastructure that provides the following:

- Supports developers to build applications in a model-driven way
- Supports administrators to manage the system landscape and to make use of the hardware resources in an efficient way
- Supports the users of the mobile devices to perform their tasks based on the needed information from the backend system.

In this chapter, we will discuss the challenges and how they are solved.

3.1 SAP NetWeaver Mobile 7.1 Challenges

Before getting into the capabilities details of SAP NetWeaver Mobile 7.1, let us first look into the challenges to mobilizing information and the required functionalities to face these challenges at a high level. Then it will be easy to understand the capabilities of the SAP NetWeaver Mobile 7.1 platform. The challenges include:

- Numerous synchronizing devices and multiple sources of information
- Long synchronization times

- Data volume to be sent to the devices
- Data consistency
- Real-time user experience
- Frequently changing organizational structure
- Manageability of the system landscape
- Model-driven application development

3.1.1 Numerous Synchronizing Devices and Multiple Sources of Information

End user productivity

Mobile scenarios are all about end user productivity. Information needs to be provisioned to the end user anywhere and anytime. This means every user is going to carry his own personal device that needs to have this information regardless of the connectivity — online or offline. In this scenario it is obvious that the number of devices requesting the data is large since every end user will need access. Also, the information that is going to be provisioned could come from multiple sources or systems such as SAP ERP and SAP CRM. Information that needs to be provisioned should also be a relevant subset based on subscriptions or profile of the user. In this scenario achieving the scalability is a real challenge.

If every device is going to synchronize against a multitude of sources then each individual source of information should be scalable and also should be capable of filtering out the relevant subset. In this scenario the need for a middle tier that can provide consolidated data to every end user with appropriate filtering is obvious. This middle tier will make the multitude of sources of information transparent and will be capable of filtering out the information that is required by every user.

3.1.2 Long Synchronization Times

Since we are talking about end user productivity, synchronization time is another challenge that needs to be addressed. Even though there is a middle tier that is going to provision information in a harmonized fashion, if it starts filtering the data during synchronization, then the synchronization time will increase dramatically.

Therefore, there is a need for the precalculation of the data that need to be provisioned to the individual users. This also means there is a need for an event-driven architecture where the changes made in the source systems are sent immediately to the middle tier, and the middle tier calculates who needs to get what immediately and prepares and stages the data immediately so that whenever the device synchronizes, it will be a simple exchange of data from the staging area, much like a file transfer. This process would dramatically improve the response time.

Precalculation of data distribution

3.1.3 Data Volume To Be Sent to the Devices

The size of the data being exchanged between the server and the device is another challenge that needs to be addressed. In a mobile scenario, only a relevant subset of data will flow down to the device, which is determined by subscriptions. Even then, data volume on the wire will increase dramatically if the server communicates gross data instead of net data. A side effect of an event-driven design is that if the same object is getting updated multiple times, that object could flow down to the same device as multiple messages.

To address this, the net data needs to be communicated; that is, only the modified fields should be communicated. This is called *net field* communication. There is also a need for *semantic compression* so that multiple updates on the same object are not communicated as different messages, which increases the data volume on the wire. Instead, a single message with all of the changes is prepared and sent to the device.

Semantic compression

3.1.4 Data Consistency

In an occasionally connected landscape a lot of consistency issues need to be addressed because it is an asynchronous communication, unlike in the online scenario. Following are the fundamental issues that need to be addressed:

- **Object identity**
  In an occasionally connected scenario, an object cannot be guaranteed to have a system-wide unique identity under all circumstances. That is, if a sales order is created locally on the mobile device, it cannot be guaranteed that a unique order number for

that object will be created. In this scenario the middle tier should be able to fill the gap by correlating the request and response, thereby responding with a unique id generated by the source or the owner system. In essence, the middle tier needs to have *key mapping* to map the local key with the global key and the capability to correlate request and response.

- **Conflict handling**
  In a distributed scenario such as a mobile scenario, it is possible that changes could be made to the same object in parallel in multiple systems. In this scenario it should be possible to detect conflicts. This conflict detection should be configurable to accommodate first one wins (at object level and row level), server wins always (at object level and row level), or last one wins scenarios. Once a conflict is detected, it should be possible to resolve it either centrally on the server or locally on the client.

- **Supporting tentativeness**
  Whatever changes happen on a device in an offline mode are tentative. It is possible that these changes could get rejected either because of owner system validation failure or because of conflict. In this case the middle tier should support a protocol where every change that comes from the device is responded to with either a confirmation in the case of success or a rejection in the case of failure so the device can update the status locally, and it should provide an option to resolve the error or conflict either locally on a device or centrally on the server.

3.1.5 Real-Time User Experience

Mobile scenarios should cater to both connected and disconnected users. If the user is always connected, there should be a real-time synchronization experience for the end user. In essence, the user should be able to feel the seamless online-offline behavior when he is using the application.

Background synchronization

Therefore, the background synchronization needs to be done at a regular time interval. Otherwise, a notification from the server to the device in order to trigger the synchronization is required so that user will feel that he is online without having to synchronize manually.

3.1.6 Frequently Changing Organizational Structure

In an occasionally connected scenario the user will only get the subset of information that he needs. This subset is often determined by the organizational structure, such as the organizational hierarchy or territory to which the user belongs. This organizational structure is subject to frequent change, and subscriptions that are applied to find out what data the user need will also change often. For example, an employee could be transferred from one territory to another. In this scenario data relevant to the new territory should be made available to the user and old data needs to be deleted. The challenge is to realign the filtering criteria and performance of data realignment to reflect the changes immediately.

It is necessary to automatically align the filtering criteria or subscriptions based on the information available from the source system such as SAP CRM, which keeps track of all employee-related information. Whenever an attribute of the employee object such as the territory changes, this should automatically be reflected in the subscription that is being applied for filtering the data. There should not be any double effort from an administration point of view. Also, changes in the subscription should result in fast recalculation, which means a high-performing, scalable algorithm that can cater to these real-time requirements is needed.

Realignment

3.1.7 Manageability of the System Landscape

If the number of devices in an occasionally connected landscape is substantial, manageability becomes a real challenge. The following points give a brief overview of the challenges faced by the administrator, and these challenges have to be handled through tools:

- **Inventory of devices**
  An inventory that can be searched to find specific device and access all its attributes is needed.
- **Device tracking**
  It should be possible to track all of the devices with their particular status, for example, list of installed applications, synchronization statistics, monitoring of exchanged messages, and so on.

- **Fast rollout**
  It should be possible to roll out multiple devices every day making it possible to scale up to thousands of devices in the landscape.

- **Phased upgrade**
  If an application is upgraded, it will not be possible to do a big-bang upgrade of all of the devices in the landscape. It should be possible to upgrade a set of devices in a landscape on a daily basis, which means the middle tier should be able to run both versions of the application in parallel.

- **Message tracking**
  It should be possible to track all of the messages flowing through the system and search based on some error condition to find out what happened. Also, there is a need to reprocess the failed messages in bulk if necessary.

- **Device recovery**
  It should be possible to restore the data on a device if the device gets corrupted or lost.

3.1.8 Model-Driven Application Development

Invariably, occasionally connected clients have business logic running on local devices. To achieve this, an application is developed that will be deployed to the local devices. In this case it should be possible to develop the application in a model-driven way.

Therefore, there is a need to develop the mobile application through a model-driven paradigm and possibly reuse the business logic that is defined on the online application

3.2 SAP NetWeaver Mobile 7.1 Capabilities

In Section 3.1, we described the challenges and required functionalities of a platform that helps mobilize data from various backend systems. Figure 3.1 describes various components that are part of the SAP NetWeaver Mobile 7.1 platform, which helps solve the challenges described in the previous section.

SAP NetWeaver Mobile 7.1 Capabilities | 3.2

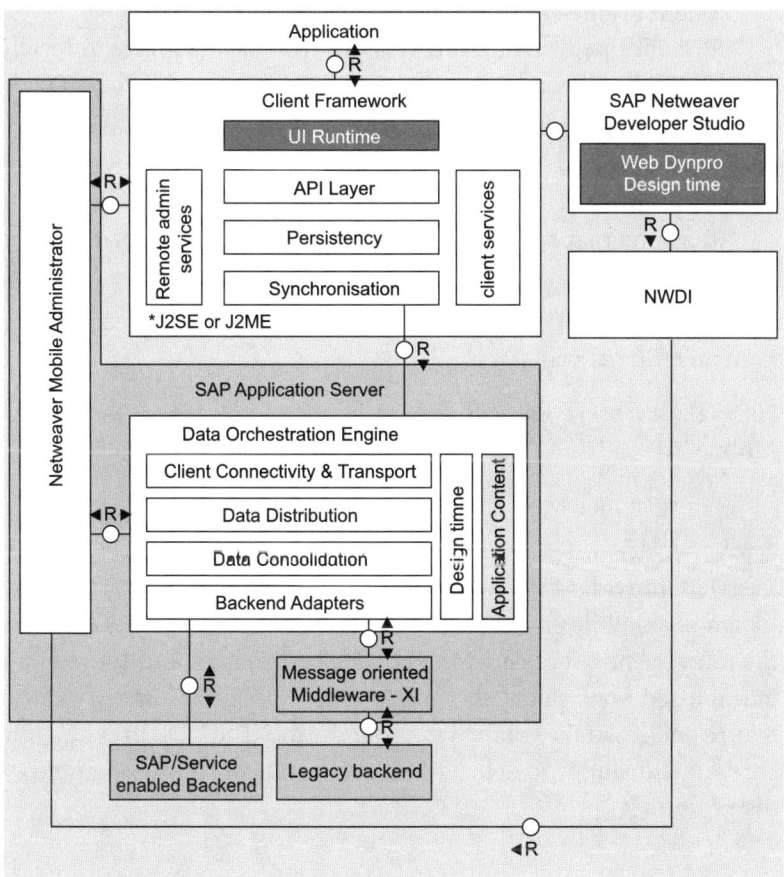

Figure 3.1 Components of NetWeaver Mobile Platform

SAP NetWeaver Mobile 7.1 contains three core components:

- **Data Orchestration Engine (DOE)**
  This is the middle tier server part that helps mobilize data from various backend systems and filters out the data relevant to a specific user based on subscriptions.

- **SAP NetWeaver Mobile Client Platform**
  This software resides on a target device. An application running on the client can be developed using SAP NetWeaver Developer Studio, which provides integrated development environment (IDE) functionalities for developing mobile applications. Also, it contains two core runtime parts:

3 | SAP NetWeaver Mobile Challenges and Capabilities

Runtime
- **Client Framework Services (CFS)**
  Provides persistency and synchronization capability to locally stage the data and synchronize the changes with the DOE. It also provides supporting services such as user management, deployment, logging, and tracing.
- **UI Runtime**
  Runtime that renders the application on to the screen.

▶ **SAP NetWeaver Mobile Administrator**
This provides set of tools and capabilities to manage the landscape in an efficient way

Let's take a closer look at these core components of SAP NetWeaver Mobile 7.1.

3.2.1 DOE

The DOE provides the capabilities that help resolve most of the challenges of a mobile environment. This is the middle tier that provides the relevant subset of data to target devices from various sources in a harmonized way. Being the middle tier, this is the core of performance and scalability of the whole landscape. The DOE provides two core functionalities to achieve the goal: data consolidation and data distribution.

Data Consolidation

Consolidated data store (CDS)
The DOE consolidates data from various sources and stores a replica of that data in its own store, called the *Consolidated data store* (CDS). The basic entities that are used to define the schema are called *data objects*. Data objects are definitions of the business objects relevant to a mobile scenario, such as sales order and customer. A design time tool is available to define these objects, and tables in CDS are automatically generated for storage whenever these objects are activated.

Backend adapter
Also, it will be possible to define references across objects because it is necessary in most business scenarios. For example, the Sales Order data object refers to the Customer data object. The Data Consolidation module keeps the runtime references across the object instances intact even if the instances of the business objects are coming from different sources. Backend adapters are used to provide a loose coupling between the data source and the DOE. Backend adapters pro-

vide a means to connect to the source system and provide transformation functionality to transform backend or source structures to the data object format. Figure 3.2 depicts the CDS.

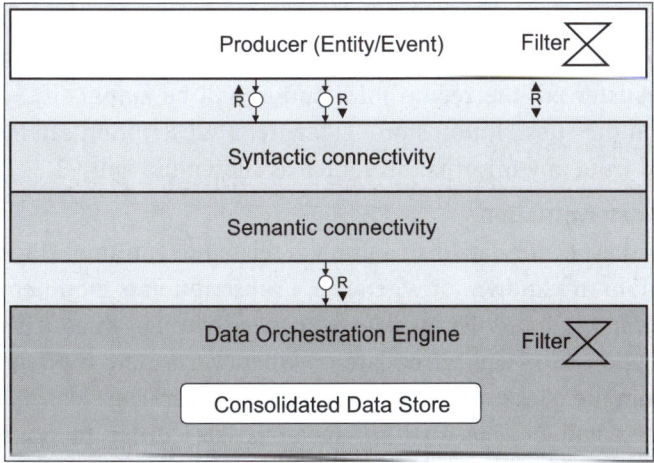

Figure 3.2 Data Consolidation

Data Distribution

In the mobile scenario, relevant data needs to be distributed to all of the devices. Devices do not need and cannot hold all of the data in the backend system, so strong data distribution capabilities are needed. Data distribution consists of two components:

- **Subscription management**
  The relevant subset of data for a user is determined through subscriptions, but in the case of thousands of devices it is impossible to imagine that the administrator is maintaining this information on a device-by-device basis. This increases the TCO. Therefore, the DOE supports a paradigm of subscription generation based on rules. Subscriptions are generated out of the information that is already available in the system landscape. For example, sales order information has to be distributed to the users based on the region where they belong, and every user has a device. In this scenario, based on the user information available in the backend, a receiver inventory that stores all of the receiver-specific information can be automatically generated from the system, containing users, and user-specific attributes that are region-specific. Then a simple rule is defined that declares that Sales_order.region = receiver.region.

Rule-based approach

3 | SAP NetWeaver Mobile Challenges and Capabilities

In this case subscription and receiver inventory will be automatically updated with the identities of all of the receivers and the information about what individual receivers want. From the administrator's point of view, there is no need to maintain user-specific subscriptions any more for mobile devices. Whenever a new user is added, a receiver will be automatically created, and whenever a user is transferred, the region information will be automatically updated in the subscription store. Likewise, a subscription can be generated from any information source as shown in Figure 3.3.

▸ **Receiver determination**
The second aspect of data distribution is related to runtime. Once subscriptions are known, or whenever a subscription is modified, this runtime engine will calculate who needs to get what. This happens upon subscription update or whenever a new message comes from the backend system. For example, a receiver determination step will be executed whenever a sales order message (update, create, or delete) comes from the backend system, whenever region information is updated, or whenever a new user is created in the backend system. To handle thousands of devices, the algorithm is pruned for dealing with a mass volume of updates. This process is described in Figure 3.3

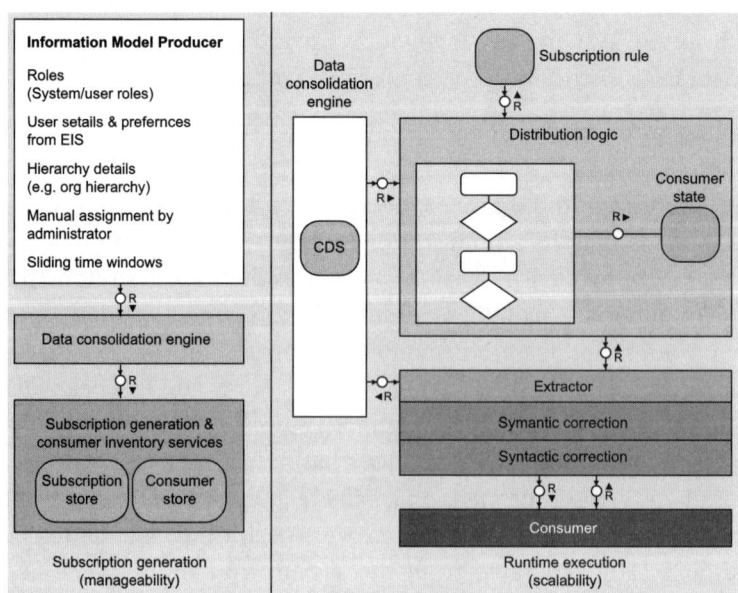

Figure 3.3 Overview of Data Distribution Architecture

Openness

Openness is one of the key capabilities of the DOE. The DOE is a runtime engine that provides data to multiple devices, consolidating the data from various backend system. It not only plays a role in distributing the data, but it also plays a key role in deploying the application to individual devices. It is the heart of SAP NetWeaver Mobile, which connects to backend, devices, and device management capabilities. Thus, it is important that these areas are opened up so that the DOE can be used in multiple scenarios and landscapes. Figure 3.4 describes the three areas that are opened up:

Data distribution and application deployment

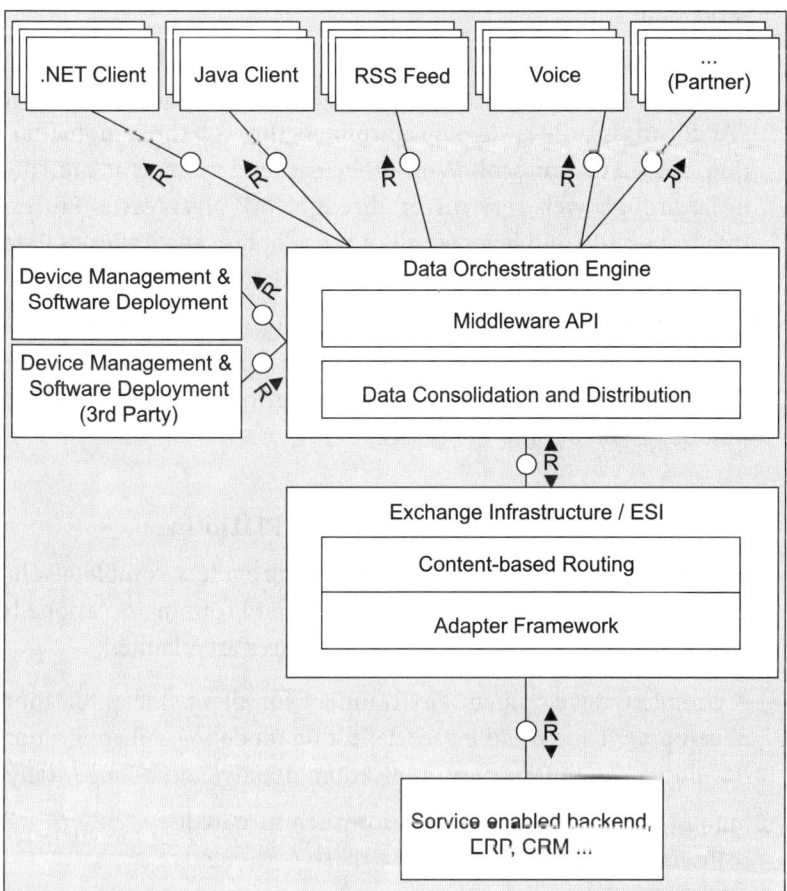

Figure 3.4 Openness of the SAP NetWeaver Mobile 7.1 Platform

3 | SAP NetWeaver Mobile Challenges and Capabilities

SyncML, RSS
- **Client connectivity**
  A multitude of possibilities are available when it comes to devices, programming models, and connectivity options. Therefore, this area is opened up so that the DOE is completely device, programming model, and connectivity independent. It can be used for a Java client, .NET client, devices enabled through synchronization markup language (SyncML), or even online really simple syndication (RSS) feed types of scenarios that uses the core capability of data orchestration from the DOE. The DOE has a standard channel to connect to an SAP NetWeaver Mobile client, but it is possible to plug in custom handlers for other devices and protocols on the server side

- **Data Consolidation**
  The DOE can connect to any kind of backend system. With the SAP Business suite system it can connect through the remote function call (RFC) protocol. With other backend systems it can connect through web services or through SAP NetWeaver Process Integration (PI) and leverage all of the adapter capabilities of PI to connect to any third-party or legacy backend system.

- **Device Management**
  The DOE is opened with multiple APIs to connect to any available third-party device management software to manage the application deployment onto the devices

3.2.2 SAP NetWeaver Mobile Client Platform

The SAP NetWeaver Mobile Platform will provide a complete solution for developing, debugging, deploying, and running occasionally connected applications. The following features are planned:

- A complete development environment for client-side application development and middleware definition modeling. An application developer can build a new application, deploy, and debug locally.

- Support for peripheral integration such as barcode scanners and printers. The application can use these peripherals.

Client Framework Services (CFS)
- A client-side framework will enable the application to run on individual devices with its own persistency and synchronization. This is the core of the client and is called Client Framework Services (CFS).

To develop the application, SAP NetWeaver Developer Studio provides a mobile perspective to develop occasionally connected mobile applications. For laptop-based applications, the standard Web Dynpro functionality is optimized for less memory consumption and higher performance for a single user standalone mode. Utilizing the SAP GUI for Java as a unified rendering component, the Web Dynpro runtime runs as a normal *Java 2 Standard Edition* (J2SE) program on the *Java Virtual Machine* (JVM) without the need for a web server, application server, or a servlet engine. Swing-based Java GUI makes the client experience richer with faster rendering time. On personal digital assistants (PDAs), the application runs on an Abstract Window Toolkit (AWT) or a Java Server Pages (JSP)-based UI.

Web Dynpro, Abstract Window Toolkit

Client Framework Services

CFS are a set of services required by other client components to run. These are reusable services and work on both PDAs and laptops. Services can be categorized in following groups:

- **Mobile Middleware Client Services**
  - **Transport layer:** The transport layer implements low-level (byte-level) transport protocol between NetWeaver Mobile Client and the DOE that supports checkpoint restart functionality.
  - **Synchronization dispatcher:** The synchronization dispatcher dispatches the message to the appropriate consumer.
  - **Client synchronization service:** The client synchronization service uses the transport layer for data transport between mobile client and middleware and implements a synchronization service for mobilized business objects, which ensures that only delta information will be transported between the DOE and NetWeaver Mobile Client
  - **Error and conflict handling service:** The error and conflict handling service detects errors during the synchronization and applies the appropriate conflict handling service, if necessary.
  - **Persistency service:** For occasionally connected scenarios this service is used to persist the data locally on the mobile device and to maintain the offline state of the information.

- **Mobile System Administration and Monitoring Client Services**
  - **Deployment service:** The deployment service is used when an application is deployed to the device from the server.
  - **Configuration service:** The configuration service is used for remotely controlling the configuration of the device.
  - **Logging and tracing service:** The logging and tracing service is used to upload log files and traces from the mobile device to the server for central monitoring.
  - **Alert service:** The alert service is triggered if an alert is sent from the mobile device to the server.
  - **Agent framework:** The agent framework is used to manage the agents that are deployed to the mobile device.

3.2.3 SAP NetWeaver Mobile Administrator

Smooth management of the entire system landscape

Because the SAP NetWeaver Mobile platform supports so many mobile devices, the effort to manage them is very high. Therefore, the scope of Mobile System Administration and Monitoring is to ensure smooth management of the entire system landscape, starting from setting up of the devices by distributing applications, then configuring data distribution, managing and monitoring the daily processes, and, finally, tracking and handling errors.

SAP NetWeaver Mobile Administrator is the single point of user interface for configuration, administration, and monitoring of the mobile system landscape and providing the manageability for numerous mobile devices. The SAP Mobile Administrator provides the following monitoring capabilities:

Communication sessions

- **Monitoring client communication**
  This functionality enables the administrator to monitor the client communication sessions. When a device connects to the DOE and starts synchronizing data, a session is created. The session ends when the device is disconnected.

Logs and traces

- **Monitoring external client logs**
  The information about the various operations that are performed on a client device is stored in the log and trace files, which are maintained in the XML file format on the client. These files are sent to the DOE when the client synchronizes data with the DOE. The DOE converts the data in these files to a format it understands

and stores this data in the monitoring framework. In addition, the DOE analyzes the data and notifies the administrator if it encounters any errors or inconsistencies.

- **Monitoring logs and traces**
  This functionality enables the administrator to monitor the logs and traces created for the operations that are performed on the middleware server.

- **Monitoring messages**
  The DOE uses messages to exchange information with the mobile devices. The message store contains all of the messages received by the DOE for processing. In addition, the message store provides various options for troubleshooting messages and subsequently reprocessing them. As a result, if some messages are not processed successfully, the administrator can analyze them and perform the required troubleshooting tasks before you reprocess them.

  Reprocessing messages

- **Monitoring the DOE using Computing Center Management System (CCMS)**
  Using CCMS, the administrator can monitor some aspects of the DOE, such as:

  Computing Center Management System (CCMS)

  - Hardware configurations of the DOE and various backend systems connected to the DOE
  - Alerts triggered by the client devices, backend systems, or other systems that are connected to it
  - Information related to the system health of the DOE

- **Monitoring the workload and performance statistics of the DOE**
  This functionality enables the administrator to monitor the resource usage for data object messages that are processed by the DOE. The data can be monitored on a daily, weekly, or monthly basis.

  Performance statistics

The administrative activities you can perform using the SAP NetWeaver Mobile Administrator include:

- Rolling out devices by using setup packages or software packages. You use setup packages if the users of the client devices need initial data to perform their activities immediately after the device setup is complete. This is because in a setup package, you can include data along with the relevant mobile components that are

  Software packages, setup packages

required for the devices to be productive. You use software packages if the users of the client devices do not need initial data to perform their activities immediately after the device setup is complete.

Single device tasks
► Performing administrative tasks that are applicable to a single device, such as assigning mobile components to a device, assigning rules to a device, assigning device profiles to a device, and extracting data for a device.

Multiple device tasks
► Performing administrative tasks that are applicable to multiple devices, such as assigning a mobile component to multiple devices, extracting data for multiple devices, and disabling devices.

► Deploying agents on the device to set or retrieve values of specific attributes for a client device.

► Archiving data such as logs and traces, alerts, and messages in the message store.

► Other tasks, such as delta generation, data carrier synchronization, device reassignment, and periodic tasks.

To manage all of these scenarios the administration and monitoring is divided into set of services as shown in Figure 3.5. The administration and operations set of services help in maintaining configuration information used in initial rollout and subsequent management of mobile deployment. The upgrade and deployment set of services centrally manage deployment of mobile applications and mobile devices and upgrade the landscape to a higher version. These services are designed for mass operations to reduce the TCO. These services and associated processes for managing the lifecycle of the mobile application are covered in Chapter 6, *Mobile Application Lifecycle Management*.

3.3 Summary

In this chapter, we presented the challenges of mobile platforms and the key capabilities of the DOE that are required to overcome them. The main design goal of the DOE is the ability to mobilize business processes with a minimized total cost of development by providing a model-driven design time and with a minimized TCO by providing the functionalities of the SAP NetWeaver Mobile Administrator along with a fast and scalable design for data consolidation and data distribution.

In Chapter 4, we will describe in detail the capabilities of the DOE design time.

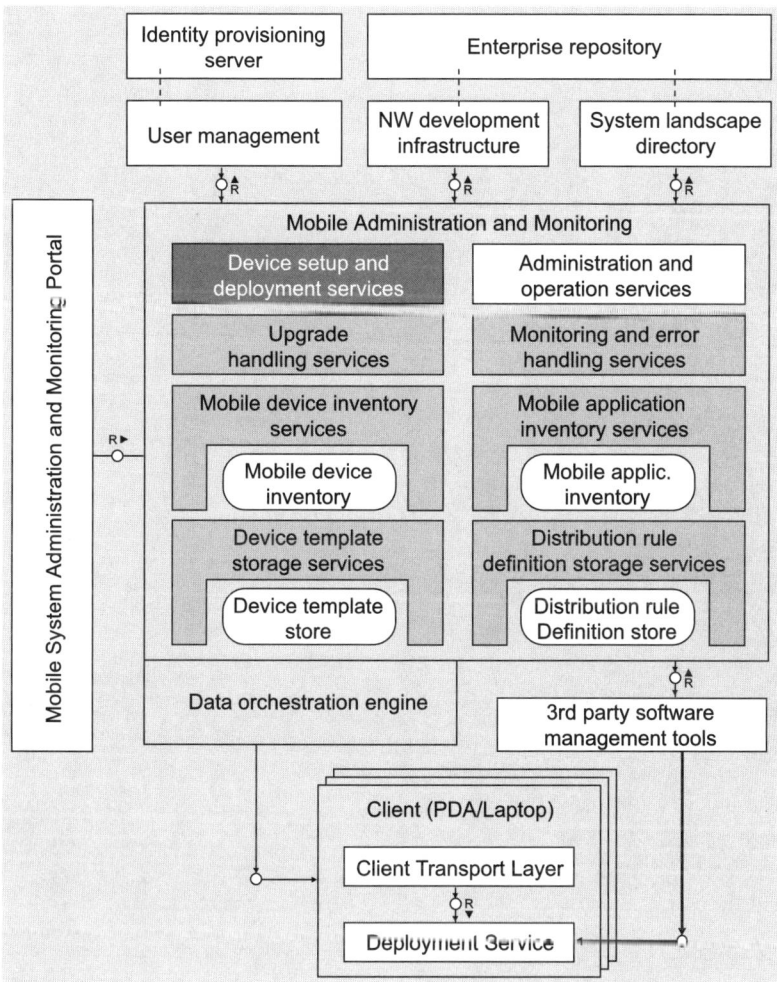

Figure 3.5 Overview of NetWeaver Mobile Administrator Capabilities

This chapter explains the concepts around the meta models and the design time tools of the Data Orchestration Engine (DOE).

4 Data Orchestration Design Time

Development of mobile applications using SAP NetWeaver Mobile 7.1 starts with model definitions at the DOE. These models describe the data that are exchanged between the backend system, the DOE, and mobile devices. Also, models in the DOE describe the subscriptions for the mobile devices based on which data will be filtered before distributing to the device. This chapter describes the concepts and details behind the modeling of DOE design time objects.

4.1 DOE Design Time Conceptual Overview

The DOE design time, also called the Data Orchestration Workbench, provides the tools for modeling the content of the DOE. Content that is developed using the Data Orchestration Workbench forms metadata, which are executed at runtime. Let's briefly recap the main concepts of the DOE.

4.1.1 A Brief Recap of the DOE

A mobile system landscape consists of one or more backend systems, which are the source or target of the business-relevant data, and many mobile devices, which exchange information based on messages with the backend system. The message exchange is managed by the DOE. The mobile device users can personalize the data, and based on their preferences, data are replicated to the devices. For instance, the user using the mobile device Device1 could have the preference "I want sales orders by region LA". The DOE, which is always connected to the backend systems, consolidates the data from the backend systems and does the data distribution based on the con-

Message-oriented middleware (MOM)

figured preferences. The DOE is a Message-Oriented Middleware (MOM) that facilitates the communication between the backend systems and the various mobile devices. Figure 4.1 depicts the high-level architecture of the DOE.

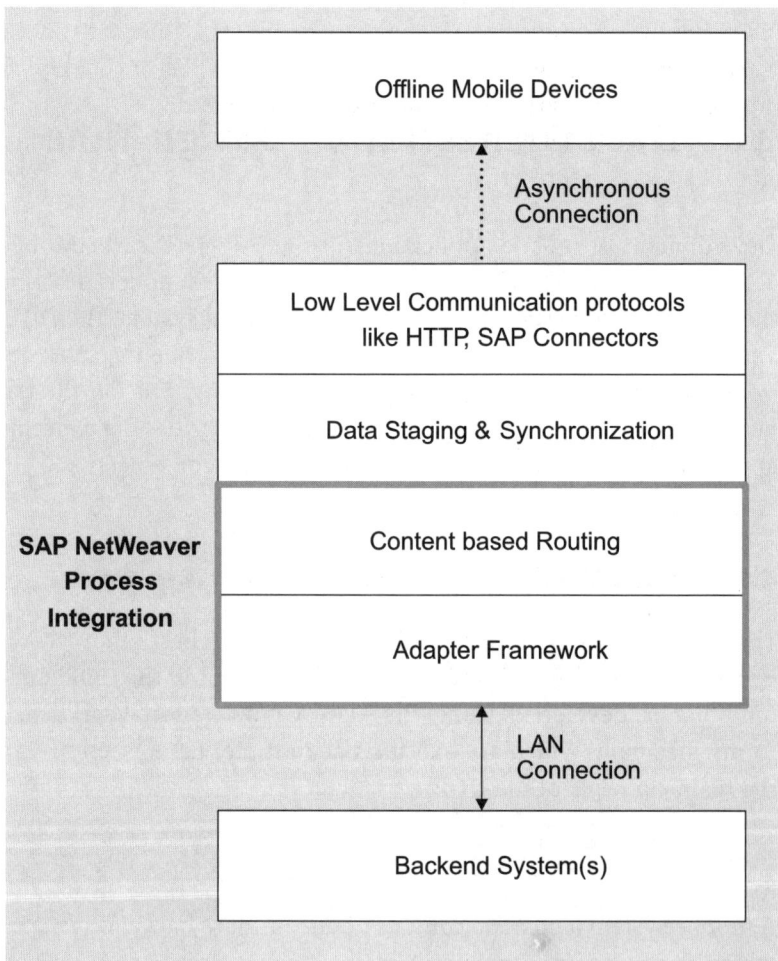

Figure 4.1 Middleware Infrastructure Necessary to Enable Occasionally Connected Mobile Devices

To enable this data exchange between backend systems, the DOE, and mobile devices, some sets of modeling concepts or meta models are important to understand. Let us briefly look at the meta model concepts of the DOE.

4.1.2 Meta Model Overview

Application data flow across the backend systems, the DOE, and the mobile devices as messages. The messages that are exchanged between the DOE, the backend systems, and the mobile devices have to be interpreted by all of the three components. That means the DOE requires a schema that defines the content of the message that corresponds to a business object. The messages that are pushed or pulled in the DOE are staged and distributed to the receivers, which is also part of the DOE's core functionality. To achieve this functionality, two basic representations are needed:

- Representation of a business object, which can be staged in the mobile middleware. This representation is called a *data object*.
- Representation of the distribution model, which forms the basis for the definition of distribution rules such as "Sales order by Region LA".

The representation of the business objects, which are required by the mobile application, and the appropriate distribution model has to be provided by the owners of the business objects (i.e., by the applications or for customer-specific objects by the customer). The DOE provides tools to import the information into the DOE server. An easy setup routine generates the metadata and services from the incoming data so that after some initial customizing by the applications, the DOE can handle the new data objects.

Messages as Instances of Data Objects

Core services in the DOE consume the messages, which are instances of data objects. The schema defined for the data objects could be different from their counterparts in the backend system (the business objects) and the client application, so the messages need to be transformed during the exchange. Because the number of mobile devices might be huge, it is recommended that you keep the schema definition close to the mobile client to reduce the mapping overhead.

Message Subscription

The messages, which are stored in the DOE message store, are distributed to the devices based on preferences of the mobile user.

Message transformation

4 | Data Orchestration Design Time

These preferences are called subscriptions. The subscriptions specify the messages in which a specific device is interested.

Dependencies Between Messages

Typically, dependencies exist across various business objects in an application. For instance, the business object Sales Order has a reference to the business object Product in its schema. This dependency is not represented by the individual data object definition itself but has to be captured separately. Since the user of the mobile device is interested not only in the individual object but also its dependent object, the DOE provides a way to publish data objects and their dependencies as an entity called a *distribution model*.

Criteria Fields for Message Subscription

Data distribution model

The mobile device users have additional preferences such as "Sales Order by Region LA." In this example, *Region* is nothing but a field in the Sales Order data object. These fields are called *criteria fields*. By defining the appropriate criteria fields (the publishing part) and the values for those criteria fields that the individual mobile device is interested in (the subscription part), the DOE can calculate the receiving device for a specific message. Therefore, it is possible to identify the criteria fields of various data objects in the distribution model. Based on the wrapper information on the Publication object and a device rule such as "Sales Order by Region LA," data distribution is performed by the DOE. To ensure a smooth message flow, the following information needs to be captured:

SyncBO
- The schema of the data objects that represents the business object in the backend system. The Data Orchestration Workbench supports the modeling of the data object schema but also supports the import of schemas from other sources, such as the Synchronization Business Object (SyncBO) definition file. SyncBOs were the message schema used in previous versions of SAP NetWeaver.

- Criteria field identification for the given data objects. The identification of the criteria fields is the basis for the definition of the distribution rules.

- Relationships between the data objects. These relationships ensure the semantic integrity of the messages that are exchanged between the mobile devices and the backend systems.

This information is captured and stored as metadata required by the DOE. Once the data object is activated, the following objects are generated:

- The required database tables for data staging.
- The message structure required by the runtime.
- The core services (key mapping service, data staging service, rejection service, replication and realignment service, inbound and outbound handlers). They are explained in the later sections of this chapter.
- The default flow definition. This is explained in detail in later sections of this chapter.

The generated flow definition can be modified, and custom services can be plugged into the flow.

Design Time Tools for Creating a Mobile Application

To create a mobile application, the Data Orchestration Workbench provides the following design time tools:

- **Data object tool**
  Used to build data objects or to import them from other models
- **Distribution model tool**
  Used to build dependencies and to identify criteria fields
- **Flow definition tool**
  Used to modify the flow definition
- **Backend adaptertool**
  Used to provide the mapping define the semantics for consuming data from backend systems

All design time tools are accessible from a single point of entry. In the next section, we discuss the basic entity of the DOE, the data object.

4.1.3 Data Object

A data object represents a business object and makes it possible to stage data relevant for mobile applications in the DOE. It has a hierarchical structure, in which each level in the hierarchy is called a *node*. An example of a data object is shown in Figure 4.2. Every node

4 | Data Orchestration Design Time

has a schema or set of attributes linked to it. Each data object is associated with a software component and a version. Software component and version (SWCV) is a grouping entity in the DOE. Every model defined in DOE belongs to one SWCV.

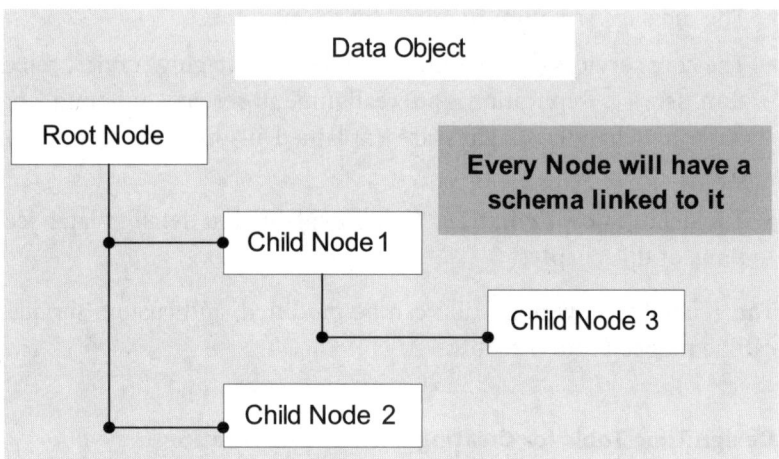

Figure 4.2 Structure of a Data Object

Flow Definition   Every data object has a flow definition attached to it. The flow definition describes how the services are executed in a sequence at runtime. The flow definition can also be edited to plug in a custom service if the scenario demands some additional functionality, such as data enrichment. Depending on their usage, data objects are divided into various categories, as follows.

> **Note**
> The flow definition varies depending on the category of the data object.

Categories of Data Objects

There are several categories of data objects:

- **Standard**
  This is the primary category. Data objects defined with this category are used to transfer data between backend systems and mobile devices.

- **Device local**

  This category is used to process data that are exclusively created by the mobile applications and stored locally on the mobile devices. Data of this category are never communicated to DOE. This data object is not relevant for DOE or backend systems.

- **Receiver generation**

  This category is used to generate logical devices. Data that are fetched from the backend system using these data objects are used to fill the device inventory. We will see this in detail in the upcoming sections of this chapter.

- **Subscription generation**

  This category is used to generate subscriptions for devices.

- **Hierarchy generation**

  This category is used to generate hierarchies to group devices and can help in efficiently managing the mobile landscape.

An example of a Purchase Order data object is shown in Figure 4.3.

Purchase Order Header	Node Details
Orderid	String
Created Date	DateTime
Created Time	Date Time...
Status	String
...	...

↓ Occurs 1 to n times

Line Items	Node Details
Line ID	String
Product Name	String
Product ID	String
Quantity	double
...	...

Figure 4.3 Example of a Typical Data Object

Let us now look at how data objects are integrated with the backend system data source or business object.

4.1.4 Backend Integration

BAPI Wrapper — Backend systems are the source and the target of data that are mobilized. Usually all of the data in the backend systems may not be relevant for the mobile scenario. Even the schema of the business objects in the backend could be very different than that of the data objects. The backend integration functionality of the DOE provides the tools for integrating data objects with the backend system. To do this, backend systems need to have BAPI wrappers. BAPI wrappers are the set of RFC-enabled function modules with certain semantics, so that the DOE can access the backend to fill the data object content or to update the backend with data object content.

Data access from and to the backend is divided into three distinct phases, which are shown in Figure 4.4.

- **Initial download**
  This is the process of setting up the DOE with the initial set of data from the backend system. These are the baseline data and contain a replica of all of the data that are relevant for the mobile scenario from the backend system. Data can either be replicated in bulk or as single instances.

- **Delta download**
  This is an operational process in which all of the changes that happened in the backend systems are replicated to DOE. These changes can either be pushed from the backend or pulled by the DOE. Push is the recommended approach, as it is the better performing and scalable solution.

- **Delta upload**
  This is the process of replicating changes from the devices to the backend. Changes that happened in the device are communicated to backend through Create or Update or Delete BAPI wrappers.

Backend adapter — To link BAPI wrappers to data objects, backend adapters need to be developed in the DOE. Every data object should have a backend adapter if it needs to communicate to the backend system. Once the data object is defined and backend integration is enabled for it, it is possible to define how the data object will be distributed to the mobile devices. This filtering of data objects is defined through a modeling concept called the distribution model. Let us briefly look at the concepts behind the distribution model.

DOE Design Time Conceptual Overview | 4.1

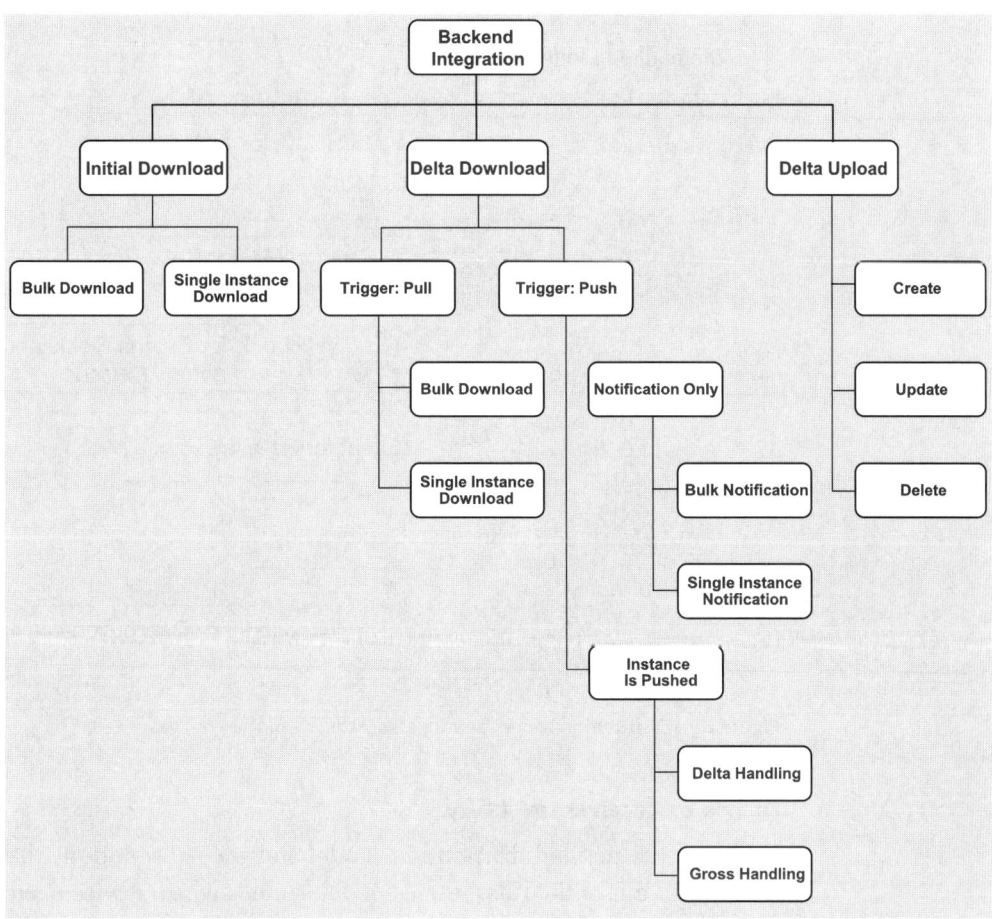

Figure 4.4 Backend Integration Semantics

4.1.5 Distribution Model

The distribution model defines how the data are distributed to various devices. The distribution model consists of a set of data objects that are distributed to devices. It has a hierarchical structure, in which each level in the hierarchy is a data object and there is only one root data object. Rules can be defined for the root data object, and these rules are evaluated to find out which device needs to get what data. Later, all of the other data object instances related to this root in the dependency tree are also distributed to the devices. Figure 4.5 shows the structure of a distribution model.

4 | Data Orchestration Design Time

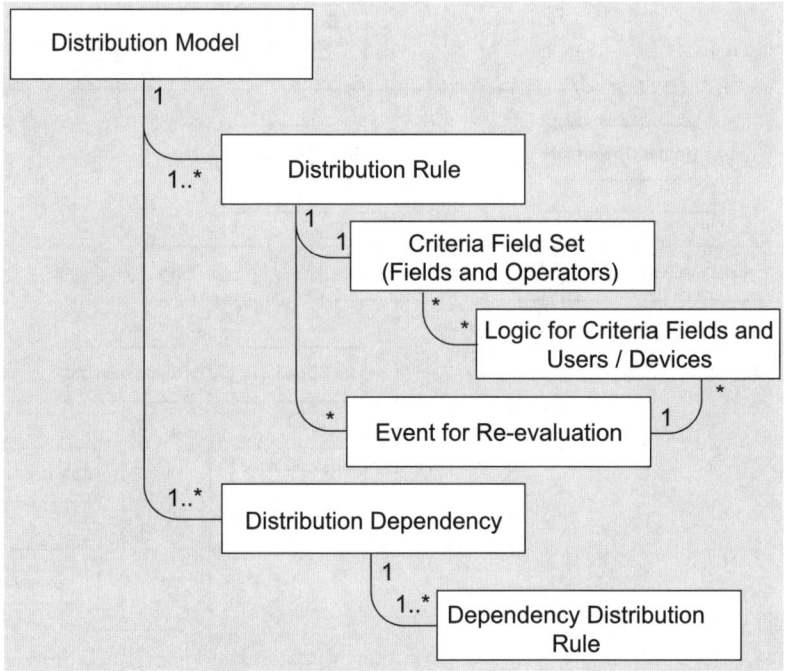

Figure 4.5 Distribution Model and Related Artifacts of the NetWeaver DOE

Device or Receiver Inventory

Based on the defined distribution model and the subscriptions that are created out of the rules, the DOE determines which device needs to get what data.

Receiver meta model (RMM)

This means the DOE also has a receiver inventory in which the definitions of all of the devices are stored. These definitions are referred to as logical devices, as they are simply identifications of the target. These logical devices have a set of attributes, which can contain values for them (e.g., Sales_order.header.region = Device.region). This is a simple rule, which says that the sales order should be distributed to the devices where the region field of the sales order matches the region attribute of the device. It should be clear now that the set of attributes that is required for achieving a particular scenario can vary from scenario to scenario. Therefore, this attribute maintenance is made customizable in a way that, depending on the scenario, inventory can be enriched with more attributes. This customization is achieved through the receiver meta model (RMM). As the number of

DOE Design Time Conceptual Overview | 4.1

devices or receivers increases, it becomes impossible to create and maintain receivers manually. In most of these scenarios, customers usually have external systems that can provide information about the receivers, for instance the backend system or an external device inventory system.

Relationship Between Device and User

An example of such a use case is the mobile device user. In most cases, the relationship between device and user is one to one, that is, one user uses only one device. The mobile device users have to be defined in a system and then need to be imported in the mobile middleware as well. In such cases, it should be possible to generate the receivers for the messages sent by the mobile middleware while the users are being downloaded or created. Of course, the relationship between users and devices may not be one to one (for instance, if the devices are shared between different users), and then such an approach to identify a device by its user may not be useful for the receiver generation. A similar example is the equipment number. Each company has an inventory management system in place to track and manage the equipment that is bought and issued to employees. This could be a full-fledged inventory management system or just a simple Microsoft Excel sheet. Thus, we can assume that each mobile device can be identified by a unique equipment number. In this case, it should be possible to generate the receivers from the mobile middleware using the equipment identification of the external inventory management system.

Receiver Generation Data Object

Looking at both of these scenarios, SAP software provides mechanisms to do the receiver generation in both of the above cases. However, these are only two scenarios, and customers can come up with more scenarios of managing devices and providing the information about the receivers for the messages sent by the DOE. Therefore, it is important to make it possible to model the receiver generation. Since the model entities in the DOE are data objects, a simple way to achieve this is the concept of *receiver generation data object*. This is a new category of data object that has its own set of flow definition, modeling possibilities, and services getting generated. If the receiver

Inventory management system

generation is modeled like a data object, it can be simply considered like the initial download from the backend to the DOE.

Distribution Rule

The DOE has to provide an easy way of administering the data distribution model. The main objectives in design have to be the following:

- Low TCO for the customer
- Self-explanatory data distribution logic
- Full flexibility regarding easy customizing and enhancement of distribution rules

Publish and subsribe

The customer's distribution logic may be very complex. To provide maximum flexibility, the subscription concept of the DOE is based on a rule-based approach. Note that this is only the outside view of the publish and subscribe concept. The fact that the subscriptions are organized in distribution rules should not affect the internal processes of receiver determination in any way. A distribution rule makes a general statement about which devices will get which instances of a given data object. Distribution rules consist of the following:

- **Data objects**
  A main data object always underlies each distribution rule. For a given data object type, multiple distribution rules can be active at the same time. This data object is the root of the distribution model.

- **Criteria fields and operators**
  The criteria fields define the set of data object node attributes, based on which the data object can be distributed. Apart from specifying the criteria fields, the operators for these criteria fields also need to be specified. The criteria fields can be of certain data types only. For instance, Binary Large Object (Blob) fields cannot be used for distribution. The operators supported are =, NE, <, >, <=, and >=.

- **Device assignment logic**
  The device assignment logic is based on the publish and subscribe paradigm. We will discuss the device assignment logic in the next subsection.

▶ **Execution plan information**
The execution plan of a distribution rule basically defines the point in time when the distribution rule should be triggered. There are the following options:

- Manually
- By a periodical job
- Event based

4.1.6 Device Assignment Logic

The device assignment logic defines the ways in which the set of device subscriptions can be calculated. The approach to get all of the device assignments to a distribution rule is to get the device and criteria association for a particular data object via a different calculation mechanism, so that there is no need to statically provide these assignments.

The idea is to provide mechanisms that can be defined within the design time environment to reduce the efforts of the administrators. Ideally, if the distribution rules are defined appropriately, administrators would be required to only perform initial download from the backend system and activate appropriate distribution rules, and all of the device subscriptions would be automatically generated. This is one of the key features required for scalability of distribution definitions for numerous devices.

Thus, the device subscription information (i.e., device 1 should get data object A, where the field F of data object A should have a value of 1) is not required to be statically provided by the administrator, but is provided by any of the following mechanisms:

▶ **Data object association**
A specific category of data object called a subscription generator would be created that could be mapped to the Criteria fields. This type of data object supports standard types of backend integration possibilities along with specific types of backend adapters provided by default. These backend adapters would internally provide the device subscription information. We will describe the subscription generation data object in the following subsection.

- **Device attributes**

  This approach refers to the set of attributes maintained in the device inventory. Examples could be:

  - The applications deployed on the device
  - Properties of the device, especially information such as version, vendor, and device type
  - Attributes of the device as maintained in the mobile administrator
  - Attributes inherited from groups or user or role assignments) and any combinations thereof

The device assignment forms the key part of the distribution rule because, based on this, a whole set of services would be generated to calculate the device subscriptions. Any of the device assignment logic can address a single device or groups of devices or all devices. The subscription generation data object plays a key role in generating these subscriptions of mobile devices. Let us briefly look at the concept behind the subscription generation data object.

4.1.7 Subscription Generation Data Object

The subscription generation data object is a data object of a specific category created for providing device binding for a distribution rule. The basic requirement for such a type of a data object is to enable the generation of device subscriptions from an external system.

Device binding   The subscription generation data object is not distributed to any device but is used only to get the information about device subscriptions. The attributes of a subscription generation data object provide either the unique receiver identification (ID) or a set of attributes that uniquely identify a receiver or a device. Ideally, the data object node attributes are also present as attributes within the device inventory or receiver store. Apart from this, the rest of the attributes within the data object provide criteria field values. The data object node attributes can be linked to criteria fields of any distribution rule at the time of distribution rule modeling. One device subscription generation data object can be associated with a set of distribution rules.

The association captures the information about the fields that provide the device identification. This could be one field or a set of fields. The device information is stored in the device inventory. Any attribute that identifies a device is maintained in the RMM. Thus, if the device subscription generation data object provides the device subscription information, it should have fields that provide information that can uniquely identify a device in the receiver store or device inventory. Let us look at the information that can be in the device inventory:

- Device ID (the logical identifier of the device)
- User ID
- Custom attribute (e.g., equipment number)

It is possible to associate some of the attributes of the subscription generation data object node attributes to the device attributes defined in the RMM. Let us look at an example of a subscription generation data object:

- Root node
- User: linked to device attribute user
- Region: mapped to criteria field region in a Sales Order data object node
- Field3
- Field4

In this case, whenever a message comes from the backend for this data object, a subscription is generated for the device that has the corresponding user, and the criteria value is set to the Region attribute value. This subscription is automatically generated without administrator intervention.

Concepts behind the DOE modeling notions should be clear to you by now. Let's look at modeling of data objects and backend adapters in the Data Orchestration Workbench next.

4 | Data Orchestration Design Time

4.2 Modeling Data Objects and Backend Adapters

All of the objects developed in the DOE are modeled through a tool called the Data Orchestration Workbench. Following are the primary objects that are created using this tool:

- Data objects
- Backend adapters
- Distribution model with rules and dependencies

SWCV All of the objects that are modeled in this workbench are grouped under an SWCV. This is a modularization unit under which objects can be grouped. It is also possible to have derivation dependencies across SWCVs to control the visibility of the objects. In this chapter, we will see how SWCVs, data objects, and backend adapters can be created and managed using this tool. Figure 4.6 explains the general layout of the Data Orchestration Workbench. The Data Orchestration Workbench can be started using Transaction SDOE_WB.

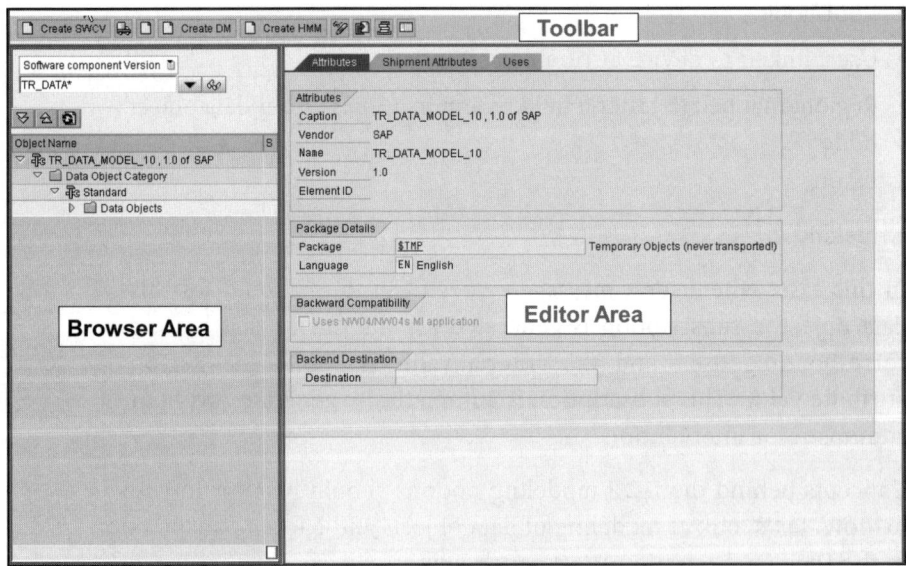

Figure 4.6 SAP NetWeaver Data Orchestration Workbench Layout

4.2.1 SWCV

SWCVs can be created using the toolbar in the Data Orchestration Workbench. All of the attributes of the SWCV can also be managed through the same tool. As explained earlier, this is the grouping entity, which helps group and modularize all of the design time objects in DOE. SWCVs have the following attributes, which are shown in Figure 4.7:

- **Name**
  Defines the name of the SWCV

- **Vendor**
  Specifies the name of the vendor who created the SWCV

- **Version**
  Indicates the version of the SWCV

- **Element ID**
  Only relevant for SWCVs imported from the System Landscape Directory (SLD)

- **Backend Destination**
  Specifies the RFC destination of the SWCV

- **Uses application based on NW04/NW04s**
  To be checked for applications on the compatibility layer

- **Data Object Package**
  Defines the package in which the objects of the SWCV are automatically saved

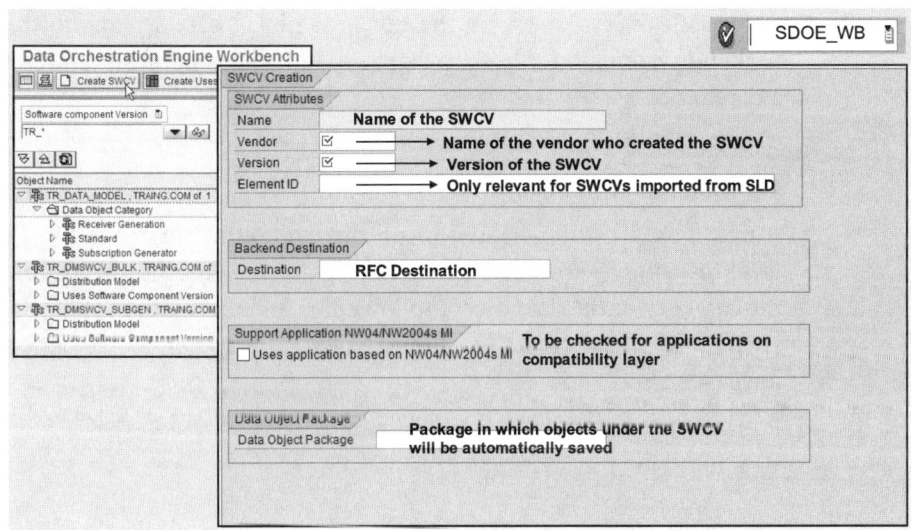

Figure 4.7 Attributes of an SWCV

4 | Data Orchestration Design Time

It is also possible to define relationships between SWCVs. By defining relationships, it is possible to reuse the objects that are defined in the parent SWCV in other SWCVs. An example is shown in Figure 4.8.

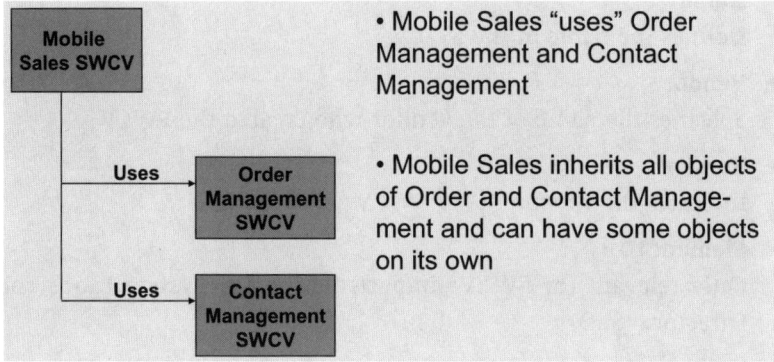

Figure 4.8 SWCV Inheritance Example

4.2.2 Handling Data Objects

Data projection

As mentioned in Section 4.1.3, data objects represent business objects that are relevant to the mobile scenario. In most of the cases, a data object is a projection of the actual business objects that exist in the backend system. This means the schema of the data objects may not match one to one with the business object data schema in the backend system. Refer back to Figure 4.2 for the general structure of a data object.

Creating and Managing Data Objects

A data object can be created using the context menu at the SWCV level or using the toolbar. Then it brings up a pop-up to determine the category of the data object followed by an editor where all of the attributes of data object can be managed. The attributes are as follows (see also Figure 4.9):

Modeling Data Objects and Backend Adapters | 4.2

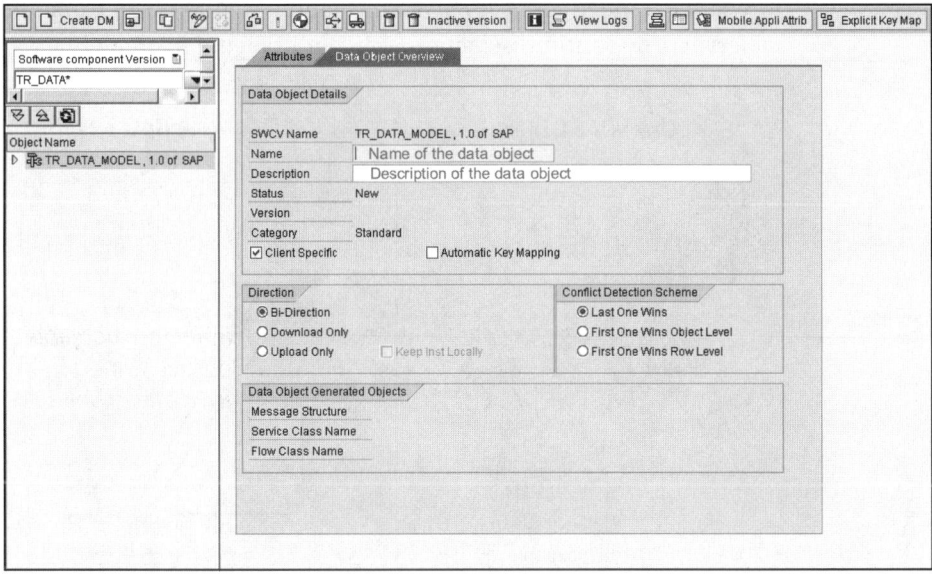

Figure 4.9 Data Object Overview in the Data Orchestration Workbench

- **Direction**

    A data object can be bidirectional to specify that messages can be exchanged in both directions, from device to backend and vice versa. It can also be unidirectional. If it is upload only, data are exchanged from device to backend only. If it is download only, data are exchanged from backend to device.

    Unidirectional, bidirectional

- **Client specific**

    On activation of data objects, runtime services and tables for storing the data are generated. If the data object is client specific, the data are stored in client-specific ABAP tables, which means different clients (MANDTs) in WebAs can connect to different backend systems for different scenarios. If it is not client specific, the data are stored client independently. This client should not be confused with the physical devices, which are also referred to as client devices.

- **Conflict detection scheme**

    It is possible to configure the conflict detection scheme. It can be *first one wins* on object level, *first one wins* on row level, or *last one wins*. *Last one wins* means there is no conflict detection at all. Whoever changes the instance last wins the conflict. If there is no conflict and if there is no business error, every change from the client

    Conflict resolution

93

4 | Data Orchestration Design Time

will be replied back by a confirmation (C) message from the server. The runtime behavior is shown in Figure 4.10.

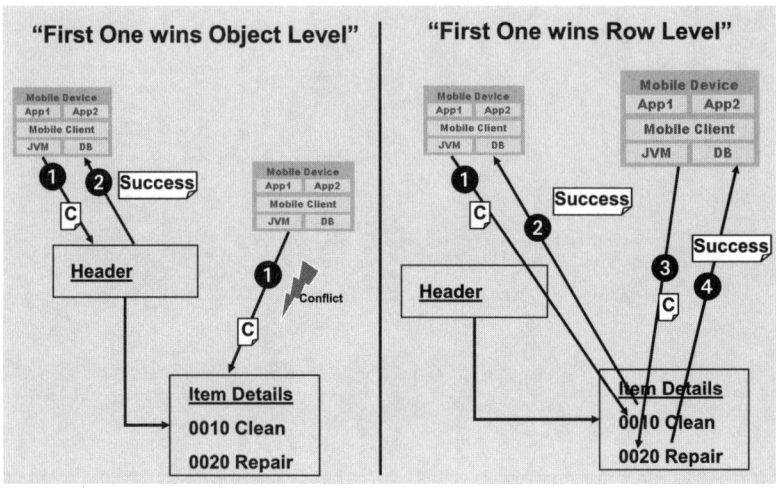

Figure 4.10 Conflict Resolution Schemes

Creating and Managing Nodes

Nodes have a database representation

Nodes can be created using the context menu at the data object level or using the toolbar menu items. There can be only one root node for a data object, but it can have multiple child nodes at different levels. A node has a set of attributes that are the fields representing the schema. Each and every node that is created as part of a data object has a corresponding database table. This table is generated on activation of the data object and stores the data coming from the backend and devices.

These tables are called the *consolidated data store*. Every node has two system fields, called Synckey and Psynckey. The Synckey represents the primary key of the table and is managed automatically by the DOE. The Psynckey is created in case of child nodes as reference to the parent node. There are also business key fields that can be declared by the developer of the model. Figure 4.11 shows the node overview screen of the data object in the Data Orchestration Workbench.

Modeling Data Objects and Backend Adapters | **4.2**

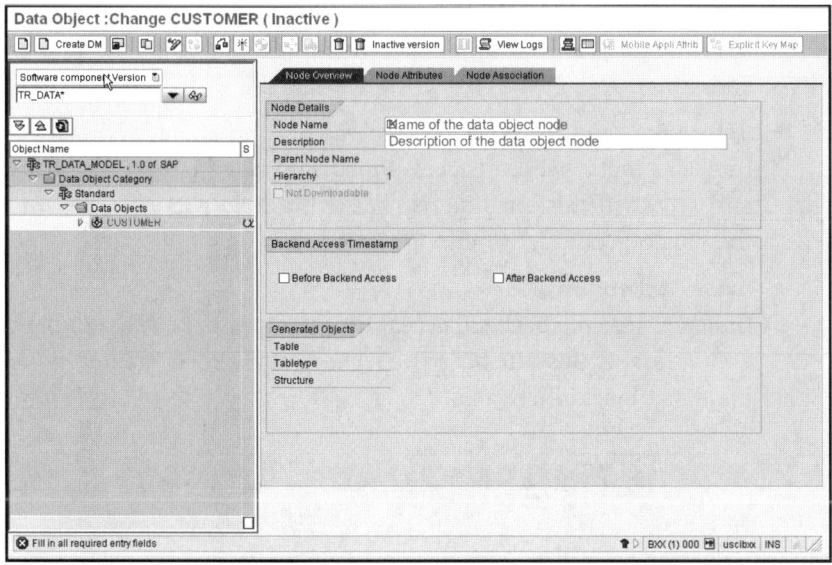

Figure 4.11 Data Object Node Overview in the Data Orchestration Workbench

The following node attributes are available (see also Figure 4.12):   **Node Attributes**

▶ **SyncKey**
DOE-specific keys are created in each node of the data object.

▶ **PsyncKey**
If the node is a child node, it needs to contain the immediate parent node's SyncKey field.

▶ **Backend Field**
Specifies that this field corresponds to a field in the backend system.

▶ **Backend Key Field**
Specifies that this field corresponds to a key field in the backend system.

▶ **Text Memo (CLOB)**
Specifies that this field corresponds to a field in the backend system that contains a large amount of text data.

▶ **Binary Memo (BLOB)**
Specifies that this field corresponds to a field in the backend system that contains binary data. This binary data can be images, manuals, or multimedia files, which can be downloaded or uploaded from the client or backend.

4 | Data Orchestration Design Time

- **Group Field**
  Specifies the association of two or more fields (e.g., for amount and units).

- **Before Backend Access**
  Indicates that a backend access timestamp is to be set before backend access. If this attribute is checked, a field gets created when the data object is activated.

- **After Backend Access**
  Indicates that the backend access timestamp is to be set after backend access. If this attribute is checked, a field gets created when the data object is activated.

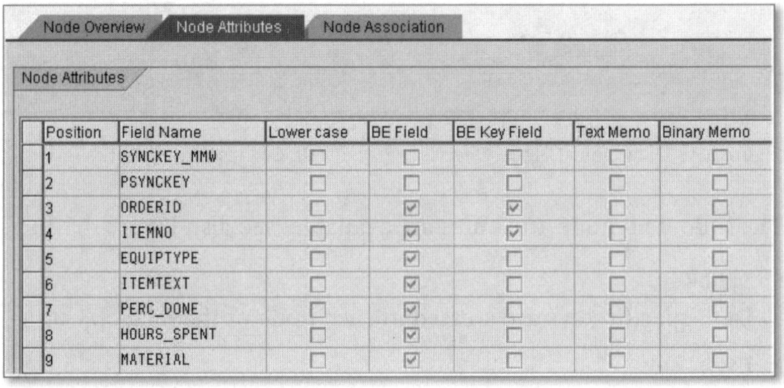

Position	Field Name	Lower case	BE Field	BE Key Field	Text Memo	Binary Memo
1	SYNCKEY_MMW	☐	☐	☐	☐	☐
2	PSYNCKEY	☐	☐	☐	☐	☐
3	ORDERID	☐	☑	☑	☐	☐
4	ITEMNO	☐	☑	☑	☐	☐
5	EQUIPTYPE	☐	☑	☐	☐	☐
6	ITEMTEXT	☐	☑	☐	☐	☐
7	PERC_DONE	☐	☑	☐	☐	☐
8	HOURS_SPENT	☐	☑	☐	☐	☐
9	MATERIAL	☐	☑	☐	☐	☐

Figure 4.12 Node Attributes Definition View

Mobile Application Attributes

Data objects that are defined in the DOE are used for creating mobile applications as well. In this case some attributes that would be interesting for mobile applications are running on the mobile devices. These attributes are also captured in the Data Orchestration Workbench and are as follows (see also Figure 4.13):

- **Lifecycle flags for the node**
  These flags indicate what operations are possible at the node level, for instance, whether the rows in this node can be created, updated, or deleted. NetWeaver Developer Studio, which is used for developing mobile applications, consumes these flags and allows only the relevant operations to be enabled by the developer.

▶ **Indices on the client**

Like the DOE, the mobile application generates one table per node. Data in these tables are queried during runtime, and it is possible to define custom queries by the mobile application developer. In this case there is a need for defining indices on the locally generated table to optimize the performance. Indices at the field level can be defined using the flag, and you can also provide a name for the index. It is possible to define clustered indices if the underlying database running on the client supports them.

▶ **Lifecycle flags for the node attributes**

It is also possible to control the operations at the node attribute level. Data that are stored in the mobile device can be in two possible states: the global state if it is in sync with the server or the local state if the data are locally modified. By choosing the flag NE-GState, it is possible to specify that the attribute is not modifiable in the global state. By choosing the flag NE-LState, it is possible to specify that the attribute is not modifiable in the local state. It is also possible to mark some attributes as mandatory by selecting the Required flag.

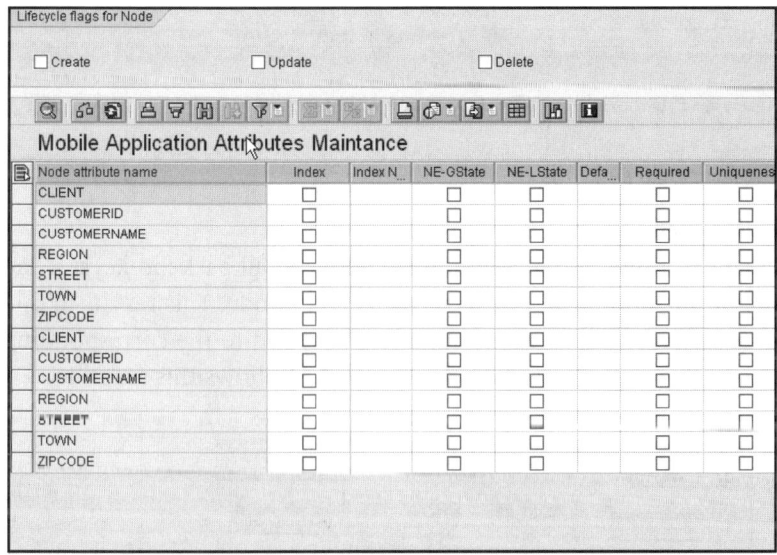

Figure 4.13 Mobile Application Specific Attributes Maintanence for the Data Object

A data object can have reference to other data objects. For instance, the Order data object may refer to the Product data object. These ref-

Node Association

erences are captured as associations at node level. This is used to maintain the backend- and SyncKey-foreign key relationship at node level. An association wizard helps create these associations. See also Figure 4.14 for the corresponding screen in the Data Orchestration Workbench.

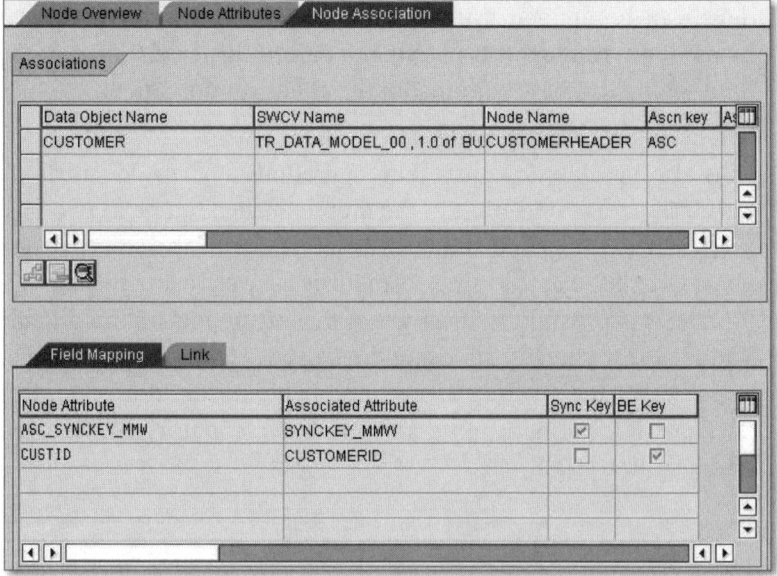

Figure 4.14 Data Object Node Association Maintanence

There are three kinds of association:

- **Complete association**
  This is a one to one relationship between all backend keys of the associated node and fields of the current node. This results in one SyncKey of the current node being mapped to the corresponding SyncKey in the foreign node. Figure 4.15 shows this scenario.

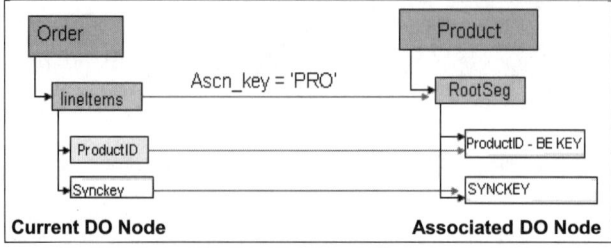

Figure 4.15 Example of a Complete Association

▶ **Partial association**

One data object node row can point to multiple target data object node rows. This means only the subset of the backend keys of the target node is available in the referring node. In this case it is not possible to find exactly one row per association; it will result in multiple rows. As a consequence, associated SyncKeys are to be maintained in a separate table. This table is generated and managed by the DOE. This generated node is called a *shadow node*, and this node is not visible for application development. See Figure 4.16 for an example of a partial association.

Support of multiple languages

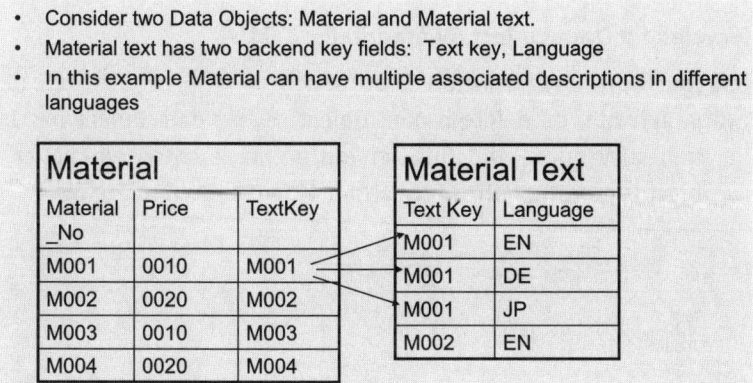

Figure 4.16 Example of a Partial Association

▶ **Extract association**

An extract association is used when some field values need to be replaced with some other local values dependent on device attributes. It has the following three parts:

▶ **Field association**

To map backend keys between associated nodes to uniquely identify the instance.

▶ **Replacement association**

To pick up the value to be replaced in the current node from the associated node field.

▶ **Defining an extract rule**

This is necessary to find out what device attribute the value needs to be picked based on which field will be actually replaced. An extract rule is defined as part of the distribution model. See Figure 4.17 for an example of an extract association.

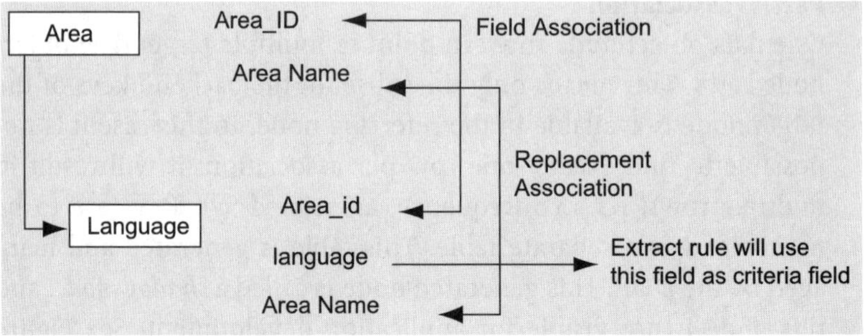

4 | Data Orchestration Design Time

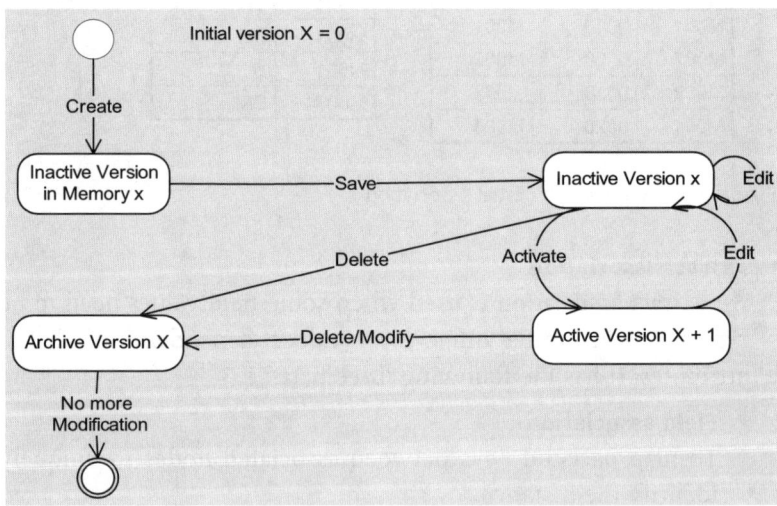

Figure 4.17 Example of an Extract Association

Lifecycle of a Data Object (Metadata)

Versioning of data objects

Using the Data Orchestration Workbench, it is possible to create, modify, activate, or delete a data object. Every data object has its own internal version, and this version is incremented whenever a data object is modified after activation. This is shown in Figure 4.18.

Figure 4.18 Lifecycle of a Data Object

On activation of the data objects, runtime services and tables are generated. It is also possible to only generate a data object in case the data object is already active. Generation of a data object does not increment the internal version of the metadata. Figure 4.19 shows the **Activate** button in the Data Orchestration Workbench.

Modeling Data Objects and Backend Adapters | 4.2

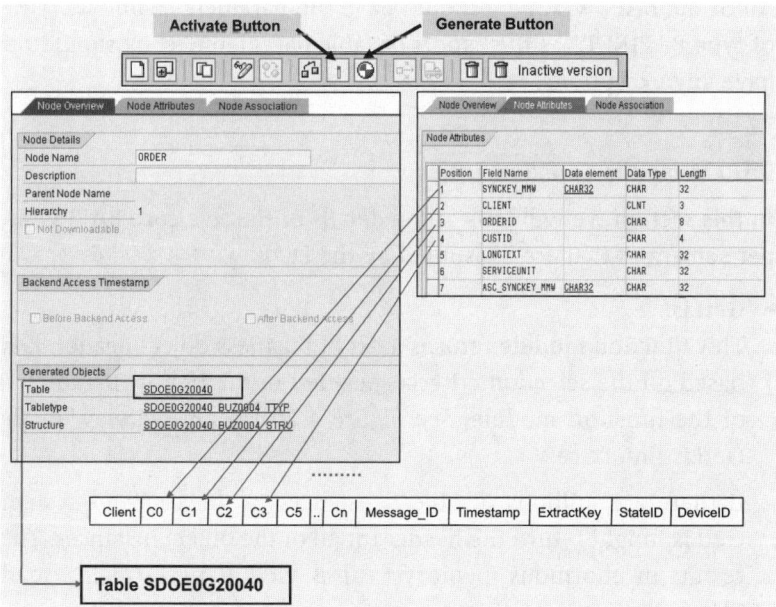

Figure 4.19 Activation of a Data Object

4.2.3 Backend Adapters

Backend systems are the sources of the data that are consumed by mobile devices and also validate the data that are created or modified by mobile devices. Data are exchanged in the form of data objects between the DOE and the devices. Backend adapters help integrate backend data with the data objects. Backend adapters connect data objects to the backend through a set of services. Currently RFC function modules are supported natively, and web services can also be called using these RFC function modules as proxies. These RFC function modules follow certain semantics for retrieving and updating data in the backend system. They are called BAPI wrappers. Five core semantics are important for consuming and updating data in the backend system for every data object. These semantics are:

Integration with the backend system

- GetList
- GetDetails
- Create
- Modify
- Delete

All of the BAPI wrappers should have the parameter name RETURN of type BAPIRET2 as the export or table parameter. They should not have any exceptions.

BAPI Wrapper Core Semantics

In this section we will look at the details of the five core BAPI wrapper semantics that are consumed by the DOE:

- **GetList**
  This function module returns a list of business object header data, based on the selection criteria specified in the Import parameters of the function module. See Figure 4.20 for an overview of the GetList interface.

  Performance Considerations — If there are millions of object instances in the backend system, GetList might return the header for all of the object instances. This results in enormous memory load as well as performance load. The DOE has to wait until GetList returns. To improve this situation, it would be possible to model GetList as bulk enabled. In this case, the backend system returns only sets of header items controlled through the backend package size configuration. Instead of one GetList call, the DOE makes multiple GetList calls to get all of the header keys and parallelizes the fetching of details while calling GetList.

- **GetDetail**
  This function module returns one header data as an Export parameter out of the header data list based on the object key(s) specified in the Import parameters. It also returns one or more lists of item entries associated with the header data. See Figure 4.21 for an overview of the GetDetail interface.

  Performance Considerations — GetDetail BAPI wrappers return one instance by taking one set of keys as input. If there are millions of object, it will result in millions of calls to the backend system. Therefore, there is a provision to support GetBulkDetail instead of GetDetail. GetBulkDetail returns a set of business object instances from the backend system by taking multiple keys as input. This package size can be controlled through configuration. Thus, if there are one million instances in the backend, and if the package size is configured to 200, it will result in 5,000 calls to the backend system instead of 1 million calls.

4.2 | Modeling Data Objects and Backend Adapters

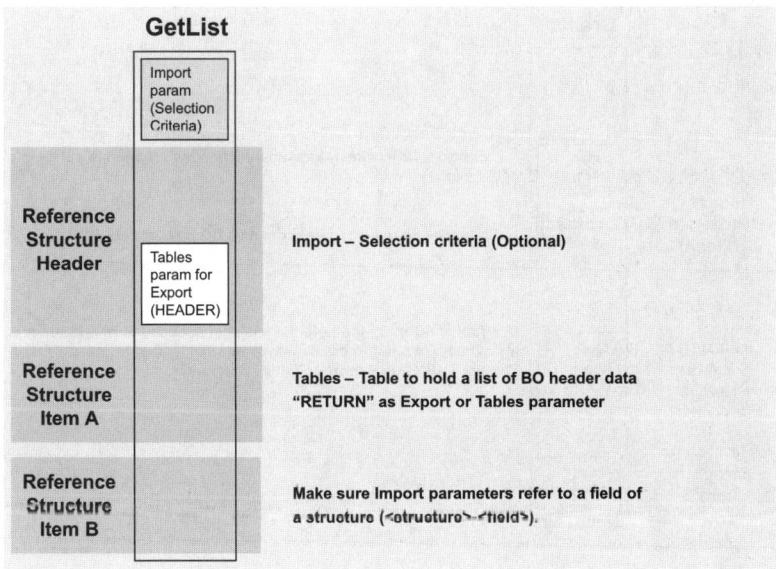

Figure 4.20 BAPI Wrapper Core Semantics for GetList

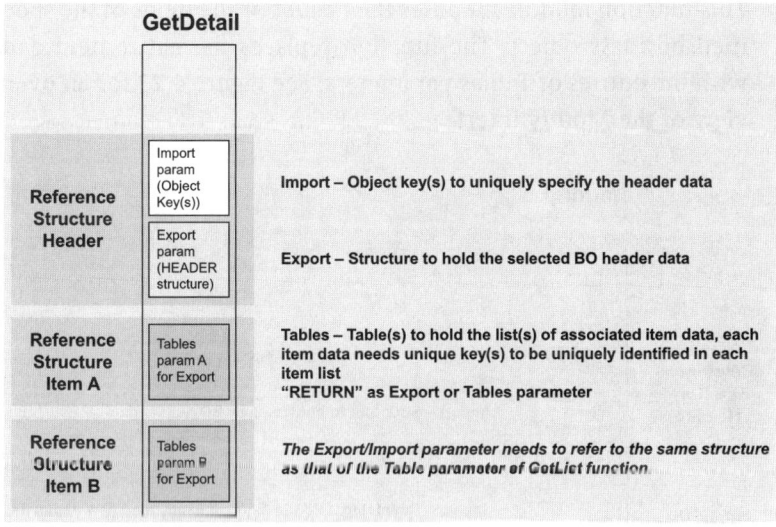

Figure 4.21 BAPI Wrapper Core Semantics for GetDetail

▶ **Create**

This function module creates a single business object and returns object key(s). See Figure 4.22 for an overview of the Create interface.

103

4 | Data Orchestration Design Time

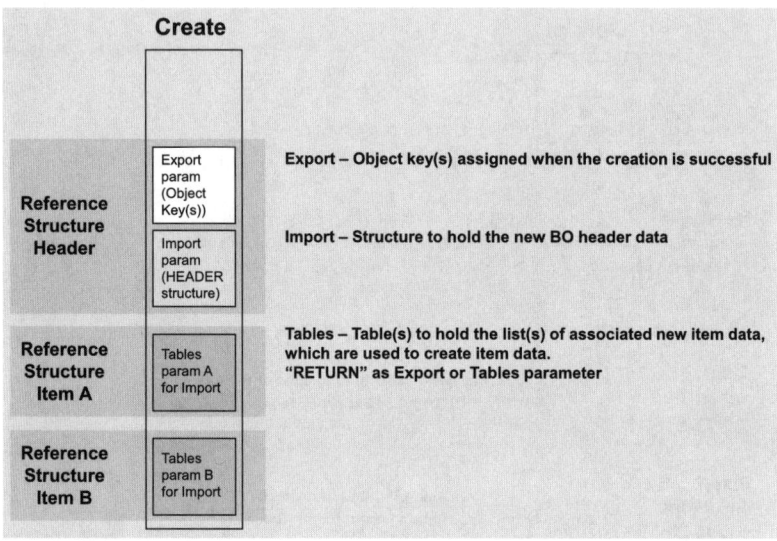

Figure 4.22 BAPI Wrapper Core Semantics for Create

▶ **Modify**

This function module modifies the header or the items of the specified business object. The function replaces the entire item data with the entries of Tables parameters. See Figure 4.23 for an overview of the Modify interface.

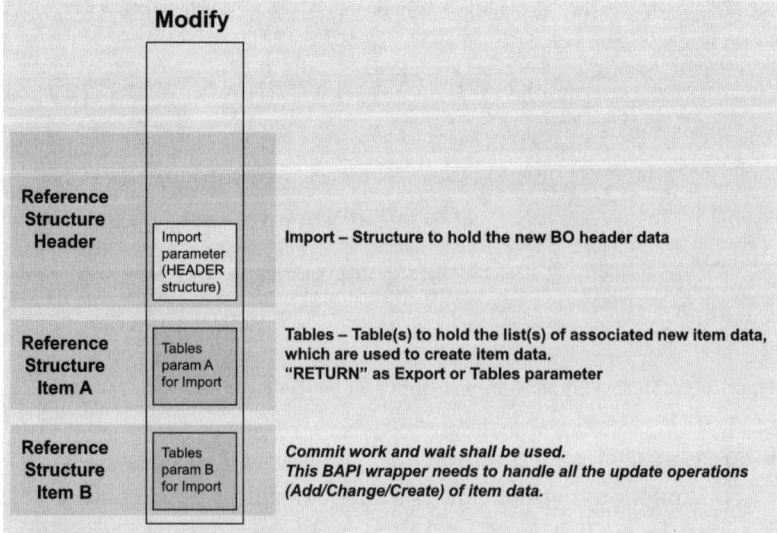

Figure 4.23 BAPI Wrapper Core Semantics for Modify

▶ **Delete**
This function module deletes the specified business object instance, including the items. The importing parameter of this function module takes the object keys.

Creating and Managing Backend Adapters

Backend adapters can be created for a data object using the context menu at the data object level. It is possible to define multiple backend adapters for the same data object, but only one backend adapter can be active at runtime for the given data object and given client (MANDT) if the data object is client specific. Every backend adapter has the following mandatory header attributes:

▶ **Adapter Name**
The name of the backend adapter.

▶ **Synchronization Type**
This specifies whether the data object is DOE triggered (pull) or backend triggered (push). Push is recommended over pull. Details of this type will be explained in the next section

▶ **Backend BO Name**
This has to be provided if the adapter is backend triggered.

▶ **Version**
This is the internal version managed by the tool to support modifications.

▶ **BAPI Wrappers**
This is the set of BAPI wrappers provided in backend system for accessing data.

Only one active backend adapter per data object

Figure 4.24 shows the corresponding screen of the Data Orchestration Workbench.

A mapping tool is provided in the backend adapter editor to map the fields of the nodes to the fields of the BAPI wrapper parameter structure. Based on this mapping, the data object is mapped to the BAPI wrapper structure before updating the changes to the backend. In the same way, return parameters of the BAPI wrapper are mapped to the data object structure during runtime.

Mapping Tool

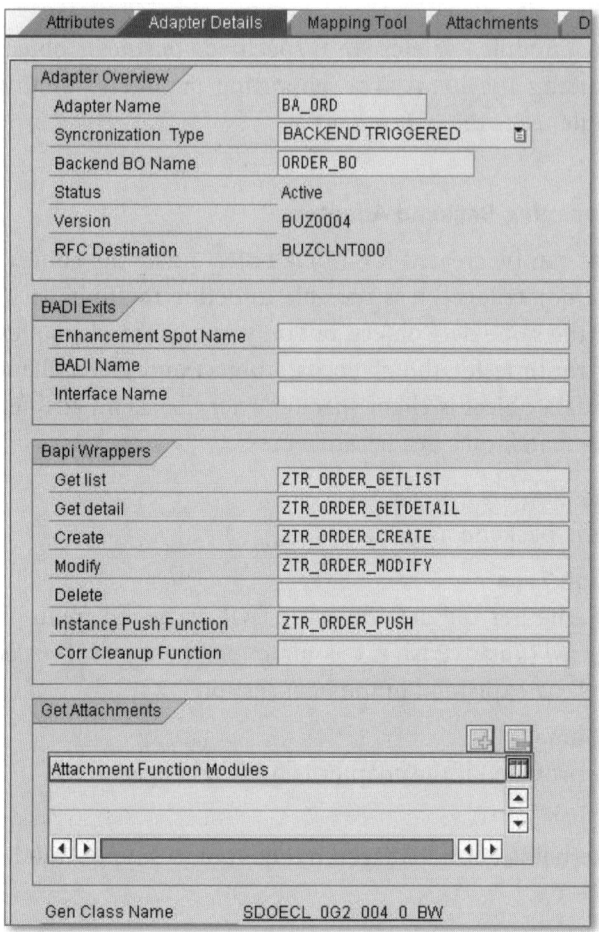

Figure 4.24 Backend Adapter Details Overview

If there is a need for complex mapping, then instead of using this field-to-field mapping tool, a Business Add-In (BAdI) exit can be implemented, which can contain complex logic for mapping. At runtime, the DOE calls this BAdI instead of the generated mapping to map the structure. Figure 4.25 shows the mapping screen in the DOE.

In the following subsection, we will describe the backend triggered backend adapter.

Modeling Data Objects and Backend Adapters | 4.2

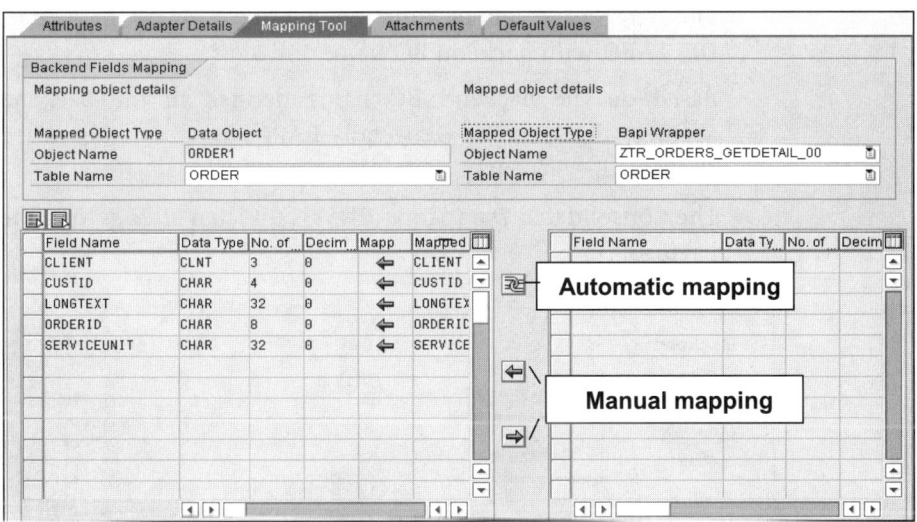

Figure 4.25 Definition of Mappings Between the Data Object and the BAPI Wrapper Structures

Backend-Triggered Backend Adapter

A backend-triggered backend adapter can also be called a *push adapter*. In this scenario, the backend pushes the changes to the DOE. Otherwise, the adapter is a *pull adapter*, and the DOE has to download the complete set of instances every time and then compare them to find out the deltas. Thus, the pull approach is extremely costly, so it is recommended to use push adapters. There are two push categories:

Push adapter vs. pull adapter

- **Key push**
  In this approach, keys of the modified object instances are pushed by the backend system to the DOE, and then the DOE calls getDetail or getBulkDetails to fetch the complete payload. Keys can be pushed to the DOE either through the standard intermediate document (IDoc) interface or through RFC function modules. The complete runtime process using IDoc is explained in Figure 4.26.

  IDoc

  The steps involved in a key push using IDocs are listed below:

  - IDocs of message type MEREP_DELTABO (basic type: MEREP_DELTABO01) are received by the ALE framework of the DOE server.

4 | Data Orchestration Design Time

- This triggers a call of function module SMMW_BE_CALL_DELTABO with backend BO name and keys.
- Based on the backend BO name defined in the backend adapter, the relevant GetDetails BAPI wrapper is identified and called.
- The Consolidated Data Store (CDS) is updated after getting the payload.

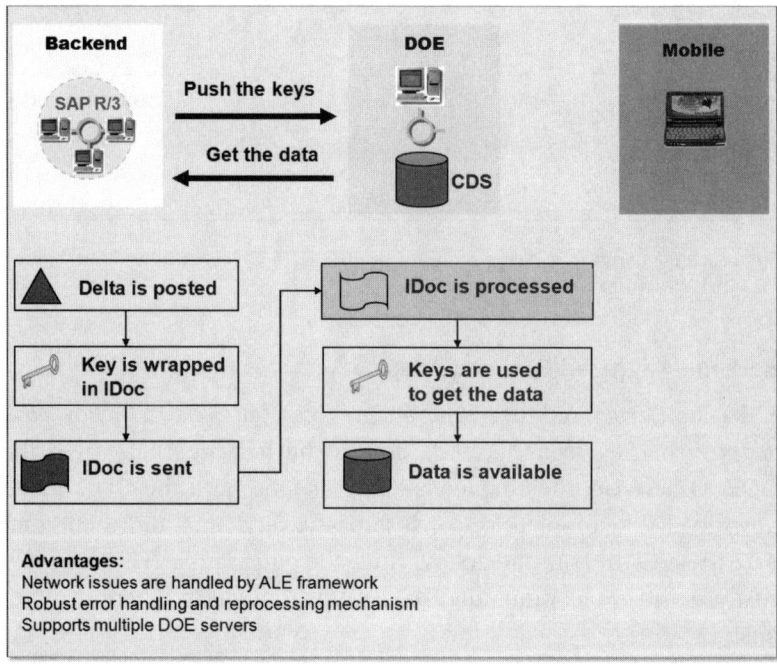

Figure 4.26 Backend Integration Based on Key Push Followed by Data Fetch Triggered by DOE

- **Instance push**
  In this approach, a complete payload is pushed by the backend system, so there is no need for the DOE to call GetDetail. The complete payload can be pushed using an RFC-enabled function module, which is generated in the DOE. The name of this function module is provided by the developer of the backend adapter. See Figure 4.27 for the corresponding screen of the DOE.

Modeling Data Objects and Backend Adapters | 4.2

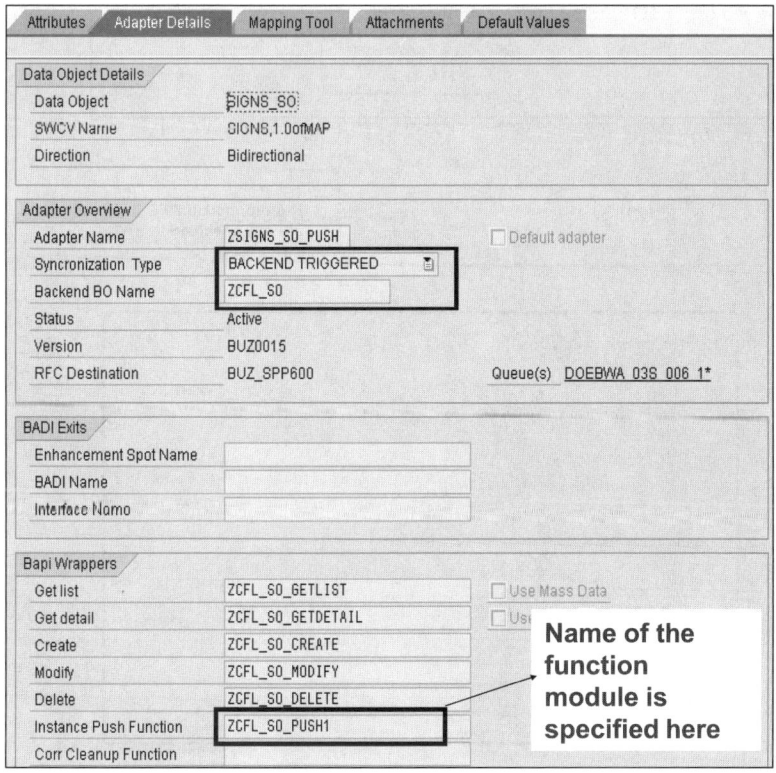

Figure 4.27 Backend Integration via Complete Instance Push to DOE

Importing BAPI Wrappers

The DOE automates the process of creating a data object and its backend adapter if the BAPI wrappers are already known and available in the backend system. Figure 4.28 shows what the wizard in the DOE looks like.

Import via wizards

The direction of the data object is automatically determined based on the set of BAPI wrappers that are provided. The DOE will be able to detect the backend keys of the root if GetDetail contains the key field names as the importing parameter or if the key field names are provided in the exporting parameter of the Create BAPI wrapper.

4 | Data Orchestration Design Time

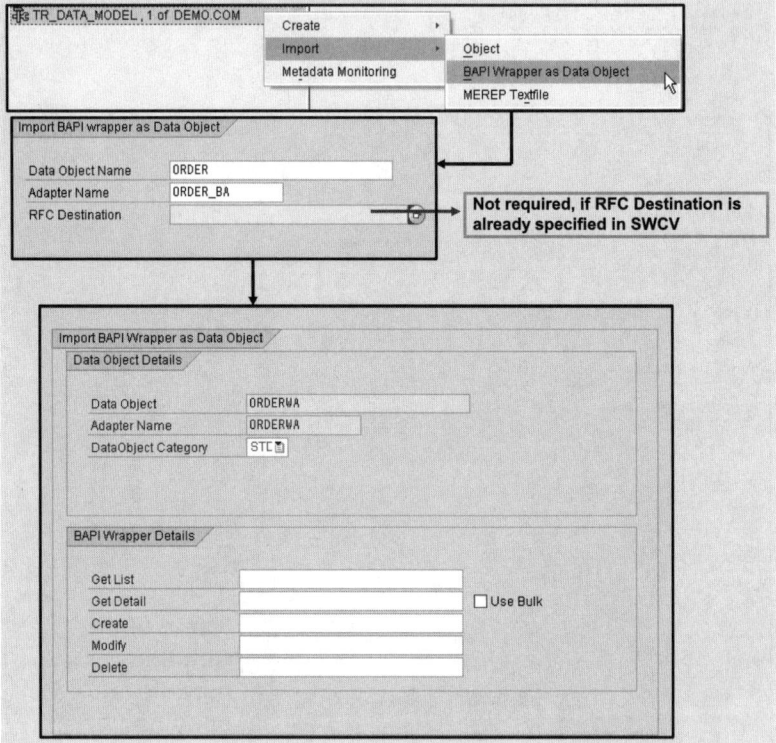

Figure 4.28 Creation of Data Object via BAPI Wrapper Import

Backend Configuration

It is possible to configure the backend adapter runtime behavior using certain parameters. These parameters can be configured in SAP NetWeaver Mobile Administrator (see Figure 4.29).

Important parameters for configurations are:

- BACKEND_DESTINATION
  Specify the RFC destination for the backend. Mandatory.
- BACKEND_MAX_PACKAGE_SIZE
  Number of backend instances to be sent as a block. Numeric value. Not mandatory. Default: 50.

Modeling Data Objects and Backend Adapters | **4.2**

▸ BACKEND_MAX_QUEUES
Indicates the number of queues (parallel processes) to which data can be posted. Numeric value. Default: 1.

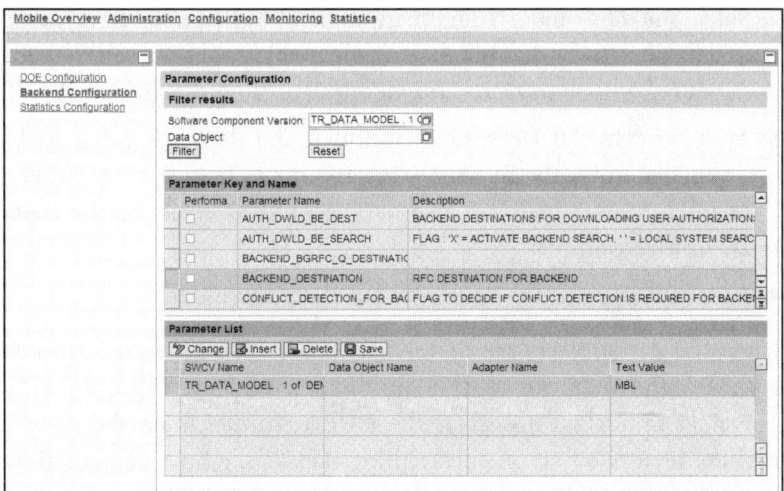

Figure 4.29 Backend Adapter Configuration Management via the SAP NetWeaver Mobile Administrator

Trigger Backend Data Load to the DOE

It is possible to trigger a data load from the backend system once the backend adapter is created and the backend destination is maintained in the configuration (see Figure 4.30).

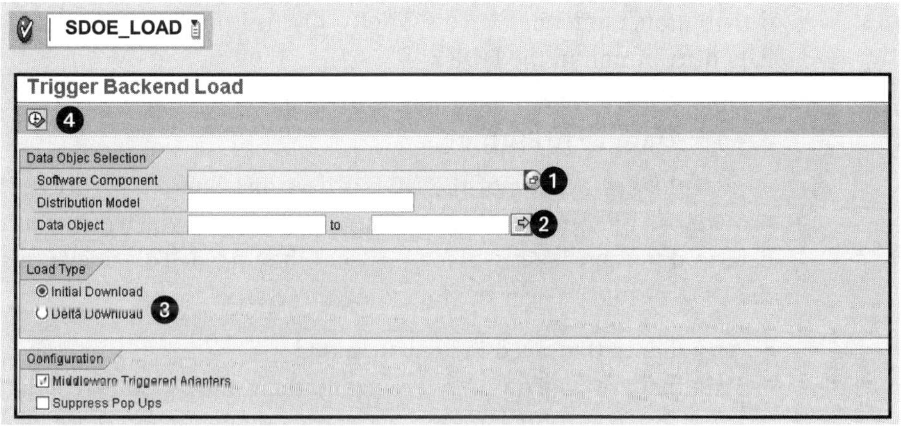

Figure 4.30 Trigerring the Backend Data Download to the DOE

111

4 | Data Orchestration Design Time

Transaction SDOE_LOAD
The data load can be triggered using the Transaction SDOE_LOAD. Use the following steps to download the data:

1. Select the SWCV from the input list.
2. Select the data object from the input list. You can also select the set of data objects for download. If the data objects are not selected, the data load will be triggered for all of the data objects in that SWCV.
3. Select the **Initial Download** option if the data are going to be downloaded for the first time. In case of a DOE-triggered backend adapter, a delta load can also be triggered by selecting the **Delta Download** option.
4. Execute the selection to trigger the data download.

Once the data objects are defined with the corresponding backend adapters, the DOE can consolidate the data and store it in the CDS. The next important aspect of the DOE is to distribute the data to mobile devices based on subscription. Let us see how data distribution can be modeled in the DOE to achieve the filtering of data to various mobile devices.

4.3 Data Distribution Modeling

Data distribution in the DOE follows the publish and subscribe paradigm. All of the data objects of the category Standard are able to be distributed to mobile devices. It is important to understand the concepts behind data distribution before getting into the details of data distribution modeling. Let us briefly discuss the concepts behind data distribution in the DOE.

4.3.1 Data Distribution

One of the key aspects of the DOE is data distribution. Figure 4.31 provides an overview of the data distribution logic, which distributes data to different devices based on what they need. To achieve this, the DOE needs to cover the following three aspects.

- **Actual data that need to be distributed**
  Data that are staged through data objects in the consolidated data store are distributed to the receivers. Modeling of these data objects and their connectivity to the backend systems was explained in the previous section.

- **Set of receivers that need to receive the data**

    The DOE has a receiver or device inventory where it stores the set of all receivers that are the consumers of data. In this inventory it stores the definitions of devices in the landscape, including all their attributes. Also, it is possible to add custom attributes depending on the scenario. For example, it is possible to add a Region attribute to the device definition template, which can then be used in creating the subscriptions. These enhancements to the device or receiver inventory can be made through a model-driven tool called the RMM Definition tool.

    RMM Definition tool

- **Subscriptions for the receivers**

    Subscriptions for the receivers can be generated through a *distribution model*. A distribution model captures both rules and dependencies based on which data are distributed to the devices. For instance, it is possible to define a rule for the sales Order data object through the region node attribute: SalesOrder.header.region = Receiver.region. Then, automatically, the subscriptions are generated for the receivers, based on the region attribute. It is also possible to make the Product data object follow Sales Order data object by defining the following dependency: SalesOrder.items.productid = Product.header.productid and SalesOrder.items.ProductSyncKey = Product.header.SyncKey

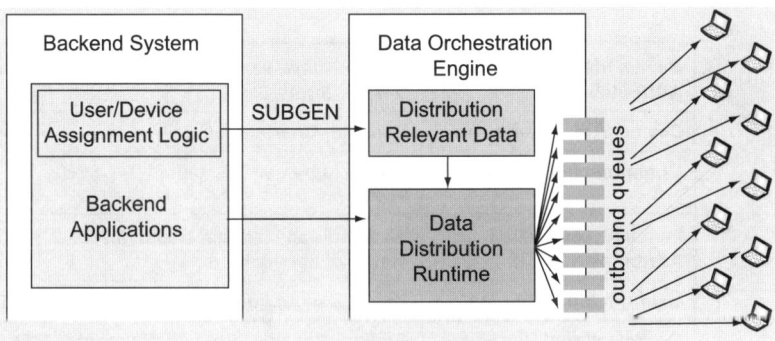

Figure 4.31 Data Distribution to Mobile Devices

4.3.2 RMM

Before getting into the details of the distribution model, it is important to understand the receiver inventory and how it can be enhanced. The RMM is a design time concept that defines the

Custom Attributes

attributes of devices on the DOE, which then can be used for managing subscriptions and managing the mobile landscape. The DOE ships an RMM called MOBILE. This RMM consists of standard attributes, which are already shipped with the DOE. It is possible to add more custom attributes depending on the scenario that needs to be handled. Attributes are divided into the following three categories:

- **Standard**
  These attributes are available as part of the DOE and are completely managed by the DOE.
- **Category**
  These attributes are defined for managing various categories of devices. They are shipped as part of the DOE and managed by the DOE.
- **Custom**
  These are the attributes added depending on the requirement of a particular scenario. Any application developer can add these attributes.

Typical Attributes in the RMM

Figure 4.32 shows the typical set of attributes in the RMM.

Standard	Device Identification Attributes	Device Name, ID, Description, Custom Search Terms, …
	Device Status Attributes	Enabled, Operational, …
	Communication Attributes	Queue to be used, Physical Device ID, Protocols, …
Category	Installed Application Attributes	Installed applications, Deployment status of applications, …
	User related Attributes	Users, Language,
	Organizational/Hierarchy Attributes	Region, Org Hierarchy Assignment
Custom	Attributes for Distribution Orchestration	Criteria Fields, e.g. Country, Region, Territory ID

Figure 4.32 Typical Attributes of a Receiver Meta Model

Currently, the DOE only supports the MOBILE RMM. Therefore, custom attributes should only be added to the MOBILE RMM. We'll look at managing custom attributes next.

Managing Custom Attributes

Figure 4.33 shows the process of adding and managing custom attributes. Custom attributes can be added to the MOBILE RMM using Transaction SDOE_RMM01 as follows:

1. Select the **MOBILE** RMM.
2. Click **Display**.
3. Click **Customize**.
4. Add a new customizing group, or if you want to use an existing customizing group, select the appropriate customizing group.
5. Add or modify the custom attributes needed for the scenario.
6. Activate or generate the MOBILE RMM by using the Activate or Generate toolbar icons.

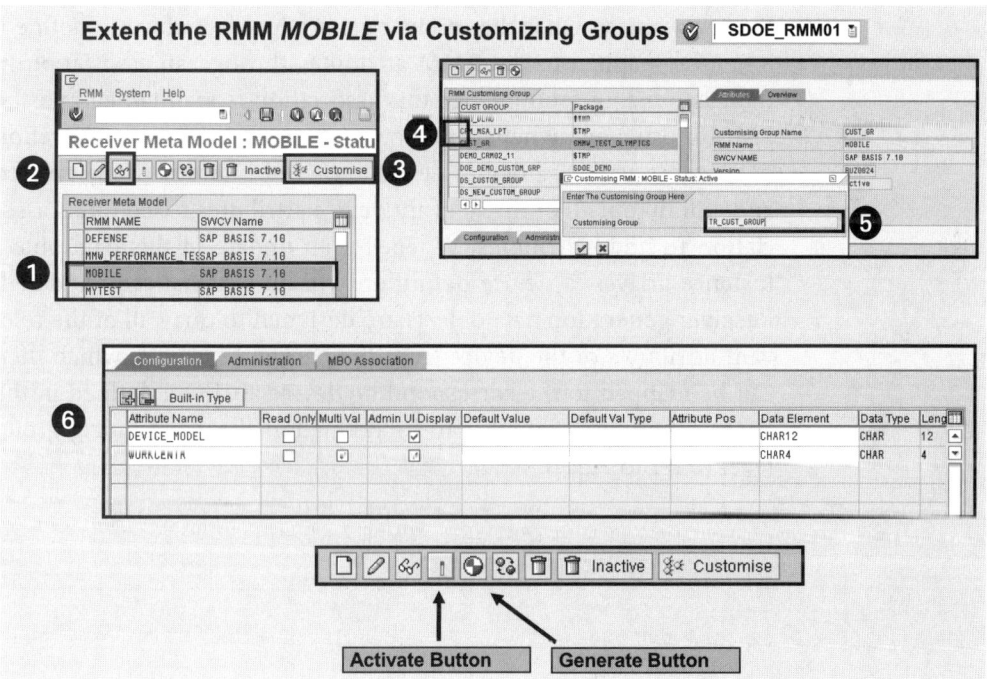

Figure 4.33 Management of Custom Attributes

4 | Data Orchestration Design Time

Receiver Generation

SAP NetWeaver Mobile Administrator

A typical mobile scenario could have thousands of devices in the field needing data. This means all of the devices should have been already defined in the inventory. These devices can be manually created in the DOE through the Mobile Administrator. Creating a device is not simply a create activity; many attributes such as name, assigned mobile components, and so on need to be managed during creation. Thus, the creation of thousands of mobile devices is a time-consuming task for an administrator. To ease the creation and the management of these devices in the device inventory, it is possible to automatically create these device definitions based on information available from the backend system. For instance, one device can be created automatically for every employee based on employee information available in the backend HR system.

This backend information can be consolidated to the DOE through a data object category called the receiver generation data object. The receiver generation data object is exactly the same as a normal data object from a definition point of view, with few restrictions. It is not possible to add more than two hierarchy levels to a receiver generation data object. Once the receiver generation data object is defined, it can be mapped to the RMM attributes through an association in the customizing group. Once this association is maintained and the RMM is activated, whenever a new instance of a receiver generation data object arrives, a device definition will be automatically created and will fill out all of the relevant device attributes based on its association to node attributes. Whenever an update of this data object instance arrives, a device definition will be automatically updated. Receiver generation data objects are designed to carry all of the relevant attributes of the device from the backend systems, which then can be mapped to the corresponding device attribute defined in the RMM. These associations can be defined at the customizing group level (refer to Figure 4.34).

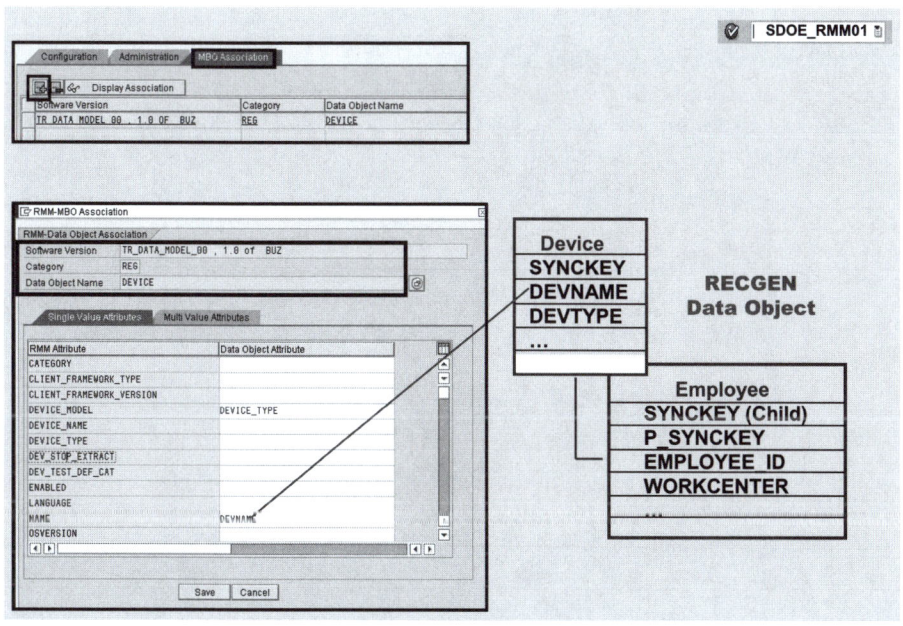

Figure 4.34 Device Attributes Defined in the RMM

4.3.3 Distribution Model

Distribution modeling is done in the Data Orchestration Workbench, which can be invoked using Transaction SDOE_WB. A distribution model contains both rules and dependencies. Every distribution model has a set of data objects, but there is only one data object in the root, and everything else follows on dependencies. Figure 4.35 depicts the structure of a distribution model.

Distribution models are created under an SWCV. An SWCV that contains at least one distribution model is called a distribution model SWCV. Figure 4.36 shows the principle of the SWCV separation, and Figure 4.37 shows the advantages of separating the data object SWCV and the distribution model SWCV.

Distribution models and SWCV

> **Note**
>
> It is not mandatory to seperate data objects and distribution layers. However, it is strongly recommended! The advantages are:
> - Modularization
> - Reusablity of data objects (including their backend integration)

4 | Data Orchestration Design Time

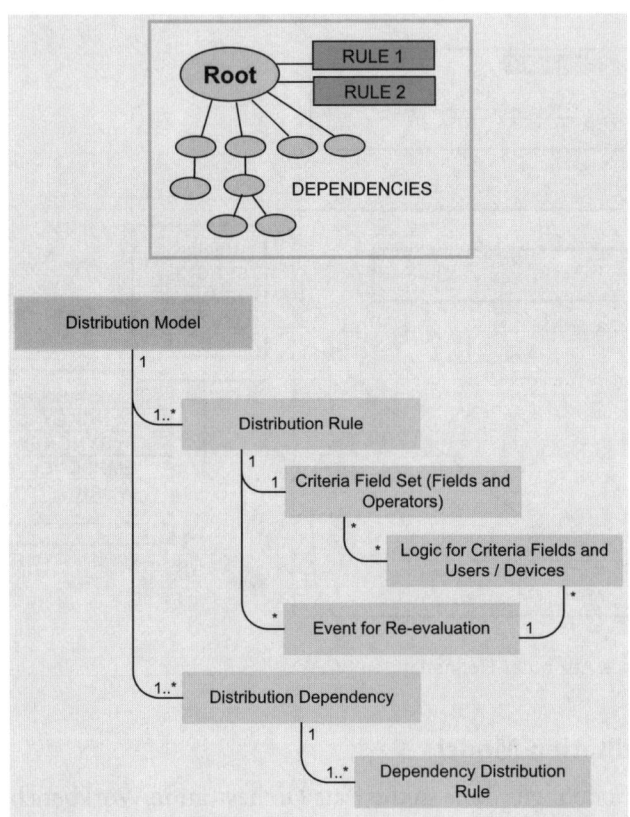

Figure 4.35 Structure of a Distribution Model

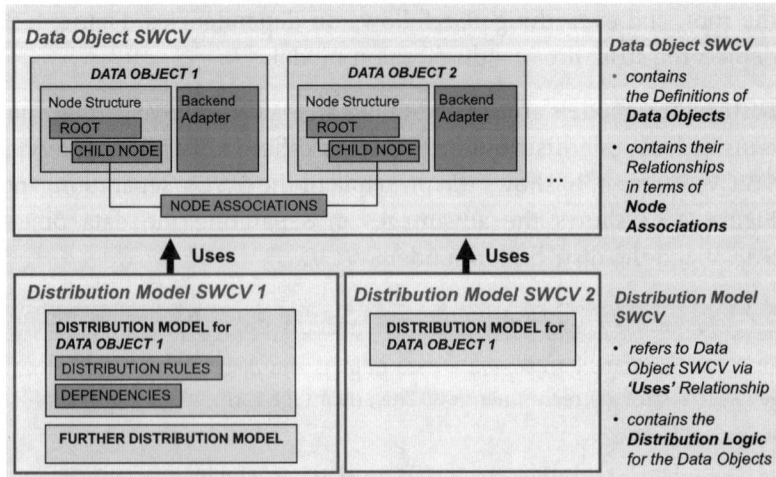

Figure 4.36 Interrelationship of Distribution Model and SWCV

Data Distribution Modeling | **4.3**

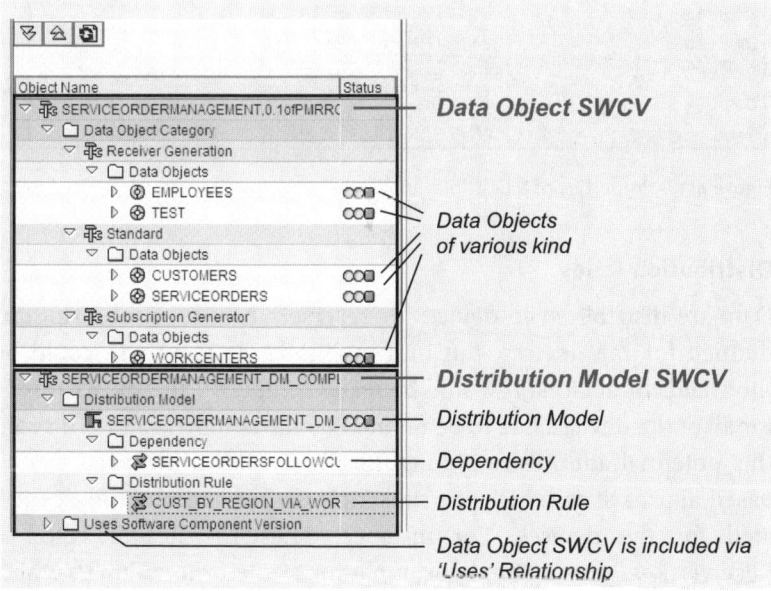

Figure 4.37 Advantages to Separating the SWCVs for Data Objects and Distribution Models

Distribution models are the entities that group and organize distribution rules and dependencies. Figure 4.38 illustrates the properties of a distribution model, which include:

- The DM always refers to one root data object.
- Distribution rules operate on the root object.
- Dependencies can be established starting from the root object to any level in the hierarchy.
- Multiple distribution models can be set up in parallel.

To create a distribution model, proceed as follows:

1. In the **DM Name** field, enter a name for the model that is unique within the DM SWCV.
2. In the **DM Description** field, enter a description for the model.
3. In the **Data Object Name** field, select the root data object.
4. The SWCV details will be filled in automatically.

119

DM Name	SERVICEORDERMANAGEMENT_DM_COMP
DM Description	Complex DM for Service Order Management
DM SWCV	SERVICEORDERMANAGEMENT_DM_COMPLEX, 0.2 of PMR
Data Object Name	CUSTOMERS
Data Object SWCV	SERVICEORDERMANAGEMENT, 0.1ofPMRROCKS

Figure 4.38 Properties of a Distribution Model

Distribution Rules

Support of organizational realignments

Data are distributed to devices or receivers based on subscriptions defined for the devices, but in a mobile landscape there could be thousands of devices. It would be really complex if the subscriptions for all of the devices had to be defined by the administrator. To avoid this potential administrative nightmare, the DOE has taken a rule-based approach in which the subscriptions are automatically generated for the devices. For instance, SalesOrder.header.region = Receiver.Region is a simple example for a rule or a policy in which the data object node attributes are mapped to the device attributes as a pattern. Then whenever a new device is created and the region attribute is set to a specific value, a subscription will be automatically generated for that device.

For instance, device 1 is created, and the region attribute is set to NORTH. In this case, a subscription will be automatically generated for device 1, with the region value being NORTH. If the device user is transferred from region NORTH to region SOUTH, the subscription will be automatically modified to Region SOUTH for device 1, and a delete message for the old region and an insert message for the new region will be prepared for that device. As a result, the device gets the latest data when it synchronizes next time.

Every rule has the following two important aspects:

- **Instance determination logic**
  This logic determines which instances need to be selected. Based on this, rules can be divided into two categories:
  - **Bulk rule**
    This kind of rule does not contain any criteria fields. All of the data object data are distributed to the assigned devices
  - **Intelligent rule**
    This kind of rule contains some criteria fields selected from the nodes of the data object that needs to be distributed, and the

criteria values can be bound to the device either manually, dynamically via a subscription generation data object, using the date time pattern, or through device attributes.

▶ **Device-binding logic**
This determines which devices need to get the selected data. The device identification can be done either manually, through a subscription generation data object, or through device attributes.

Figure 4.39 shows the various modeling options.

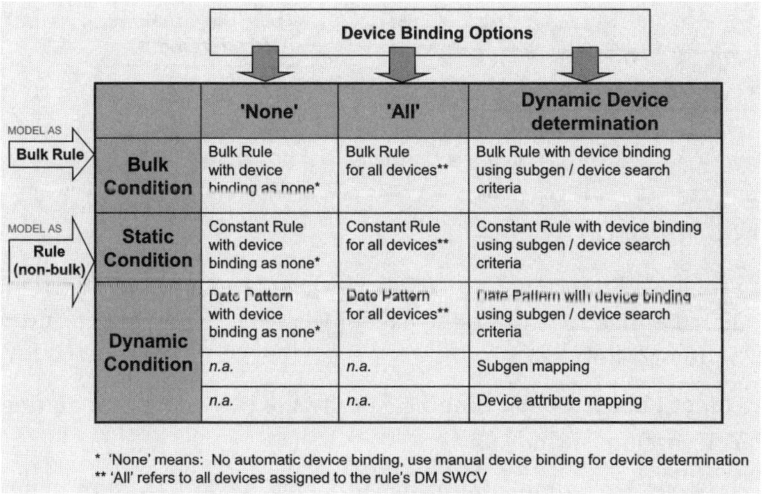

MODEL AS		Device Binding Options		
		'None'	'All'	Dynamic Device determination
Bulk Rule	Bulk Condition	Bulk Rule with device binding as none*	Bulk Rule for all devices**	Bulk Rule with device binding using subgen / device search criteria
MODEL AS Rule (non-bulk)	Static Condition	Constant Rule with device binding as none*	Constant Rule for all devices**	Constant Rule with device binding using subgen / device search criteria
	Dynamic Condition	Date Pattern with device binding as none*	Date Pattern for all devices**	Date Pattern with device binding using subgen / device search criteria
		n.a.	n.a.	Subgen mapping
		n.a.	n.a.	Device attribute mapping

* 'None' means: No automatic device binding, use manual device binding for device determination
** 'All' refers to all devices assigned to the rule's DM SWCV

Figure 4.39 Modeling Options in Distribution Modeling

Bulk distribution rules can be created by using either the context menu option or the tool bar menu option at the distribution model level. Bulk distribution rules are the simplest way to model data distribution. They capture all of the instances of the data object, and device binding has to be chosen. They can be modeled to be distributed to all of the devices or they can be left at NONE, so that the administrator can assign them to the appropriate devices. Figure 4.40 shows how to start the wizard, which helps in creating the bulk distribution rule.

Creating Bulk Distribution Rules

4 | Data Orchestration Design Time

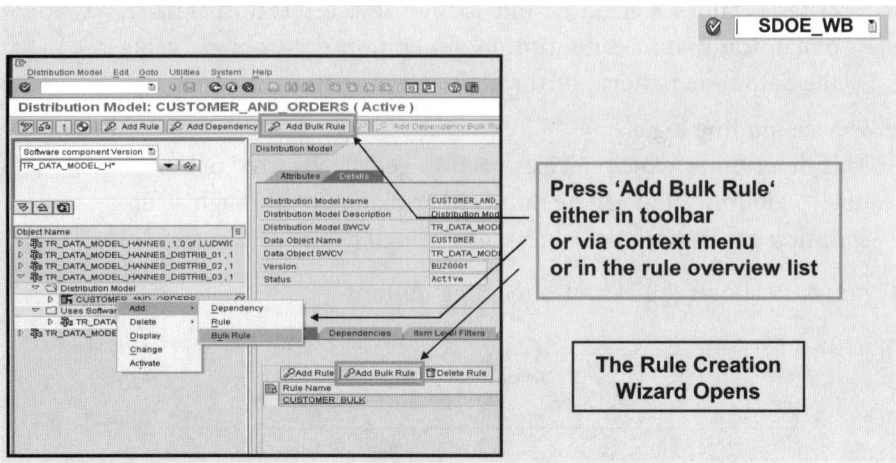

Figure 4.40 Bulk Distribution Rule Creation

Then, proceed as follows:

1. Provide a **Rule Name** and a **Description**. The **Data Object** field is already filled in because the data object is known from the Distribution Model.

2. Under **Choose Device Binding**, specify the Device Binding setting. Your options include:

   ▶ **None**: The administrator has to assign devices to rules manually (no automatic device binding)

   ▶ **All**: Automatic device binding to all devices assigned to your DM SWCV

   ▶ **Selective**: Specified via Device Binding. Restricts the binding to a set of devices.

For Selective Device Binding, you can specify:

▶ **SubGen Data Object**: Bind all devices where attribute is provided by a SubGen data object.

▶ **Search Criteria**: Bind all devices where attribute OP value (OP: eq, ne, le, lt, ge, gt, bt)

> **Note**
>
> Device binding always refers to enabled devices and is assigned to your DM SWCV only.

122

Data Distribution Modeling | **4.3**

Before getting into the details of an intelligent rule, it is important to understand the concept of a subscription generation data object. This is a category of data object that is useful in generating the subscriptions. This is useful in scenarios where some of the attributes of devices are not directly available as device attributes; rather, they are indirectly available through some other business object in the backend system. Let us take a small example shown in Figure 4.41. There is a need to model a rule at the Customer data object level in such a way that customer instances reach the end user device based on region and work center attributes. The RMM has only a work center id, but the "region to work center id" mapping is available in a separate WorkCenter data object. This data object becomes a subscription generation data object, and the rule is defined as follows:

Subscription Generation Data Object

- **Criteria Field**
  Region attribute in the Customer data object
- **Criteria field value**
  Customer.Region = WorkCenter.Region
- **Device binding**
  WorkCenter.WorkCenterId = RMM.WorkCenterId

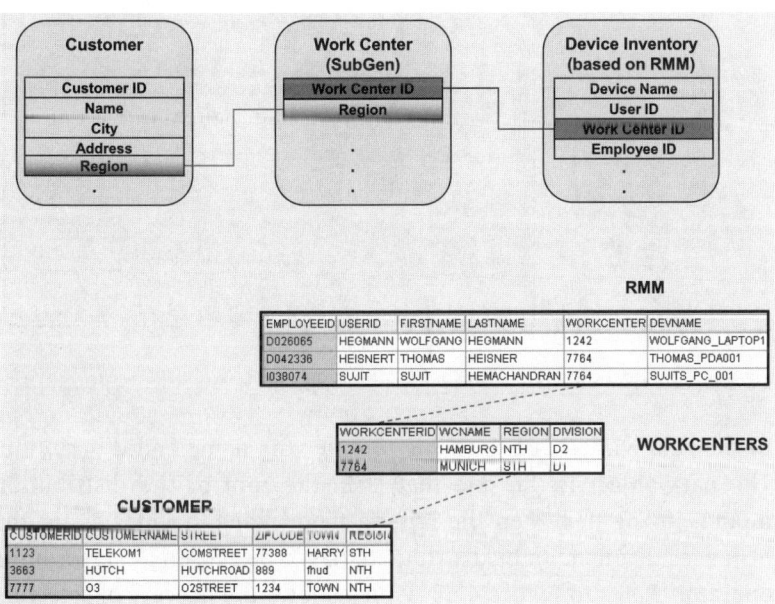

Figure 4.41 Example of Subscription Generation

4 | Data Orchestration Design Time

Creating an Intelligent Distribution Rule

An intelligent distribution rule can be created in the same way as a bulk distribution rule. It can be either created from the context menu or from the tool bar menu. Refer to Figure 4.42 for instructions on how to create an intelligent distribution rule:

1. Open the **Rule Wizard**, either from the toolbar or via the context menu.
2. On the first screen, enter the name and a description.
3. As with bulk rules, the rule will automatically refer to the root object defined with the distribution model (in our case: CUSTOMER).

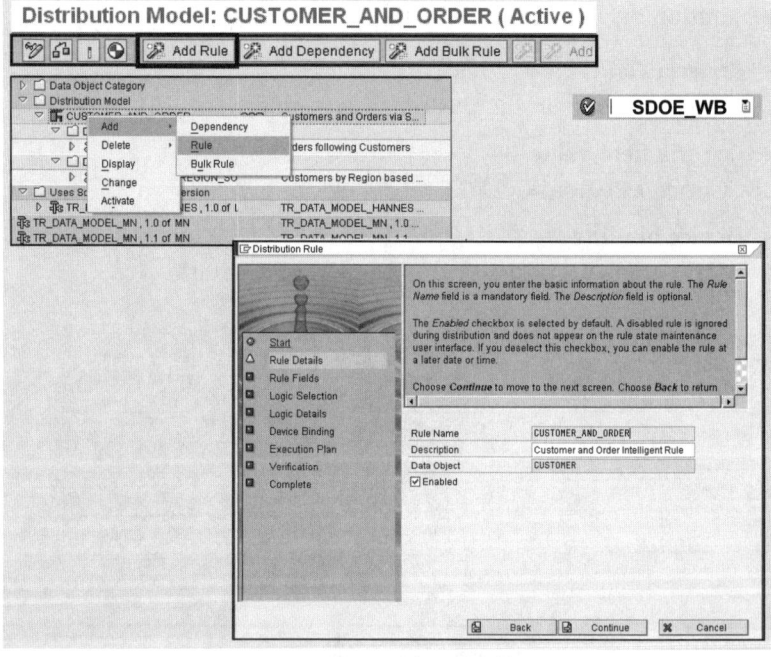

Figure 4.42 Creation of an Intelligent Distribution Rule

In the rule wizard, it is possible to enter the name and description. The data object is the one that is in the root of the distribution model. In the next step the criteria field, which decides about the instances that need to be distributed, has to be chosen along with the operator. Refer to Figure 4.43, which shows the process of selecting criteria fields:

4.3 Data Distribution Modeling

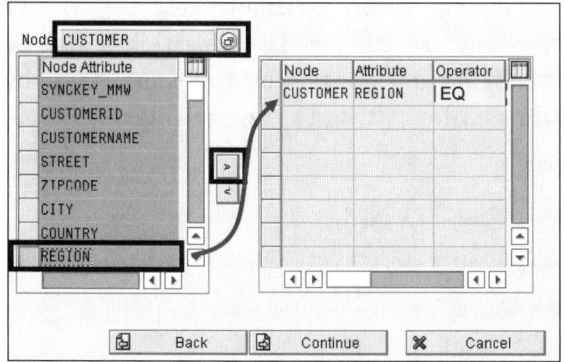

Figure 4.43 Selection of Criteria Fields for Distribution Rule Modeling

1. Select the node first. Use the value help for node selection.
2. The list of nodes is displayed.
3. Choose the attributes you need to make the criteria relevant by shifting them to the right.
4. Specify the operator to be used for criteria evaluation (EQ, BT, GT, GE, LT, or LE).

In the next screen (see Figure 4.44, part 1), the appropriate mapping type has to be chosen. One of the following mapping types is possible:

- **Subscription generation mapping**
  This means criteria field values are provided by the subscription generation data object and device mapping can be provided through the same.

- **Device attribute**
  This means criteria field values are selected from the device attribute maintained in the RMM.

- **None**
  This means the rule can be manually assigned to the devices through NetWeaver Mobile Administrator portal.

Always select "MOBILE" as **Receiver Category Type**. The field **Software Component Version** is filled automatically. In case you chose **Subgen Mapping** from the radiobutton group, specify the respective **Sub. Gen Data Object Name**.

125

4 | Data Orchestration Design Time

In case of Subgen Mapping, **Device Attribute Mapping** is also required. This defines how the subgen data object shall link to devices attributes. Specify the device attribute you want to link by providing an **Operator** and the **Attribute Low** containing the link (see Figure 4.44, part 2).

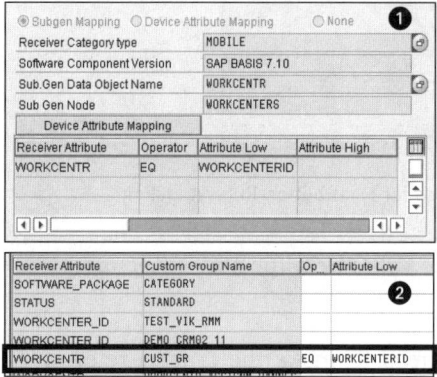

Figure 4.44 Mapping Type SELECTION in Distribution Modeling

It is also necessary to map criteria fields to the actual values. This is determined based on the kind of mapping that is selected and the data type of the field. It is possible to map the criteria fields to the following items:

- **Subscription generation data object node attributes**
  For instance, Customer.Region = WorkCenter.Region.
- **Device attributes**
  For instance, Customer.Region = RMM(Mobile).Region.
- **Constant values**
  For instance, Customer.Default_address = 'X'.
- **Date pattern**
  For instance, if the field is of type Date, then it is possible to define a date pattern. Order.CreationDate is between Today and the last 30 days. With this approach, it is possible to achieve a sliding time window for the data that are being distributed to the devices.

Support of flexible date patterns

Likewise, criteria field values can be mapped to every field individually or to a group of fields. Refer to Figure 4.45 for the details.

In the previous wizard step, we linked the subscription generation data object to the device attribute WORKCENTR, as once again displayed in Figure 4.45. Now, we have to link the criteria field CUSTOMER.REGION:

1. On the wizard screen, mark the criteria field and press option **SubGen**.

2. On the **Assignment Details** screen, choose the **SubGen Object** attribute which provides the values for the criteria field, in our example WORKCENTR.REGION.

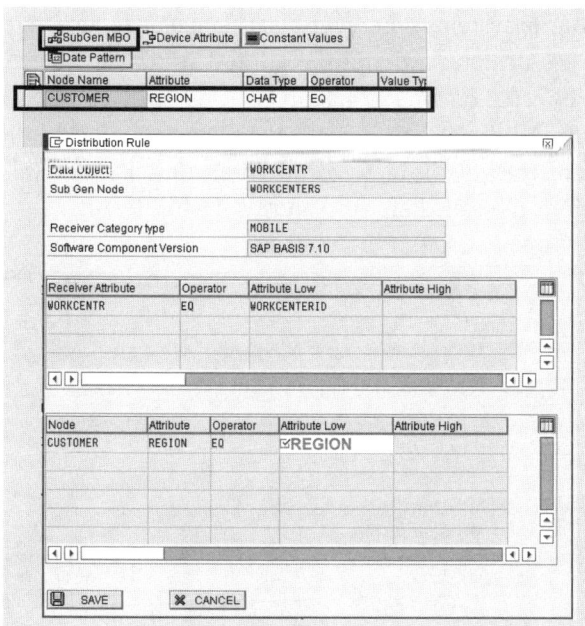

Figure 4.45 Mapping of Criteria Field Values in Distribution Modeling

Finally, it is possible to determine when subscriptions are going to be generated. This subscription generation step is called *rule evaluation*. Rules, by default, are evaluated under the following circumstances:

▶ **On arrival of a message**
If the criteria field values are mapped to subscription generation data object node attributes, rule evaluation will be triggered whenever a message for that subscription generation data object arrives into the DOE.

4 | Data Orchestration Design Time

> ▶ **On addition, deletion, or modification of device definition**
> If the criteria fields are mapped to device attributes, any modification to these attributes that happens because of addition, deletion, or modification of device attributes will trigger a rule evaluation.

> ▶ **On an interval defined by a custom job**
> If a custom date pattern is defined, it is be possible to define a custom job that will trigger rule evaluation on a regular interval determined by the custom job.

Rule Activation   Once the distribution model is created with rules, the rule needs to be activated to enable this rule for runtime execution. This step has to be done in all of the systems wherever this rule needs to be active. By default, rules are deactivated, and the administrator has to activate them to take effect at runtime. This can be done through the SAP NetWeaver Mobile Administrator. This activation step triggers the initial evaluation of the rule, which results in an initial set of subscriptions for various devices. Refer to Figure 4.46 for details.

Figure 4.46 Activation of the Distribution Rule via SAP NetWeaver Mobile Administrator

Distribution Dependencies

Rules alone are often not enough to determine which data need to be distributed to which device. This can also be directed because of the referential integrity across the data objects that are captured through associations. If some data objects need to be distributed because of these relationships, they are captured through this dependency in the distribution model.

Figure 4.47 gives an example of a dependency. The Order data object has an association to the Customer data object. In the distribution model, it is possible to make the order dependent on the customer. This means that whenever the customer is distributed to a device, the related order will simply follow the customer to the same device.

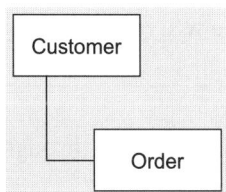

Figure 4.47 Example of a Dependency in a Distribution Model

A dependency can be created using the context menu or using the toolbar menu option at the distribution model level in the Data Orchestration Workbench. Figure 4.48 shows the process of defining the dependency. After the **Add dependency** option is selected, a wizard starts. In the first step, the wizard captures the metadata with respect to the dependencies listed below:

▶ Name
▶ Description
▶ Distribution model — (will be automatically filled)
▶ Distribution model SWCV — (will be automatically filled)

Creating Dependency

In the next step the wizard captures the real dependency information:

▶ **Leading data object**
In our example it is the Customer data object.
▶ **Following data object**
In our example it is the Order data object.
▶ **Link type**
This specifies which data object in the dependency holds the association. In a dependency two objects are involved. One is the leading object, the other one is the following object. In our example

4 | Data Orchestration Design Time

the Order data object follows the Customer data object, and the Order data object holds the reference to the Customer data object, so the link type will be chosen as the following objects.

▶ **Link data object**
The actual data object name, which holds the reference. It is Order in our example.

▶ **Link node**
This represents the actual node where the association is defined. In our example, the association is defined at the Order header node of the Order data object, so the link node will be selected as order header.

▶ **Join condition**
This specifies the field-level relationship. It is captured through the source node attribute and target node attribute.

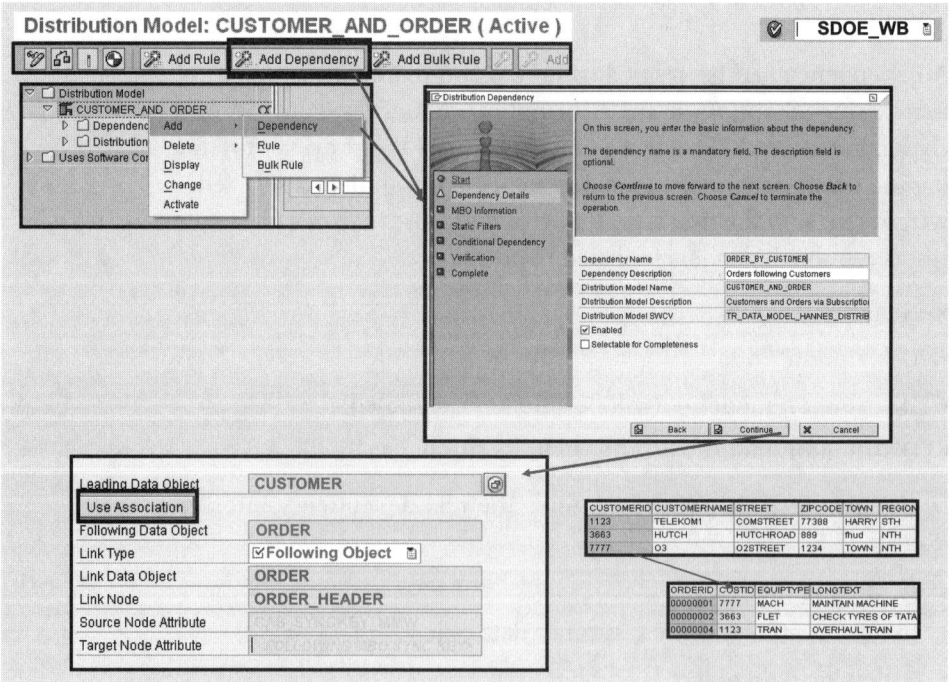

Figure 4.48 Creation of a Dependency in Distribution Modeling

> **Note**
>
> Using the **Use Association** option allows most of the entries to be automatically filled.

By following the approach shown, you can create a complete dependency network in a distribution model. It would be possible to define complex distribution hierarchies. There are also some special variants of dependencies, which are described in the following subsections.

It is possible to define a dependency with some additional conditions. For instance, let us take a scenario where we want to make orders follow customers if an order is of type Service. This can be achieved through static filtering. In the wizard step it is possible to choose any node attribute and to assign a value. This dependent object will be distributed if this value is matched. In our example, it will be distributed if ORDERTYPE matches SERVICE.

Static filtering

It is also possible to filter out the dependencies based on individual preferences of the receiver or the device. This can be achieved by defining a rule at the dependency level (see Figure 4.49). This rule creation process is very similar to normal rule creation.

Dependency Rule

Let us take the example where a dependency is defined between Customer and Order data objects. It is defined in a way that Order data will follow Customer data at runtime. But there is an additional filtering that is required at a dependency level which says that all the order data which are referring to the customer should not be distributed, orders should be distributed only if the date at which it is created falls within the last two weeks. Created date itself is captured through the node attribute called EXEC_DATE in the order header node of the Order data object. This scenario can be achieved by defining a dependency rule to the already defined dependency between customer and order data object.

Dependencies can be made conditional by excluding some dependencies based on the parent dependency. Figure 4.50 outlines an example of a conditional dependency.

Conditional dependencies

4 | Data Orchestration Design Time

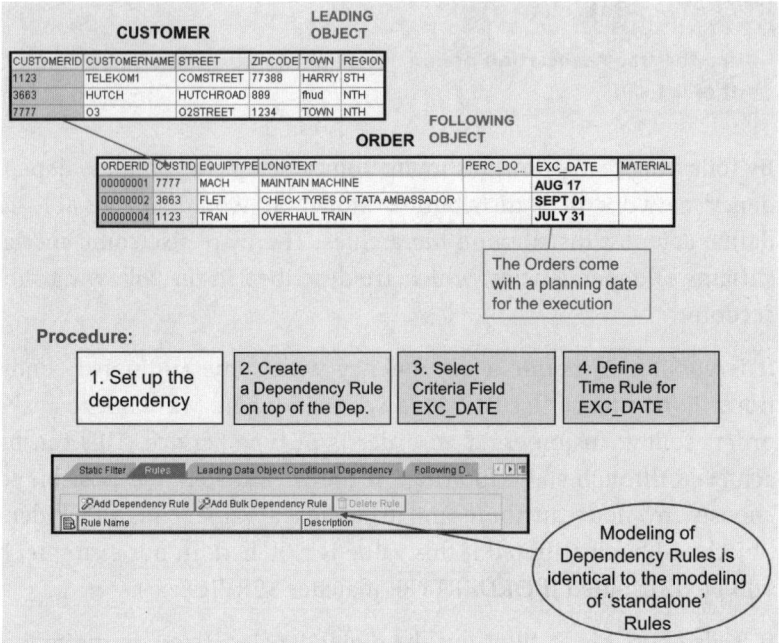

Figure 4.49 Modeling a Dependency Rule

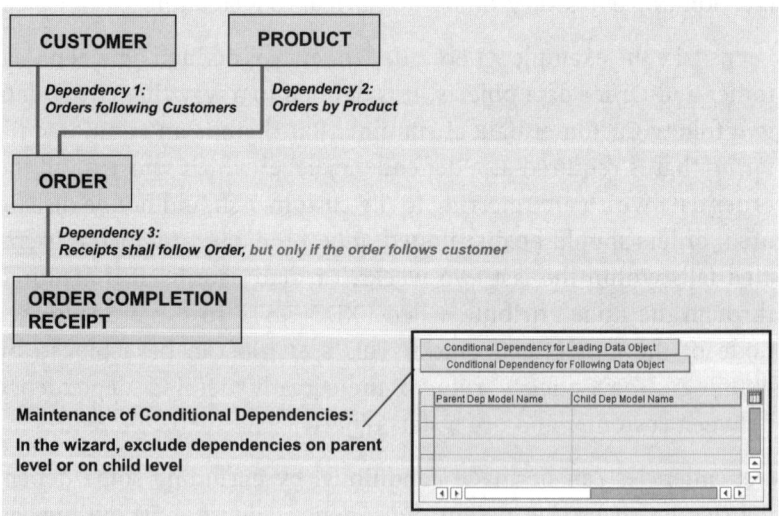

Figure 4.50 Example of a Conditional Dependency

Assigning a Data Set to Devices

Once the distribution model is created and activated, it can be assigned to devices. By default, none of the devices defined in the DOE will receive the data. Devices that receive the data are to be assigned to the corresponding distribution model SWCV. The rules and dependencies become effective for the device if that SWCV is assigned to it. Devices that are defined in the DOE are the logical definitions that can be created and managed either manually through NetWeaver Mobile Administrator or automatically through receiver generation data object association to RMM.

SAP NetWeaver Mobile Administrator

To test the distribution model that is created, the devices can be manually created, and a distribution model SWCV can be assigned to them to see whether the data is coming to the outbound queue. You can proceed as follows:

1. As described in Figure 4.51, select the **Create device** option from the NetWeaver Mobile Administrator portal.
2. Fill in all of the required fields and then go back to the **Manage device** option.

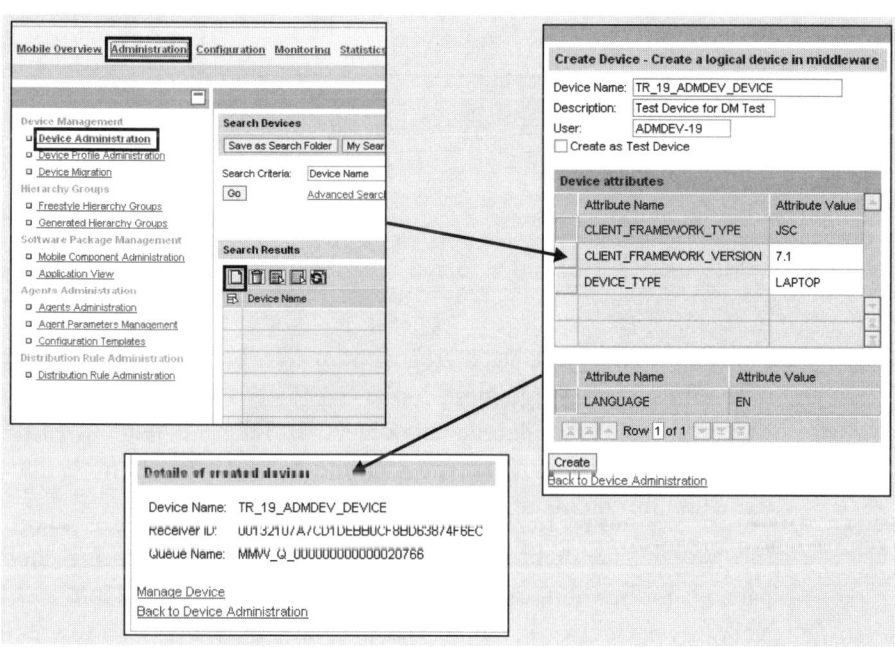

Figure 4.51 Device Creation in SAP NetWeaver Mobile Administrator for Assigning Data Sets to the Devices

4 | Data Orchestration Design Time

3. As described in Figure 4.52, assign a distribution model SWCV to the device.
4. Enable the device.

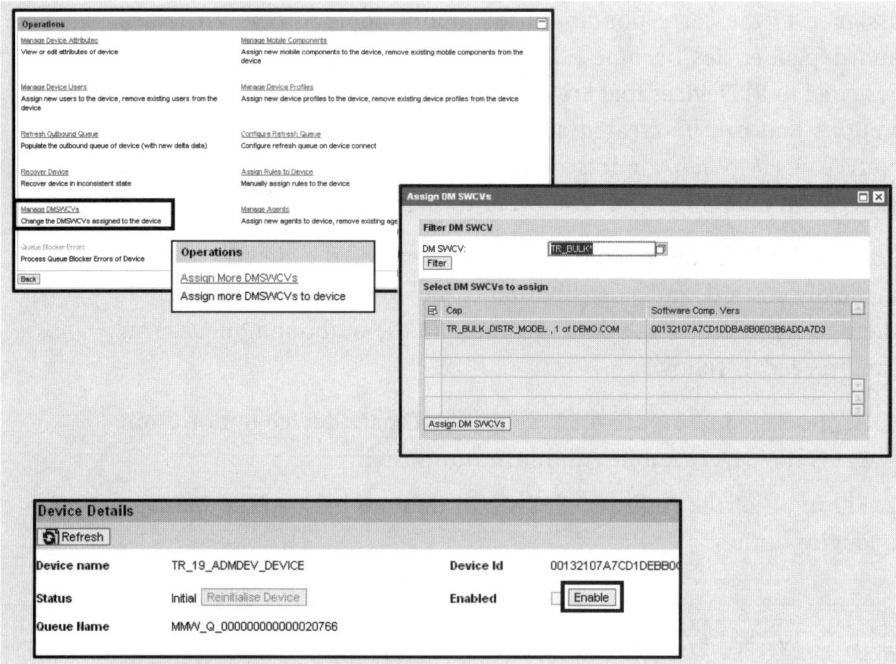

Figure 4.52 Assignment of SWCV to Devices in SAP NetWeaver Mobile Administrator

4.4 Summary

In this chapter, you learned a great deal about the design time concepts of the DOE. The Data Orchestration Workbench is the common umbrella of the design time tools. It provides the developer with powerful tools to model the data objects and their dependencies and to design an intelligent distribution model that takes care of the individual requirements of the receivers.

In Chapter 5, we will describe the design time to create the client part of a mobile application. This design time is integrated in the SAP NetWeaver Developer Studio and provides all of the tools to create the user interface and business logic of your occasionally connected mobile application.

Having presented the design time concepts of the data orchestration engine in Chapter 4, we will now introduce you in the concepts of the design time to create a mobile application in this chapter.

5   Design Time to Build Mobile Applications

In this chapter, we will describe the concepts of the design time to build a mobile application. First, we will describe the concepts of Mobile Applications for Laptop, which contains the design time to build occasionally connected mobile applications. Then, we'll describe Mobile Web Dynpro online, which is the design time to create connected mobile applications

5.1   Mobile Applications for Laptop to Build Occasionally Connected Mobile Applications

Mobile Applications for Laptop is a design time integrated in the SAP NetWeaver Developer Studio that allows you to create mobile applications and then run them in the occasionally connected mode. The applications built with Mobile Applications for Laptop target users who primarily work in the field and need to access information while they are away from the office. Typical examples are sales reps, field service and plant maintenance engineers, and delivery drivers. These users don't have access to (wireless) networks with sufficient bandwidth all of the time, and therefore run the application in the offline mode. All of the data they need to fulfill their tasks are downloaded to the device, and updated data can be synchronized with the backend system periodically, for instance, when they are back in the office or at home.

SAP NetWeaver Developer Studio

With Mobile Applications for Laptop, it is possible to create fully fledged client applications. Even complex business scenarios can be implemented. Therefore, a laptop is the primary mobile target device for these applications.

5.1.1 Integration

Mobile Applications for Laptop consists of the design time, which is fully integrated in the SAP NetWeaver Developer Studio, and the SAP NetWeaver Mobile Client, which is installed on the mobile device to run the application. We will discuss both components in further detail.

Design Time

The design time is the environment to create, deploy, and test mobile applications. It interacts with other systems in the landscape as follows:

- **SAP NetWeaver Java Development Infrastructure**
  The design time is fully integrated in the Java Development Infrastructure of SAP NetWeaver. Due to this integration, the developer and administrator can benefit from the provided services, such as sharing application resources and managing versions and central builds of the source code, as well as deploying the applications.

- **SAP NetWeaver Portal Server**
  The integration in SAP NetWeaver Portal Server provides *single sign-on* (SSO) functionality. When the user logs on to the Mobile Client, the Portal Server generates the SAP logon tickets that are accepted by the J2EE engine.

- **Mobile middleware**
  The integration with the mobile middleware enables developers to import the data object structures in the Mobile Applications for Laptop project. The data objects define the structures of the messages exchanged between the mobile device and backend system. By importing the data object structures in the design time, the application's model classes are generated.

Single sign on

SAP NetWeaver Mobile Client

The SAP NetWeaver Mobile Client is the runtime for a mobile application that was created using the Mobile Applications for Laptop design time. It uses the Java GUI-based Web Dynpro Client for Java to run the application. You can log on to the SAP NetWeaver Mobile Client with your user ID and password and perform the following activities:

- Configure user settings and change passwords
- Run the application in disconnected mode
- Download and synchronize applications and data

In the next subsection, we describe the prerequisites to run an occasionally connected application on the mobile device.

5.1.2 Prerequisites for the Client Device

Mobile applications built with the Mobile Applications for Laptop tool run on client devices, which need to fulfill the following requirements:

- **Installed software**
    - SAP NetWeaver Mobile Client for Laptop: Specifies the runtime environment that hosts and executes the application
    - SUN Java GUI: Renders the user interface of the application
    - SAP MaxDB: Provides the persistence layer of the application data on the client device
    - SUN JRE 1.5x
- **Minimum hardware requirements**
    - Pentium 1.6 GHZ
    - 512 MB RAM
    - 1 GB Hard Disk Space

System Landscape for Mobile Applications for Laptop

Figure 5.1 shows the system landscape to develop mobile applications using Mobile Applications for Laptop. We'll look at the different components in more detail in the following sections, starting with the development workstation.

5 | Design Time to Build Mobile Applications

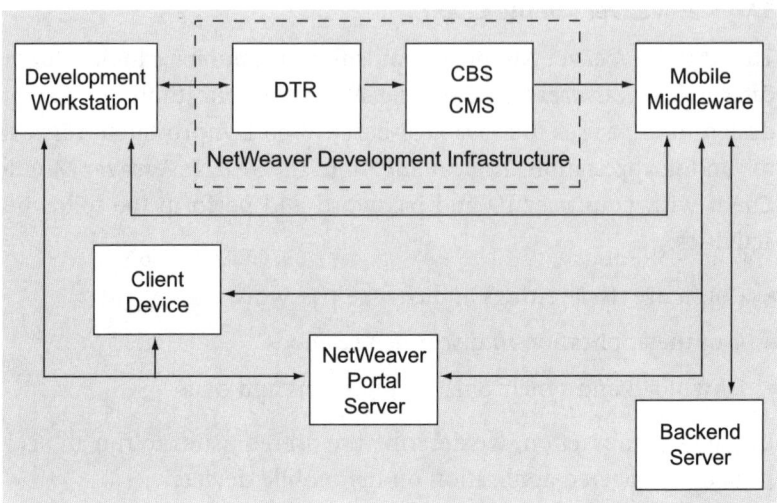

Figure 5.1 System Landscape for Mobile Applications for Laptop

Development Workstation

The development workstation is the system on which the developer creates and tests the mobile application. On the development workstation, the following software needs to be installed:

- SAP NetWeaver Developer Studio
- SAP MaxDB
- SAP NetWeaver Mobile Client for Laptop

Next, we'll look at the SAP NetWeaver Java Development Infrastructure (NWDI).

NWDI

DTR, CBS, CMS

NWDI provides the development team with an infrastructure consisting of closely coupled services to design, implement, build, deploy, and test applications. The main features include:

- *Design Time Repository* (DTR) to manage distributed development
- *Component Build Service* (CBS) to manage the central build of the source code
- *Change Management Service* (CMS) to manage the central administration of the Java development landscape

SAP NetWeaver Portal Server

The Portal Server enables users to log on to the SAP NetWeaver Mobile Client using SSO. The use of the Portal Server for user authentication is optional. The Portal Server can issue SAP logon tickets to the mobile client, which can be used to log on to the NetWeaver AS.

Mobile Middleware on the SAP NetWeaver Application Server

The mobile middleware is part of the ABAP stack of the NetWeaver Application Server and stores the replica database from the backend server. Using the ABAP stack, it is also possible to import the data objects in the Mobile Applications for Laptop project. The NetWeaver Application Server runs the J2EE engine and facilitates the followings tasks:

The SAP NetWeaver Application Server

- Deployment of the mobile application from the development workstation to the mobile middleware
- Downloading of the mobile application to the client device
- Data synchronizing between the client device and the backend server
- Accepting SAP logon tickets issued by the Portal Server

Backend Server

Depending on the application the customer wants to run, the backend system can be, for instance, an SAP ERP or SAP CRM system. In the backend system, the entire business process is implemented and offered as a service to external systems. The service can be exposed as BAPI, web service, or XI interface. Using these services, transactional data as well as master data can be exchanged between the device and backend system.

Client Device

The client device is the mobile device that enables the end user to download the data and execute the mobile application. It is possible to work with the application in disconnected mode and to connect on demand with the NetWeaver Application Server to synchronize the data with the backend. On the client device, the following software needs to be installed:

Software requirements

- JRE 1.5x
- SAP NetWeaver Mobile Client
- SAP MaxDB
- SAP Java GUI

After that, the user can log on to the Mobile Client and download the mobile application.

5.1.3 Developing a Mobile Application Using Mobile Applications for Laptop

To develop a mobile application, developers use the Mobile Applications for Laptop plug-in shipped with SAP NetWeaver Developer Studio. Mobile Applications for Laptop enables developers to create the user interface and implement the business logic for the mobile application by using declarative development techniques, such as the following:

MVC
- Model-view-controller (MVC) architecture, where the model encapsulates the business logic, the view defines the different parts of the UI, and the controller handles events, updates the model, and controls the navigation to the next view.

- Mobile Applications for Laptop design pattern, which ensures that the view layouts and business data are separated. This enhances reusability and allows you to change layouts and navigations quickly.

Meta model
As a result, the IDE generates a meta model for each entity in the project and the code that can be changed based on the specific requirements. In the next subsection, we describe the perspective of the SAP NetWeaver Developer Studio that can be used to create a mobile application.

Mobile Applications for Laptop Perspective

The SAP NetWeaver Developer Studio organizes the supported tools in different perspectives. To create a mobile application, the Mobile Applications for Laptop Perspective is used. It contains all of the views that are required to build a mobile application, including the following:

- **Mobile Applications for Laptop Explorer**
  This displays the logical structure of the Mobile Applications for Laptop Project.

- **Data Object Model**
  This is composed of a set of model classes that provide access to the application data.

- **Authorization**
  The SAP NetWeaver client supports user-specific data filtering that is defined according to the SAP authorization concept. It allows authenticated application users to read or change data, as defined by their authorization. The authorization objects are created by an administrator on the mobile middleware and assigned to roles, users, and applications. During synchronization, the authorization objects flow down to the mobile device.

  Data filtering

- **Design Time Repository (DTR)**
  This enables the development team to share application resources and manage the versioning, transportation, and replication of the source code.

Before we discuss in detail the steps that are required to build a mobile application, we provide an overview of the development process.

Development Process Flow

Figure 5.2 depicts the system landscape and the interactions of the system to show how to develop, deploy, download, and run a mobile application designed with Mobile Applications for Laptop. Figure 5.3 outlines the overall workflow to build a mobile application.

In the following subsections, the different tasks of this workflow are described in more detail, beginning with modeling the data objects.

5 | Design Time to Build Mobile Applications

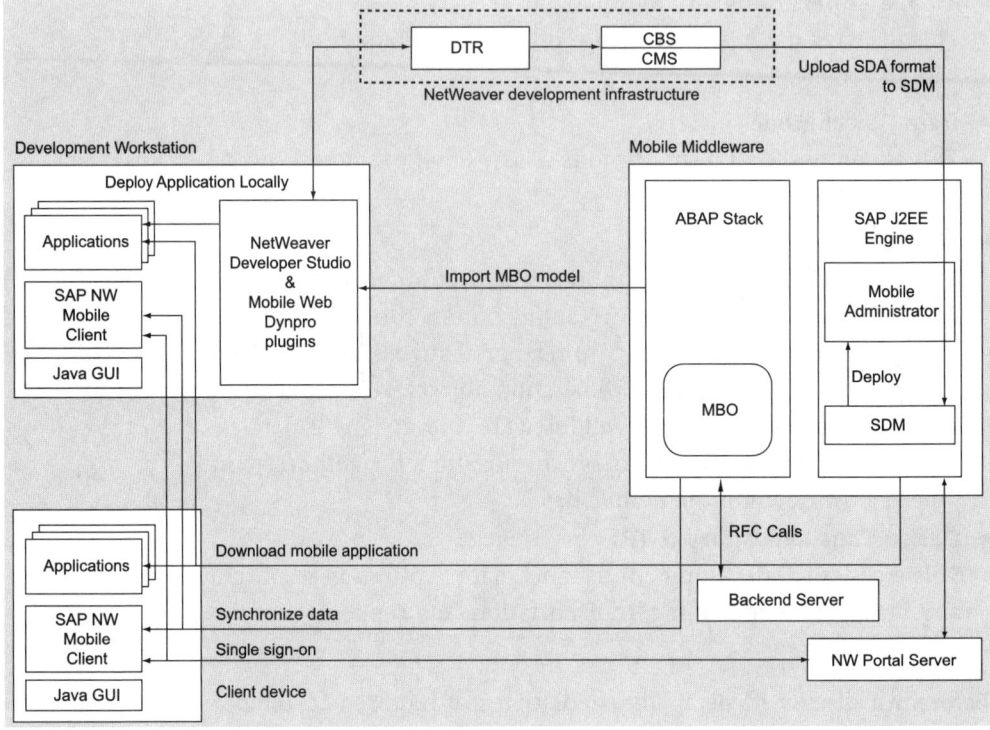

Figure 5.2 Development System Landscape for Mobile Applications for Laptop

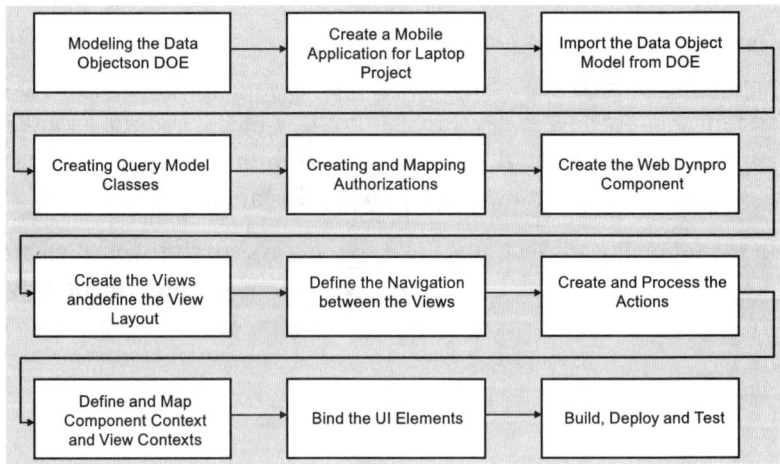

Figure 5.3 Development Process to Build a Mobile Application

Modeling the Data Objects

The data object developer defines the structure of the data objects in the Data Orchestration Workbench. The data objects define the structure of the messages that are exchanged between the mobile device and the backend system. They provide an abstraction of the business objects and their related services. A backend adapter that contains the services to be called in the backend system is attached to a data object. Using the Distribution Modeler, which is part of the Data Orchestration Workbench, it is possible to define the dependencies between the data objects, and the distribution rules of the data objects can be defined. All those settings are part of the Data Object Model, which can be imported to the Mobile Applications for Laptop Project. As a result, the application's model classes are generated and available to the Mobile Applications for Laptop developer.

Data Orchestration Workbench

After the data objects are defined in the Data Orchestration Workbench, the developer can start with the implementation of the application in the SAP NetWeaver Developer Studio.

Creating a Mobile Applications for Laptop Project

To start with the implementation of the mobile application, the developer creates a Mobile Applications for Laptop Project in SAP NetWeaver Developer Studio. This starts a wizard in which the project settings such as project name, directory, and project language can be entered. As a result, the Developer Studio perspective changes to the Mobile Applications for Laptop Perspective. In the Mobile Applications for Laptop Explorer, the project appears as the primary node of the tree structure. This structure contains all Mobile Applications for Laptop Project entities as subnodes.

> **Tip**
>
> The Mobile Applications for Laptop Project is the recommended approach for local, standalone development tasks. If the development tasks are distributed among different developers, it is recommended that you create a Mobile Applications for Laptop development component (DC) project instead.

Importing a Data Object Model

In the next step, the data objects are imported as a Data Object Model in the Mobile Applications for Laptop Project. The system, from which the Data Object Model is imported, can be configured in the Preferences page of the SAP NetWeaver Developer Studio. As a result, the following objects are created:

Model classes
- The Data Object Model and the model classes with their properties, which are displayed in the Mobile Applications for Laptop Explorer.
- The simple types used in the Data Object Model under the Dictionaries node of the project.

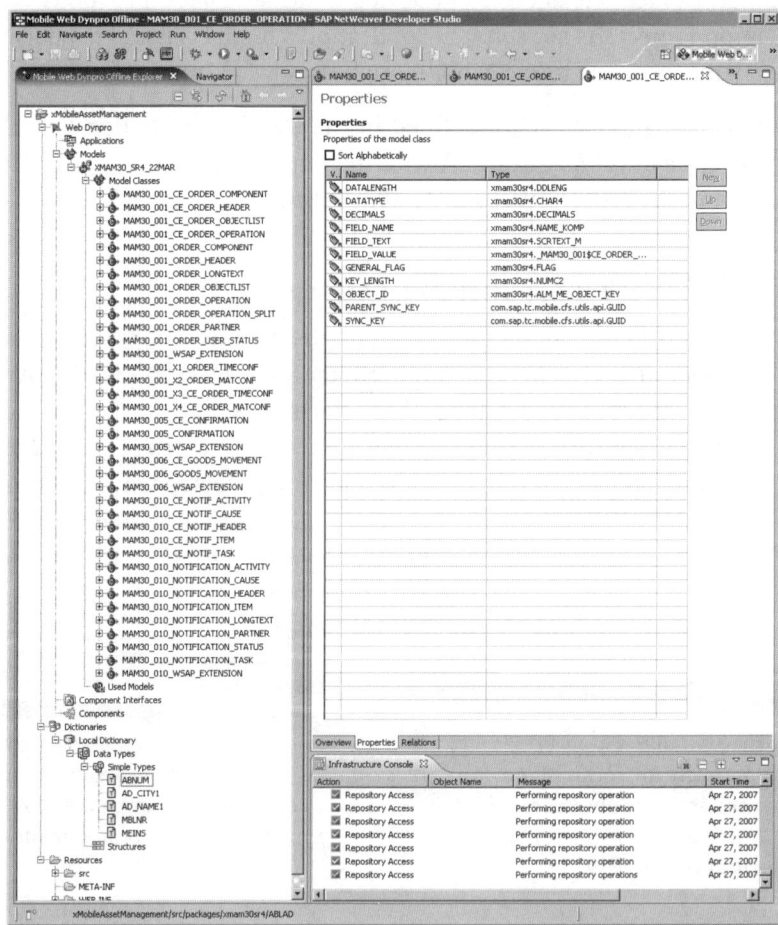

Figure 5.4 Mobile Applications for Laptop Explorer After Importing a Data Object Model

This enables the developer to

- Use the model classes in the Data Object Model for context binding in the project
- Define query and composite classes for the model that has been created
- Use the model as a Used Model in another model

Figure 5.4 shows the expanded tree of the Mobile Applications for Laptop Explorer after importing a Data Object Model.

After the data object is imported in the SAP NetWeaver Developer Studio and the model classes are generated, the developer can proceed with the creation of a query model class.

Creating a Query Model Class

Creating a query model class enables the developer to retrieve data from the local data storage on the device based on selection criteria. To facilitate this, a query or composite model class can be defined in the Mobile Applications for Laptop Project. A *query class* allows retrieval of data based on specific selection criteria. In addition, it is possible to define sort conditions to display the data in a specific order. A *composite model* class allows selection of the attributes from more than one model class and maintenance of them collectively in a composite class. For example, the query just defined requires a result object that contains properties from various model classes.

Query and composite model classes can be created by expanding the model node in which they should be created in the Mobile Applications for Laptop Explorer and then right-clicking on the **Model Classes** node. After choosing **Create Query/Composite Model Class**, the **New Query/Composite Model Class** wizard starts and a name for the new class can be entered.

Composite model class, Query class

As a result, the IDE creates the new model class and displays it in the **Mobile Applications for Laptop Explorer**. The new class can now be modeled as a query or as a composite, as follows:

- **Query model class**

  The query can be modeled in the query editor. Right-click the query node, select **Open Query/Composite Model Class Editor**, and select the **Query** tab. Now the following query details can be specified:

  - **Input Model Class**

    The input model class defines the input for the query object. It is possible to specify a model class that has been imported or a composite model class.

  - **Result Model Class**

    The result model class contains the result of the query. It is possible to specify a model class that has been imported or a composite model class.

  - **BI-DIRECTIONAL**

    This option allows navigation in the query result set in both directions. This option is enabled by default.

  - **DISTINCT**

    This option ensures that only unique rows are retrieved in the query result set. This option is disabled by default.

  Now the following query conditions can be entered:

  - **Alias**

    The alias name for a model class can be specified. The alias name can be used in the SQL query code to create the filter and the sort conditions. The syntax is as follows: Model_Class Alias, for instance, ORDER$ROOT order.

  - **Add join conditions for relations**

    This button generates the join conditions for the query if the query model classes contain related model classes. It is possible to make changes to the join condition and create the filter condition for the query, as required.

  - **Conditions**

    The SQL query to filter the query result set can be entered, for instance, order.amount > :amount, where amount is a field in the input class. Table 5.1 to Table 5.4 show the lists of supported operators and parameters.

▶ **Sort Conditions**
The sort conditions define the sort order of the query result set. The sort order for multiple attributes can be entered, separated by commas. The default sort order is ascending. The syntax is as follows: Model Class.Attribute Sort Order, for instance, order.amount descending.

> **Note**
> Using an input model class, it is possible to supply values to the query at query execution time as opposed to query compilation time.

▶ As a final step, click **File • Save**. As a result, the query is compiled. The IDE generates the QueryInput and QueryOutput relations for the query and displays them in the Mobile Applications for Laptop Explorer. The input or the result set of the query are now available for context binding in the Mobile Applications for Laptop Project.

> **Note**
> The data read from queries are read-only only if composite model classes are used as query results. If an imported model class is used as a query result, the query result object can be modified using the usual getter and setter methods of the corresponding Java Bean.

▶ **Composite Model Class**
The composite model class can be modeled in the composite class editor. Right-click the query node, select **Open Query/Composite Model Class Editor**, and select the **Properties** tab. The properties table appears, which enables the developer to add an attribute from a model class into the composite class or to delete an attribute. To add an attribute, click **Add**. The **Composite Model Class Editor** appears, which allows you to select the required attributes from the model classes, as follows:

▶ **Query Language Reference**
Table 5.1 through Table 5.4 show the lists of comparisons and logical operators and system and special parameters the Query Editor supports.

Operator	Description
=	Equal to
<>	Not equal to
<	Less than
<=	Less than or equal to
>	Greater than
>=	Greater than or equal to
IN	Search in the given list of columns
NOT IN	Search in the given list of columns except those mentioned
CONTAINS	Search columns that contain the given list of fields
LIKE	Search for a pattern (case sensitive)
NOT LIKE	Search for a pattern unlike that mentioned (case sensitive)
ILIKE	Search for a pattern (not case sensitive)
NOT ILIKE	Search for a pattern unlike that mentioned (not case sensitive)
(+)=	Left outer join
=(+)	Right outer join
(+)=(+)	Full outer join

Table 5.1 Comparison Operators

Operator	Description
AND	Used in where clause; selects a row of all conditions are true
OR	Used in where clause; selects a row if any condition is true
NOT	Used in where clause; selects a row if the negated condition is true

Table 5.2 Logical Operators

Parameter Name	Description	Syntax
Login_lang	Used to find the user's login language	:$login_lang

Table 5.3 System Parameters

Parameter Name	Description	Syntax
Null	Used to compare a value to a NULL value	:@null
This	Used to refer to the query candidate's class instance	:@this

Table 5.4 Special Paramters

After the query model classes are generated, the developer can proceed with creating an authorization definition file that can be used for data filtering.

Creating an Authorization Definition File

This step describes how an authorization file in XML format can be created in the Mobile Applications for Laptop Project and how the authorization objects in the authorization file are defined. As a prerequisite, the mobile middleware administrator has created the authorization objects in the mobile middleware and assigned the authorization objects to roles, users, and applications. Then, follow this procedure:

XML format

1. Select the resource perspective by selecting **Window • Open Perspective • Other • Resource (default)** and then select **OK**.
2. Start the New File wizard by choosing **File • New • File**.
3. In the wizard, select the required project and enter "Authorization.xml" in the **File name** field.
4. After **Finish** is selected, the IDE creates the authorization file and opens it in the edit mode, which enables the developer to enter the authorization definitions.

Figure 5.5 shows a sample authorization file.

As the next step, the authorization definition file is mapped to a business object.

5 | Design Time to Build Mobile Applications

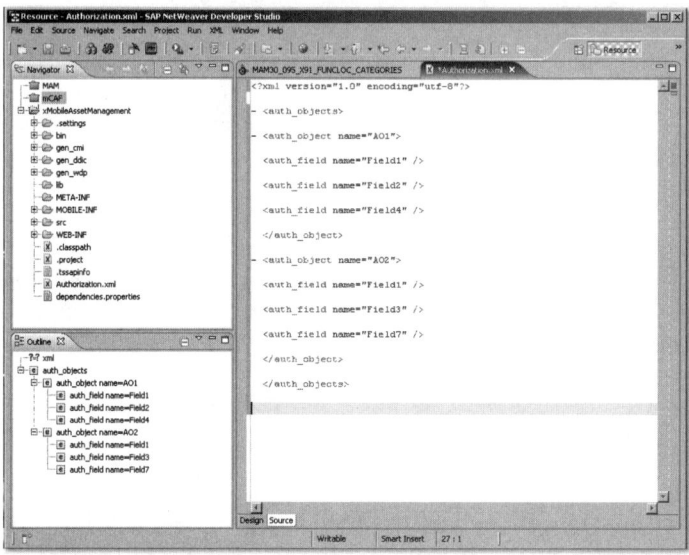

Figure 5.5 Sample Authorization File

Mapping an Authorization Object to a Business Object

In this step, the authorization file created in the previous step is mapped to the appropriate model classes in the Mobile Applications for Laptop Project. First, the authorization objects are mapped at the model class level, and, second, the corresponding attributes are mapped.

This can be achieved by selecting the corresponding model class in the Mobile Applications for Laptop Explorer. Now call the **Properties** view by choosing **Window • Show View • Properties**. In the **Properties** field, enter the required authorization objects, separated by commas (for instance, A01, A02). Enter the authorization fields on the **Properties** tab of the corresponding attribute in the **auth** field (for instance, A01.Field1).

Now all of the required steps have been completed to design the application. In the next step, the developer creates the UI of the application.

Designing the Application

The steps discussed so far are specific to Mobile Applications for Laptop applications. In this section, we describe how the user interface of a mobile application is designed.

> **Note**
>
> Designing the application is entirely based on the Web Dynpro for Java standard. Therefore, only an overview of the tasks is provided, and for further information we refer you to the standard documentation of Web Dynpro for Java, which is available on the SAP Service Marketplace (http://service.sap.com).

Web Dynpro for Java

1. **Creating a component**

    In this mandatory step, a Web Dynpro component is created that helps to better structure the implementation of the application. The Web Dynpro component contains any number of windows and views and their corresponding controllers. Additional Web Dynpro components can also be referenced. Figure 5.6 shows the structure of a Web Dynpro component. Each Web Dynpro component contains at least one global controller that is visible within the component for all other controllers. Once the data for this component controller have been created for the first time they are accessed, the lifetime extends to cover the whole period during which the component is in use. Additional controllers can be added in the form of custom controllers. The component controller is also visible also of the component and is therefore part of the interface of a Web Dynpro component. Every time there is a Web Dynpro window, another global controller — the Window controller — is added to the component.

    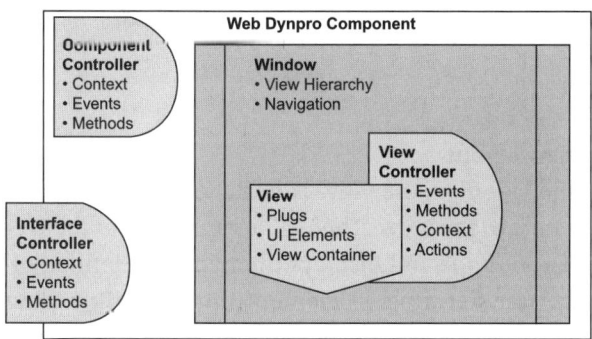

    Figure 5.6 Structure of a Web Dynpro Component

2. **Creating a view**

    A view defines the layout of the user interface in the application. The layout is made up of different user interface elements. The positioning of interface elements in one view is defined by the layout variants. In addition to these visible parts, a view also contains a controller and a context. The context manages the data to which the elements of the view can be bound. The view controller can contain methods for data retrieval or for processing user input. Figure 5.7 shows the structure of a view.

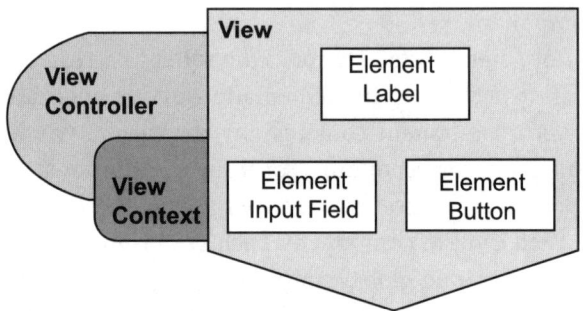

Figure 5.7 Structure of a Web Dynpro View

View set
3. **Embedding the view in a view set**
A view set is a visual frame with predefined subsections into which the views can be embedded. The Web Dynpro Framework provides the preconfigured view sets shown in Figure 5.8.

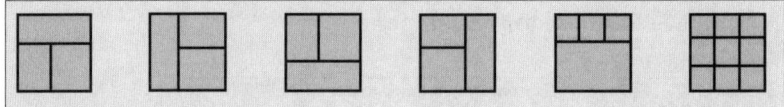

Figure 5.8 Preconfigured View Sets

View layout
4. **Designing a view layout**
In this step, the layout of the view is designed by adding appropriate UI elements to the view. The IDE organizes all of the UI elements under a root node and displays them in a predefined order in the layout. After selecting an element in the **Outline** view or **Layout** tab, the associated properties are shown in the **Properties** tab at the bottom of the screen. In the **Outline** view, there are already the **RootElement** and the **DefaultTextView** are already available. The developer can assign them the appropriate properties and create new views as child nodes of the **RootElement**. Figure 5.9 shows a simple example.

Mobile Applications for Laptop to Build Occasionally Connected Mobile Applications | 5.1

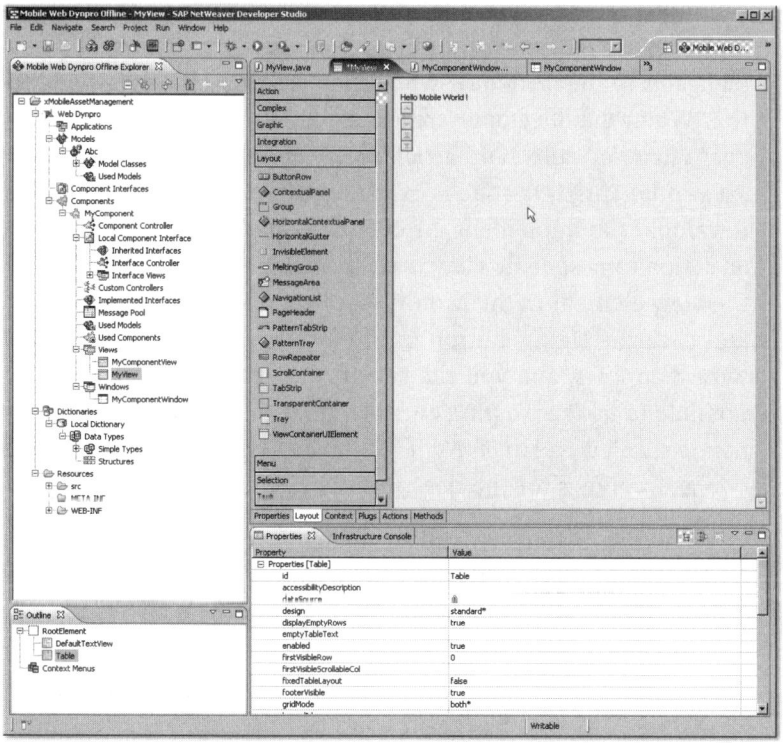

Figure 5.9 View Layout Example

5. **Defining navigation between views**

   To define navigation between views, you must perform the following:

   Outbound plug, inbound plug

   ▸ Create an outbound plug (exit point) in the view from which to navigate to another view.

   ▸ Create an inbound plug (entry point) in the view to which to navigate from another view.

   ▸ Create a navigation link to establish the connection between the two views.

   As a result, the IDE creates an event handler in the Java code with the name **onPlug<Name of Outbound Plug>** for the outbound plug.

6. **Creating an action**

   An *action* is an incident that can be recognized by the application, for example, clicking a button. When the user performs the

   Action event handler

153

action during runtime, the event assigned to the action occurs and triggers the corresponding event handler. For example, it navigates to the next view when the user clicks the specified button. When the developer creates an action, the IDE generates an event handler called and *action event handler* for the action in the Java code. This Java code is executed when the event occurs. The developer can implement the event handler if required. To create an action for a specific view in the Developer Studio, double-click the **view** element in the Mobile Applications for Laptop Explorer and click the **New...** button on the **Actions** tab. The **New Action** wizard appears, and you can specify additional information. It is possible to use an existing event handler or to create a new event handler called *onAction<Name of Action>*. Web Dynpro provides two action types for the description of actions, as follows:

- **Validating actions**: A validating action is only triggered after the data are passed to the context and some basic validations (data types, for instance) are performed. The source code of a typical event handler of a validating action could look like the code shown in Listing 5.1:

```
/** declared validating event handler */
  public void onActionSave( IWDCustomEvent wdEvent )
  {
  //@@begin onActionSave(ServerEvent)
  this.getSomeOtherContoller.Save();
  this.wdThis.wdFirePlugAddresseSaved();
  //@@end
  }
```

Listing 5.1 Implementation of onActionSave event

- **Nonvalidating actions**: The event handler for a nonvalidating action is called before the user data entered are validated and the validated data are passed to the context. Normally, they are used when the user wants to quit an application if the entries are invalid.

7. **Processing an action**
The actions that have been created in the previous step can now be assigned to a UI element. This is done by double-clicking the corresponding view in the Mobile Applications for Laptop Explorer, selecting the **Layout** tab, clicking the UI element in the

Outline View, and selecting the **Properties** tab. Under **events**, click **onAction**. Select the appropriate action from the drop-down list. In the Java editor, the generated source code can be viewed and implemented if required.

8. **Sharing data between views**

   This step describes how data are shared between the different views in a component. Data sharing can be achieved by binding the data to a UI element and then transporting the bound data to the required view. To bind the data, a value reference must be assigned between the appropriate context of the component and view controllers in which the data and UI are referenced.

   Binding data to UI elements

   The process flow to transport data between views is as follows:

   ▸ A global space is required to store the data that come from one view before they is passed on to the next. As global space, the component context can be used. To create the component context, proceed as follows. In the Mobile Applications for Laptop Explorer, double-click the **Component Controller** node under the component node you already created and select the **Context** tab. Right-click the **Context** node and select **New • Node** to create a new node, or **New • Attribute** to create a new context attribute.

   ▸ The elements of the view that contains the outbound plug are mapped to the component context. To achieve this, proceed as follows. In the Mobile Applications for Laptop Explorer, right-click the **Component Context** element and select **Open Data Modeler**. Then the created views are displayed along with the component controller. In the toolbar that appears on the left side, select **Create Data link**. Move the mouse pointer above the rectangle of the view with the outbound plug and draw a line using drag and drop to the **Component Controller** rectangle. This starts the **Context Mapping** wizard, which allows you to map the context element in the view to the context element in the component. Then assign the value attribute node in the component controller context to the root node of the view controller context using drag and drop. As a result, the new context element for the view is created.

   Component controller, context mapping

   ▸ The necessary contexts for the views that contain the inbound plugs are created. This can be done as follows. In the Mobile Applications for Laptop Explorer, double-click the required view and choose the **Context** tab. Right-click the **Context** root node and select **New • Attribute**. This starts the **Context Attribute** wizard, where you can create a new attribute. Enter a name for the view context and create a data link between the view and the component controller.

- The view context is bound to appropriate UI elements by using the appropriate properties. To do this, proceed as follows. Open the View Designer for the view that contains the outbound plug, and select the **Layout** tab. Select the input field from which you want to send the data. Select the **Properties** tab. To assign the **Value** property to the appropriate context attribute, select the property and select **Bind**. In the **Context Viewer** dialog box, select the context attribute that you created.

Now the Java code must be modified to implement dynamic transports of data between the views.

1. **Creating a Mobile Applications for Laptop application**
   In this step, you create the application. The application defines an entry point into the Mobile Applications for Laptop project. In the Mobile Applications for Laptop Explorer, right-click the **Application** node and select **Create Application**. This starts the **New Application** wizard. Enter a name for the application and specify the package name for the Java classes that the Developer Studio generates. Click **Next** and select **Use existing component**. Then select the required values for the **Web Dynpro Component**, the **Interface View,** and the **Startup plug.**

2. **Testing the mobile application**
   After the mobile application has been developed, you can test it. To test a mobile application, perform the following steps:
   - Create the executable binaries, that is, compile the Java code. To do this, right-click the project node in the Mobile Application for Laptops Explorer, and select **Build**. Depending on the builds you already made in your project, the Developer Studio builds only the modifications that have been made since the last build.
   - Create a project archive. A project archive is required to deploy the mobile application. In the Mobile Applications for Laptop Explorer, right-click the project node and select **Export**

runtime metadata. This creates the MCD.XML file that contains the metadata information about the application, the data object model used in the application, dependencies to other mobile components and the authorization mappings. The metadata are verified when you deploy the application to the mobile middleware and download the application to the SAP NetWeaver Mobile Client. To create the archive, right-click the project node again and select **Create Archive**.

- Deploy the mobile application. Before you can run the mobile application, it must be deployed. For testing purposes, it is sufficient to deploy the mobile application locally on the workstation. The deployment mechanism makes the SAP NetWeaver Mobile Client point to the binaries that are created by the Developer Studio when the project is built. Therefore, it is not necessary to deploy the application after each build. To deploy the application, right-click the application element and select **Deploy**. If you want to refresh the data persistency, select the corresponding button. In this case, all of the existing data are deleted. This might be required if you change the data model. Then click **Finish**. To make the deployment effective, you need to restart the SAP NetWeaver Mobile Client.

Runtime metadata

- Run the application. In the Developer Studio, select **Run • Run...**. Select **Mobile Web Dynpro configuration** in the **Run** window and select **New**. Enter a name for the run configuration and select the name of the project and the Mobile Applications for Laptop application that you want to run. Then select **Run**. As a result, the mobile application starts in the SAP NetWeaver Mobile Client.

- Debug the application. To debug the application, set the breakpoints in the code and select **Run • Debug** in the Developer Studio. Enter a name for the debug configuration in the **Debug** window and select the project and Mobile Application for Laptop application that you want to debug. Then select **Debug**. As a result, the Developer Studio perspective changes to **Debug**.

If the application is tested successfully, it can be deployed to the mobile middleware for the mass roll-out to the mobile devices. This is described in the next subsection.

Deployment to the Mobile Middleware

Mass roll-out — After the mobile application has been locally deployed and tested, it can be deployed to the mobile middleware from where it can be assigned to the various mobile devices. By using the Deploy Controller, the automated build process ensures that the build result is stored on the mobile middleware. Alternatively, you can upload the .archive file manually to the mobile middleware using Transaction SDOE_UPLOAD_ARCHIVE.

Now that we have described all steps required to create an occasionally connected application, we want to focus now on connected applications. Connected applications can be built using Mobile Web Dynpro Online, which we discuss in the next section.

5.2 Mobile Web Dynpro Online

Mobile Web Dynpro Online is a technology integrated into SAP NetWeaver Developer Studio that focuses on building browser-based applications that are always connected to a web server. The main objective is to extend and enhance the SAP programming model for building professional user interfaces with features that allow application developers to easily create and modify mobile applications or extend existing desktop browser applications for mobile usage. Web Dynpro as part of SAP NetWeaver provides this programming model to create professional web-based business applications and the appropriate user interfaces. To meet the requirements of mobile applications, specific user interface controls are provided for developing Mobile Web Dynpro applications for Pocket PCs as well as for BlackBerry wireless handhelds and Nokia Series 80 devices.

Browser-based applications — For Mobile Web Dynpro Online, no additional installations are necessary. Due to the full integration in SAP NetWeaver Developer Studio, the application developer can use the same development environment and programming paradigm for a mobile online application as in the case of a desktop application. In most cases, the developer adapts the layout of the user interface to the specific form factor of the mobile target device. All other functions provided by SAP NetWeaver Developer Studio can be used out of the box, such as the following:

- The application meta model
- The same development environment
- Most of the standard UI elements provided by Web Dynpro
- Functionality such as personalization, user management, and connecting to a backend system using web services
- Programming paradigms such as MVC, context mapping, and data binding

5.2.1 Overview of the Available UI Elements

Table 5.1 provides an overview of the supported UI controls for the various devices.

UI Element	Pocket PC	BlackBerry Wireless	Nokia Series 80
Button	Yes	Yes	Yes
Caption	Yes	Yes	Yes
Check Box	Yes	Yes	Yes
CheckBoxGroup	Yes	Yes	Yes
DropDownByIndex	Yes	Yes	Yes
DropDownByKey	Yes	Yes	Yes
Group	Yes	Yes	Yes
Image	Yes	Yes	Yes
InputField	Yes	Yes	Yes
InvisibleElement	Yes	Yes	Yes
Label	Yes	Yes	Yes
LinkToAction	Yes	Yes	Yes
LinkToURL	Yes	Yes	Yes
RadioButton	Only for PPC203	No	Yes
RadioButtonGroupByIndex	Yes	Yes	Yes
RadioButtonGroupByKey	Yes	Yes	Yes
TabStrip	Yes	No	No
Table	Yes	Yes	Yes

Table 5.5 Overview of the Supported UI Elements

UI Element	Pocket PC	BlackBerry Wireless	Nokia Series 80
TextEdit	Yes	Yes	Yes
TextView	Yes	Yes	Yes
TransparentContainer	Yes	Yes	Yes
Tray	Yes	Yes	Yes
ViewContainerUIElement	Yes	Yes	yes

Table 5.5 Overview of the Supported UI Elements (cont.)

5.2.2 Specific Considerations for Nokia Series 80 Devices

The individual mobile components required to run a mobile online application on these devices are:

- Mobile Extension to the Java Servlet Container in the SAP NetWeaver Application Server
- The Nokia S80 Client, which is made up of a set of renderer classes and is responsible for data and event handling

Users of Nokia Series 80 devices require a suitable wireless network that facilitates access to the SAP NetWeaver Application Server. For testing and developing mobile applications, the use of an emulator is recommended. The emulator can be downloaded at the manufacturer's website (*http://www.forum.nokia.com*). The emulator is part of the SDK, Series 80 Platform.

5.2.3 Specific Considerations for BlackBerry Wireless Handhelds

The individual mobile components required to run a mobile online application on these devices are:

WML
- Mobile Extension to the Java Servlet Container in the SAP NetWeaver Application Server
- The Wireless Markup Language (WML) client, which consists of a set of renderer classes and is responsible for data and event handling

Supported versions of BlackBerry and Mobile Data Service (MDS) are 3.6 or higher. All devices are supported as long as they have the supported software version.

In general, users of BlackBerry Wireless Handhelds already have a service contract that includes Internet access via a cellular network. These users need only ensure that all network and technical prerequisites for accessing the SAP NetWeaver Application Server are met. For testing and developing mobile applications, the use of an emulator is recommended. The emulator can be downloaded at the manufacturer's website (*www.blackberry.com/developers/*).

Device emulators

5.2.4 Specific Considerations for Pocket PCs

The individual mobile components required to run a mobile online application on these devices are

- Mobile Extension to the Java Servlet Container in the SAP NetWeaver Application Server
- The Pocket Internet Explorer client (PIE client), which consists of a set of renderer classes and is responsible for data and event handling

Pocket PC users require a suitable wireless network to facilitate the access to the SAP NetWeaver Application Server. If the mobile device is not equipped with hardware supporting wireless networks, additional hardware is required. For testing and developing mobile applications, the use of an emulator is recommended. The emulator can be downloaded at the manufacturer's website (*www.microsoft.com/pocketpc*).

5.3 Summary

In this chapter, you learned how to use the various design times offered in the SAP NetWeaver Developer Studio. You use Mobile Applications for Laptop to create occasionally connected mobile applications that predominantly run on laptops and Mobile Web Dynpro Online to create connected applications running on mobile devices. In Chapter 6, we will apply the concepts we have discussed so far. For that purpose, we provide a tutorial to create a mobile application.

This chapter describes the various aspects of the lifecycle of a mobile application built using the SAP NetWeaver Mobile 7.1 platform, covering processes spanning the development of mobile applications, their deployment, managing the mobile landscape, and eventually upgrading them to a higher version.

6 Mobile Application Lifecycle Management

A thorough understanding of the lifecycle management capabilities of SAP NetWeaver Mobile 7.1 is very important in minimizing total cost of ownership (TCO) of a mobile application. In the context of mobility, lifecycle management is an important factor in ensuring business agility, and it empowers companies to respond to business changes without disruption.

This chapter covers the following topics

- The mobile application development process
- Initial setup
- Mass device administration
- Administration and monitoring tools
- Third-party device management integration
- Patch deployment and upgrade
- Lifecycle management of mobile Web Dynpro online applications

To understand these topics better, it is essential to gain an understanding of the overall landscape of a mobile application deployed on SAP NetWeaver Mobile 7.1. Figure 6.1 shows a typical mobile application landscape.

6 | Mobile Application Lifecycle Management

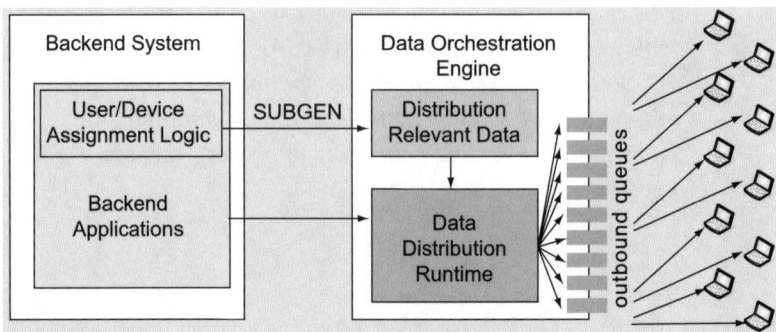

Figure 6.1 Typical Mobile Application Landscape

The typical mobile application landscape from a lifecycle management perspective consists of three broad categories of systems:

- **One or more Enterprise Information Systems, commonly known as backend systems**
  These systems could be SAP Enterprise Resource Planning (ERP), SAP Customer Relationship Management (CRM), SAP Business Suite, and so on. They can even be non-SAP systems.

- **SAP NetWeaver systems that host components such as SAP NetWeaver Data Orchestration Engine (NW DOE) as part of SAP NetWeaver Mobile 7.1 and SAP NetWeaver Exchange Infrastructure (XI)**
  These SAP NetWeaver systems are commonly referred to as middleware systems.

- **Mobile devices that connect to the SAP NetWeaver Mobile 7.1 system**
  The mobile devices can be laptops, PDAs, ruggedized handheld devices, or even smartphones.

Product availability matrix (PAM)

Note

Please see the appropriate product availability matrix for an updated list of supported mobile devices. Any discussion of the lifecycle of a mobile application should involve the totality of these systems and not just the mobile application running on the mobile devices.

To simplify the process of describing the lifecycle of the mobile landscape, a simplified view of the lifecycle is shown in Figure 6.2. The topics to be covered in this chapter fall under one or more of the stages shown in this figure.

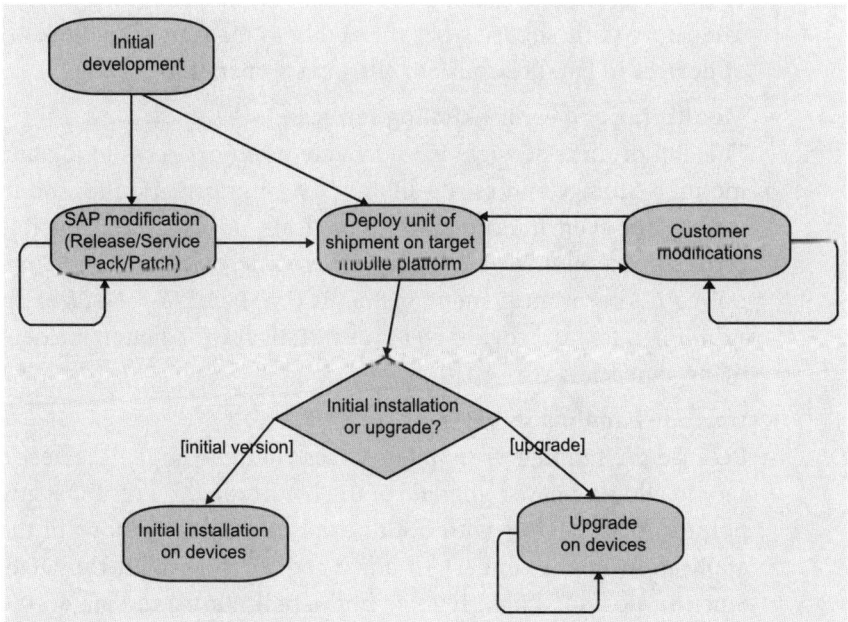

Figure 6.2 Simplified Lifecycle View

To manage all of these scenarios, especially for a large mobile deployment, the importance of administration and monitoring tools and underlying services cannot be overemphasized. Following are a list of tools and services that are available to support the various stages of the lifecycle of a mobile application. The overall architecture is shown in Figure 6.3 later in this chapter. All of these services can be accessed by the SAP NetWeaver Mobile Administrator.

SAP NetWeaver Mobile Administrator

▶ **Administration and operation services**
This set of services covers various scenarios including initial rollout and day-to-day operations that an administrator needs to carry out. The administration component of these services is accessed during the initial phase of the project or during the initial part of a mass rollout. The operation component of the set of services includes device-specific operations such as backup, reset, recovery, locking, and activation and managing the device configura-

6 | Mobile Application Lifecycle Management

tion to ensure that users are able to work with the device without interruption.

- **Device setup and deployment services**
  This includes services related to device handling such as initial device image creation and preparing the initial data set. The critical feature of these services is the ability to manage large numbers of devices in parallel, thus enabling mass operations.

- **Monitoring and error handling services**
  The aim of these services is to provide point of access to log and monitor (storage and retrieval) any sort of information for monitoring and even interpret it automatically to suggest a possible error correction flow. These services are integrated with the Computing Center Management System (CCMS) and SAP NetWeaver Administrator to provide alerts and statistics for better incident management.

- **Upgrade handling services**
  Because the number of mobile devices could be large, it is necessary to allow a phased upgrade of the landscape. As a result, at any point in time devices with both newer and older versions of the application might connect to and need to work with the DOE. Since an upgrade might involve both application and data on the mobile device, these services provide for integrated handling of both.

- **Mobile device inventory store and services**
  Large numbers of mobile devices need to be maintained in such a manner that it is easy to identify devices in a fast and efficient way, especially during the production phase. Thus, this set of services allows for maintenance of device inventory along with requisite information such as user, physical ID of the device such as the International Mobile Equipment Identity (IMEI) number, and other device-specific attributes.

- **Mobile application inventory services**
  The software logistics for mobile applications follow the standard SAP process and are based on SAP NetWeaver components. A dedicated set of services is provided to integrate the lifecycle management of mobile applications with SAP NetWeaver's standard lifecycle management. Using these services, you can maintain a centralized inventory of the various mobile applications deployed

on the mobile devices along with their associated configurations. These configurations can also be centrally modified and deployed on the devices. Additionally, this set of services acts as an interface to the SAP NetWeaver Mobile Administrator that provides information about the mobile application product, software component, and dependency information, which is available in the System Landscape Directory (SLD) and Design Time Repository (DTR). It also provides information about the application archive, which is deployed via the Change Management Server (CMS) and Software Deployment Manager (SDM).

- **Distribution rule definition services**
  As explained in Chapter 4 (Data Orchestration Design Time), the distribution of data to mobile devices via the DOE can be defined and controlled through distribution rules. The definition of these rules is a configuration task and thus is done via the Distribution Modeler, which is a key component of this set of services.

- **Device template store and services**
  The device configuration basically defines the image of the device that needs to be set up. It defines the software components that should be installed on the device along with the data that need to be distributed. The device template is the entity administrators use for managing large numbers of devices.

The following sections describe some key highlights of these tools and services and provide a process overview of the lifecycle management of mobile applications. More specifically, the next section explains the typical landscape for mobile application development and the process to be followed.

Further Information Available
For a complete description of the capabilities and usage instructions for these tools and services, please refer to the relevant help files available at *http://help.sap.com*.

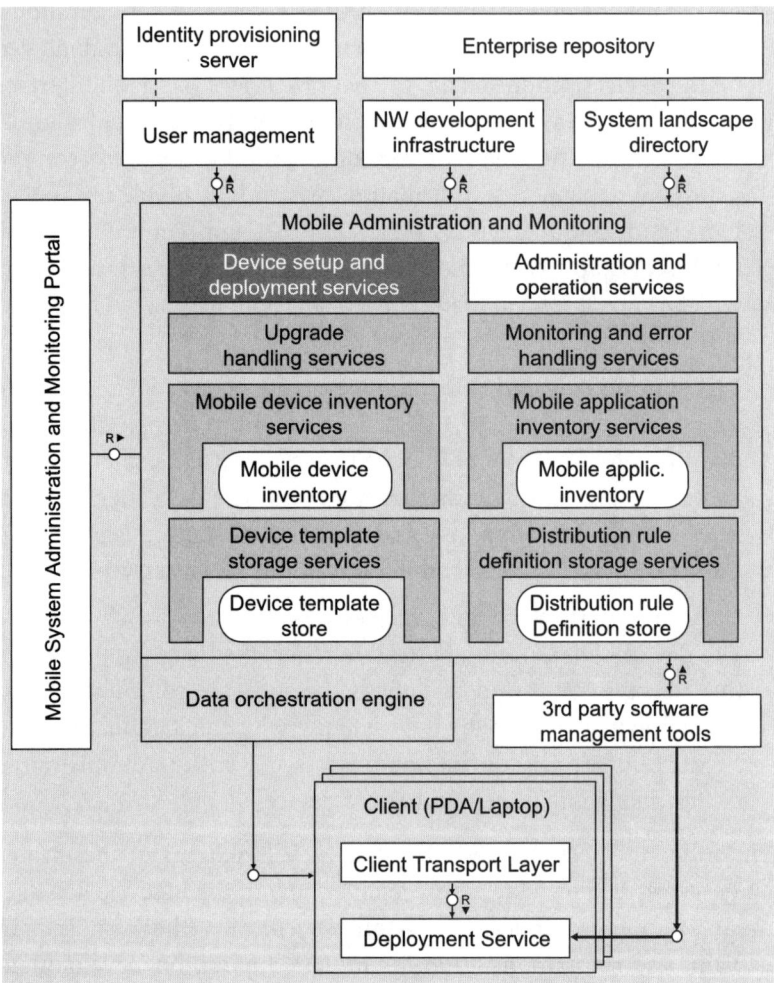

Figure 6.3 Mobile Administrator Building Blocks

6.1 The Mobile Application Development Process

The development of a mobile application that mobilizes an existing business process in the Enterprise Information System consists of the development of the mobile application that runs on the mobile devices, configuration of data distribution-related artifacts in SAP NetWeaver Mobile 7.1 DOE, and the connectivity between the Enterprise Information System and the DOE.

Figure 6.4 shows the typical landscape of systems that are used for developing, deploying, and managing mobile applications with SAP NetWeaver Mobile 7.1. The SAP NetWeaver Developer Studio is used to develop mobile applications. These applications are then deployed on to the mobile devices. The DOE includes the necessary tools and services to carry out the modeling and configurations required for setting up data exchange between the Enterprise Information Systems and the mobile applications running on the mobile devices. Some development may also be needed either on the SAP NetWeaver Mobile 7.1 platform or in the Enterprise Information Systems to set up the data exchange between these two classes of systems.

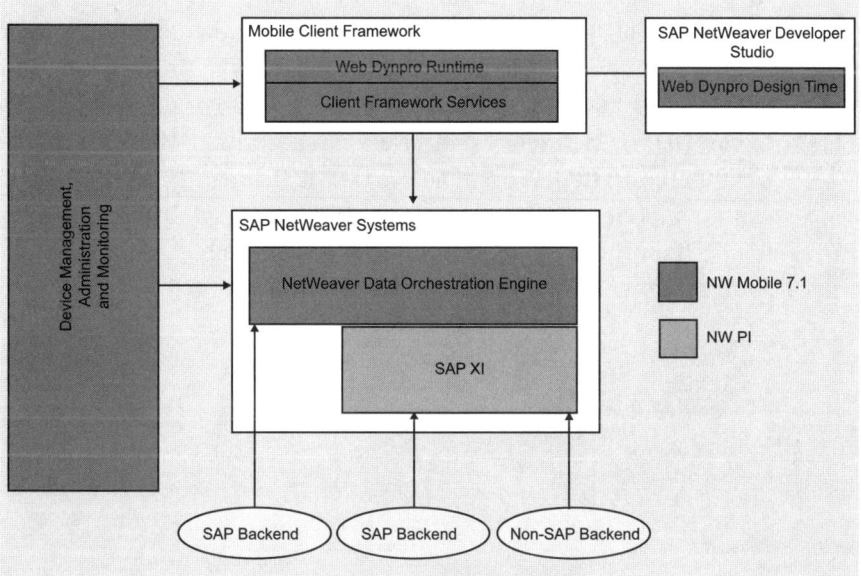

Figure 6.4 Systems Relevant to Mobile Application Development

Understanding the Design Time Meta Model

To understand the development process in the context of the lifecycle of mobile applications, it is essential to understand the design time meta model. The set of application components developed as mobile applications follows the standard SAP development paradigm of product and software components. The process starts with a definition of the mobile application product and various software components within it.

6 | Mobile Application Lifecycle Management

SAP NetWeaver Development Infrastructure (NWDI)

The Web Dynpro application development process is integrated within the SAP NetWeaver Development Infrastructure (NWDI). SAP NetWeaver Developer Studio is the development platform for mobile application development, The Design Time Repository (DTR) is used as the application development repository, the Central Build Service (CBS) is used for archive build processes for mobile applications, and the Change Management Service (CMS) is used for the shipment of mobile applications across systems.

SDA, SCA

All of the Web Dynpro user interfaces and model entities are part of some development components (DCs) because the whole process is integrated with the SAP NWDI. The build process builds the DCs in software deployment archive (SDA) files that can be packaged into a single software component archive (SCA) depending on the software component a DC belongs to. Dependencies can be defined between software components to facilitate a dependency definition and reuse of DCs. The data object definition and generation of services relevant to the DOE is defined via the Data Orchestration Workbench The Data Orchestration Workbench makes it mandatory to link a software component and version to mobile business objects as part of the design process. Based on this, the design time model for mobile applications can be visualized as shown in Figure 6.5.

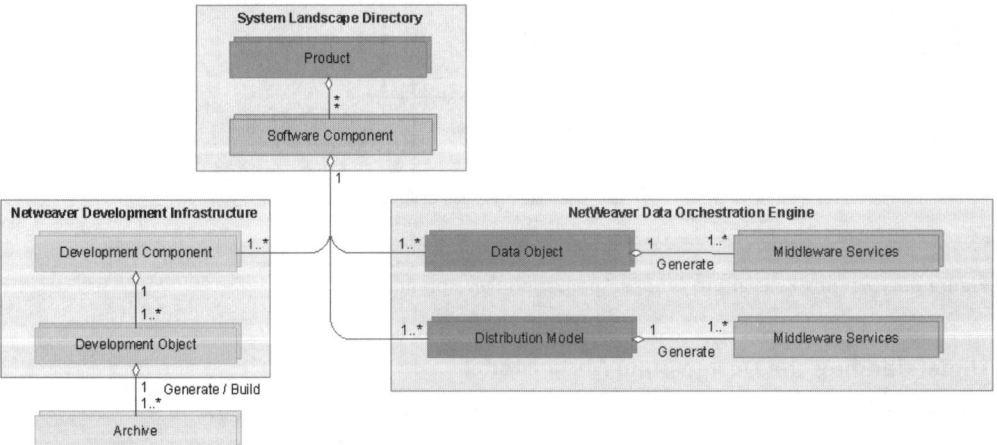

Figure 6.5 Design Time Model of Mobile Applications

The development process to be followed is shown in Figure 6.6.

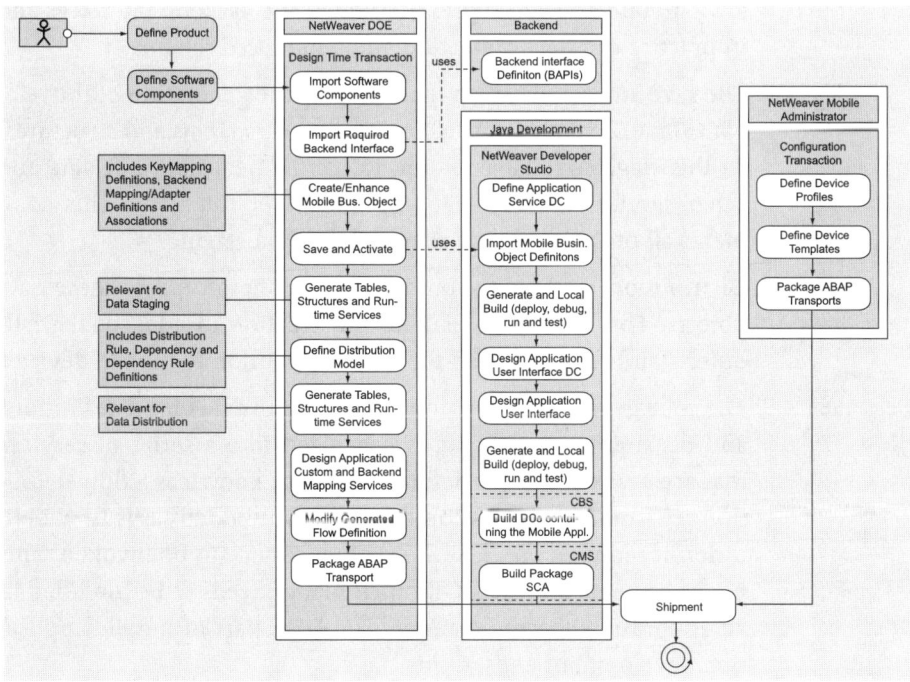

Figure 6.6 New Mobile Application Development Process Overview

The Development Process Steps

Let's go through the steps involved in the development process one by one:

System Landscape Directory (SLD)

1. The first step in the development of the mobile application is to either create a new software component or reuse an existing one in the System Landscape Directory (SLD). This software component forms the basis of the componentization of the mobile application development and thus needs to be imported into the DOE. All of the artifacts created in the process of the mobile application development on the DOE are part of one or the other software component version.

2. The next task is to identify the relevant interfaces from the backend Enterprise Information System interfaces representing the business processes to be mobilized. These interface definitions are imported into the DOE. They can be BAPIs, web services, enterprise services, and so on. These interface definitions are then used to create the so-called data objects on the DOE. These data objects

Backend adapter

are a mobile-relevant representation of the backend interfaces and in practice can be a projection and a modified schema.

3. The save and activate step then triggers the generation of the relevant Data Dictionary (DDIC) objects such as tables and structures. At this stage code is generated to handle persistence of data and other services for key mapping and other functions. This completes all of the modeling required for data staging.

4. Distribution modeling should then be done on top of these data objects. This modeling leads to the creation of additional DDIC objects and code required for data distribution to mobile devices.

Flow definition

5. The code generated, until now based on the data object definitions and distribution modeling, is organized into a series of services that are invoked in a predefined sequence known as a flow definition. The mobile application developer can modify this flow definition if required and insert a custom service to be invoked. This might be needed if the DOE functionality needs to be modified in an application-specific manner. The DOE part of mobile application development ends at this stage.

6. The next stage involves the development of the mobile application that runs on the mobile device. While the development until now happened in the DOE's ABAP stack-based tools, the subsequent development steps have to be carried out in the SAP NetWeaver Developer Studio. As with the server-side development, the client-side development also starts with the process of a component description. On the Java side this is known as a DC. In a componentized mobile application, each reusable application service needs be defined as a DC. Because this application has to have the data distributed by the DOE, the client application development reuses the data object definitions from the DOE.

SAP NetWeaver Developer Studio data object import

7. Therefore, the next step involves importing the data objects. A generate and local build step leads to generation of code to handle the data exchange between the mobile client application and the DOE. With these data objects as a data source, the mobile application developer can develop the required user interfaces and application logic as per the Web Dynpro programming model.

8. Once this development is completed and the final application version built, the Component Build Server (CBS) of SAP's Java Development Infrastructure is used to create DCs containing the

mobile applications. The Change Management Services (CMS) then consume these DCs to create deployable SCAs. The mobile client application development is now complete and ready to be shipped, together with the definition of device templates in the SAP NetWeaver Mobile Administrator.

Figure 6.7 shows the unit of the shipment of the mobile application developed according to the process described above.

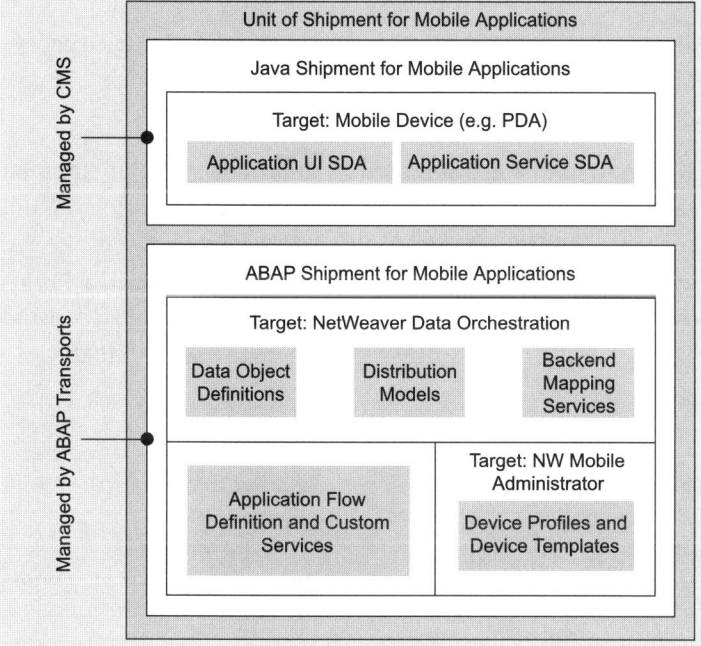

Figure 6.7 Mobile Application Unit of Shipment

It should be noted that the transport management of the mobile applications follows the same philosophy and tools as the conventional server-based applications. The ABAP transports only contain object definitions and modifications resulting from modeling. With the exception of handwritten code in the case of custom services and backend mapping services, no code or DDIC objects are transported. They are all generated in the target system based on model definitions. Furthermore, the client-side part of the mobile applications can be uploaded to the SAP NetWeaver Mobile 7.1 DOE for deployment on the mobile devices via the synchronization mechanism. These uploaded archives are then a part of the Mobile Component

6 | Mobile Application Lifecycle Management

Descriptor (MCD), which is mapped to the corresponding software component version.

Mobile Component Descriptor (MCD)

The following sections explain the processes to be followed for the deployment of this unit of shipment, or MCD. In the next section, we'll look at the initial setup of the DOE.

6.2 Initial Setup

In a connected landscape the unit of shipment reaches the target systems via ABAP Transport Management and Java Change Management Server.

Figure 6.8 shows the steps required to deploy the unit of shipment on the target landscape. The process is only meant to deploy the unit of shipment on the DOE server so that it is available within the SAP NetWeaver Mobile Administrator. After this deployment, administrators can work via the Mobile Administrator user interface to set up the DOE and download software and data to the mobile devices.

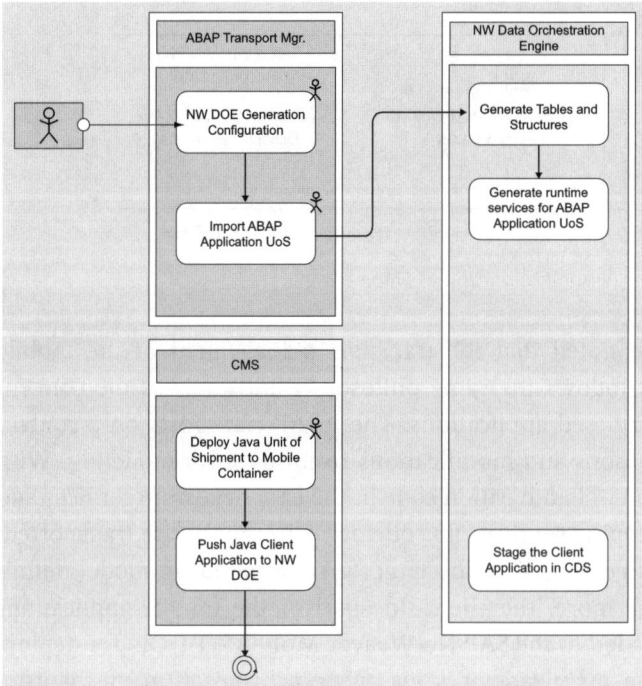

Figure 6.8 Deployment Process via ABAP Transport and CMS

It is also possible to ship the unit of shipment to the target system without using ABAP Transports and CMS, as they require a connected landscape. The unit of shipment can be transported via an offline CD installation.

Once the unit of shipment entities are deployed on the DOE, then via SAP NetWeaver Mobile Administrator, administrators can start the process of setting up DOE, that is, downloading data from the backend, setting up users and devices within the DOE, and configuring distribution rules. The complete process is shown in Figure 6.9.

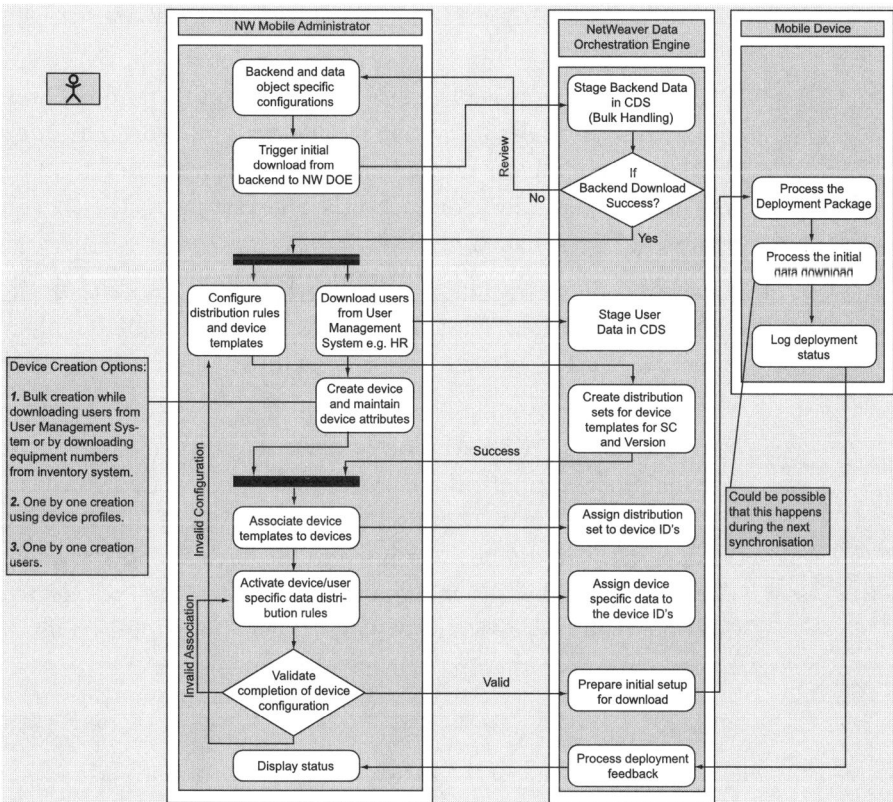

Figure 6.9 Initial Installation on Mobile Devices

Initial Installation Steps

The actions to be performed by the administrator are shown as human actions in Mobile Administrator. The internal processes triggered by these actions are also shown. Let's take a closer look:

Data staging

1. The first step is to prepare for data download from the backend Enterprise Information Systems to the DOE for data staging and eventual distribution to the mobile devices. This preparation involves configuration of filters for selecting the information relevant to mobile devices. This configuration is done specifically for each data object. If, for example, a company is rolling out mobile applications to its field force in North America but not in Europe, this information can be used to apply a filter on the Business Partner data object such that only the records for the North American region will reach the DOE.

2. Once these configurations are complete, initial download is triggered.

3. When the data are available in the DOE, the configuration of users and distribution rules to capture data relevance needs to be done. The users can either be created manually or downloaded from HR systems automatically. For each user a device is created and the device attributes maintained.

4. In parallel, the distribution rules can be configured and device templates associated with these rules. The usage of templates reduces the manual work of associating distribution rules for each device and user.

5. The next step is the association of devices to device templates so that the devices inherit the data subscriptions created automatically from the data distribution rules. At this stage the DOE has the data that need to be distributed to the devices and knows the users and their devices and the data relevance for each device. The DOE then proceeds to store the relevant data for each divice in preparation for the first synchronization.

> **Note**
> The DOE considers mobile applications as data and stores them in the queue for deployment.

6. The mobile devices with the SAP NetWeaver Mobile 7.1 client framework installed can synchronize with the DOE. On the first synchronization, the device receives a package for deployment. This package contains the mobile application that is relevant for this user. This first synchronization also carries the data that the

owner of the device needs to use the application deployed during this synchronization. For example, a company might be rolling out the xMobile Time and Travel (xMTT) application and xMobile Asset Management (xMAM) to its field force. For some users such as field service technicians, it might be required to roll out both applications, whereas for the white-collar field personnel such as consultants, it may make sense to roll out oly the xMTT. When both these users synchronize for the first time, they receive the applications they need and relevant data as explained above. The status of the synchronization is sent back to the server for remotely monitoring the success of the application and data deployment.

7. After a successful completion of the first synchronization, the device is ready to be used by the end users. — xMAM, xMTT

In the next section, we will describe how the setup of a large number of devices is supported by the SAP NetWeaver Mobile 7.1 platform.

6.3 Mass Device Administration

Organizations with a large mobile workforce require mechanisms to set up large numbers of mobile devices quickly, in parallel, and with minimum human intervention. Mass device administration addresses this need and enables setting up mobile devices including application, drivers, framework, database, add-ons, agents, and data. These mobile devices are then ready for use by end users. Mass device administration works by creating a package with all of the content necessary for a mobile device as listed above. — Ready for use

In a typical mobile application deployment scenario, each mobile device has a unique set of data that is relevant to its user. Therefore, the data portion of the package is unique for each mobile device. The software part of the package is relatively common across mobile devices to be prepared for mass roll out. SAP NetWeaver Mobile 7.1 allows for the creation of user-specific data packages and common software packages. These are combined to create a single package for download to each mobile device. The package can be transported to the mobile device either via network (HTTP) or in a physical media such as a CD, SD card, or DVD. Once the package is available on the mobile device, the installation is triggered and, if successful, the mobile device is ready for use by the end user.

It is also possible to include non-SAP software in the software package for installation on the mobile devices and to invoke specific installers for non-SAP applications. Hooks are provided to invoke these installers before and after the installation of SAP's software (including custom development) and data packages, thereby allowing customers to exercise control over the sequence in which the installation is carried out.

While these steps help in the deployment of the packages containing data and software, the configurations required on the DOE for each user can also be done efficiently for large mobile rollouts. The concepts of device class, device inventory, and device configuration set help in optimizing the efforts required to maintain mobile device- and end user-specific configurations including data distribution rules. Let's look at each in more detail.

6.3.1 Device Class

Device class is a definition of a class of actual physical mobile devices that can connect to the DOE and can be administered via the SAP NetWeaver Mobile Administrator. The device class data model is shown in Figure 6.10. A device class primarily includes:

- **Device attributes**
  Device attributes can include the following:
  - Device type, for example laptop or PDA
  - Communication protocol
  - Device vendor, operating system, and version

- **Device configuration service and parameter set**
  The set of the device configuration services that can be installed on the device along with parameters needed by these services

- **Device driver set**
  The set of device drivers that can be installed on the device

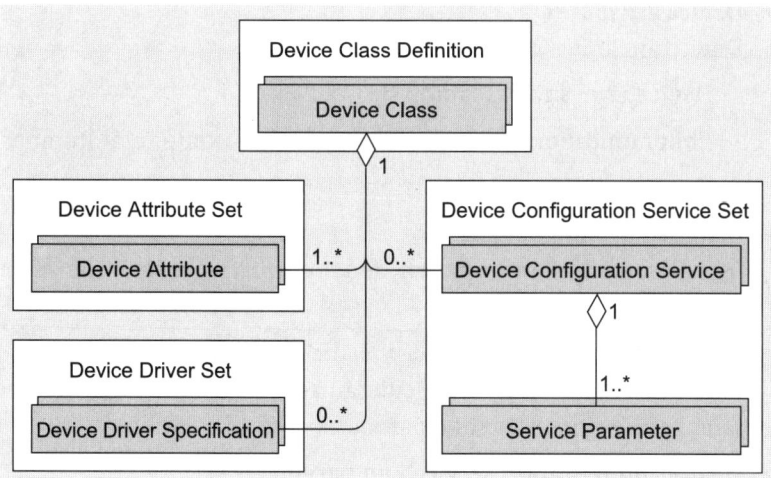

Figure 6.10 Device Class

Specific mobile devices internally identified by the device ID inherit the properties from the device class when the device class is assigned to it. Thus, all of the attributes that are maintained for that device class can be maintained for the specific mobile devices as well, without repeating the attributes for all of them individually.

Device ID

This brings us to the set of information that can be maintained for a specific mobile device in addition to that inherited from the device class. The set of information maintained for a device ID is referred to as device inventory and contains a lot of information apart from that are inherited from the device class.

6.3.2 Device Inventory

The device inventory is the catalog of mobile devices that are connected to the DOE and managed via the SAP NetWeaver Mobile Administrator. Figure 6.11 shows the device inventory data model. The information about a device stored in the device inventory includes the following:

- Device ID
  The device ID represents an actual physical device and is the identifier for processing within the DOE.

6 | Mobile Application Lifecycle Management

▶ **Device attributes**
Device attributes can include the following:
  ▶ Device type such as laptop or PDA
  ▶ Communication protocol, device vendor, equipment number
  ▶ Operating system and version, memory, processor speed

▶ **Installed product and SC**
Includes version information and information about the client framework (CF).

▶ **Employee ID and application-specific attributes**
Examples of application-specific attributes include territory and sales area for the users of a particular device.

▶ **Device configuration service and parameter set**
This includes the device configuration services that are installed on the device along with parameters with which these services are running on the device.

▶ **Device driver set**
The device drivers installed on the device.

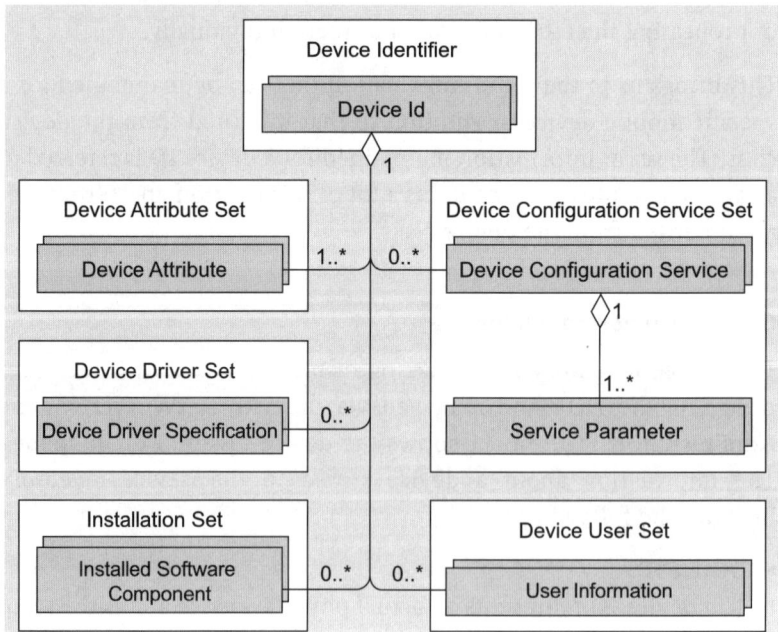

Figure 6.11 Device Inventory

6.3.3 Device Configuration

Because mobile devices primarily host various types of mobile applications, to increase the efficiency of the deployment process, a device configuration set or device template is available. A device configuration set is the set of software components that can be deployed together on a set of devices. This way, apart from assigning software components one by one to devices, it is possible to assign a single device configuration to a device, thus reducing the steps for the administrator. A device configuration set also contains device configuration services that need to be installed and a configuration parameter set that needs to be set for these services. The device configuration set can be visualized as shown in Figure 6.12.

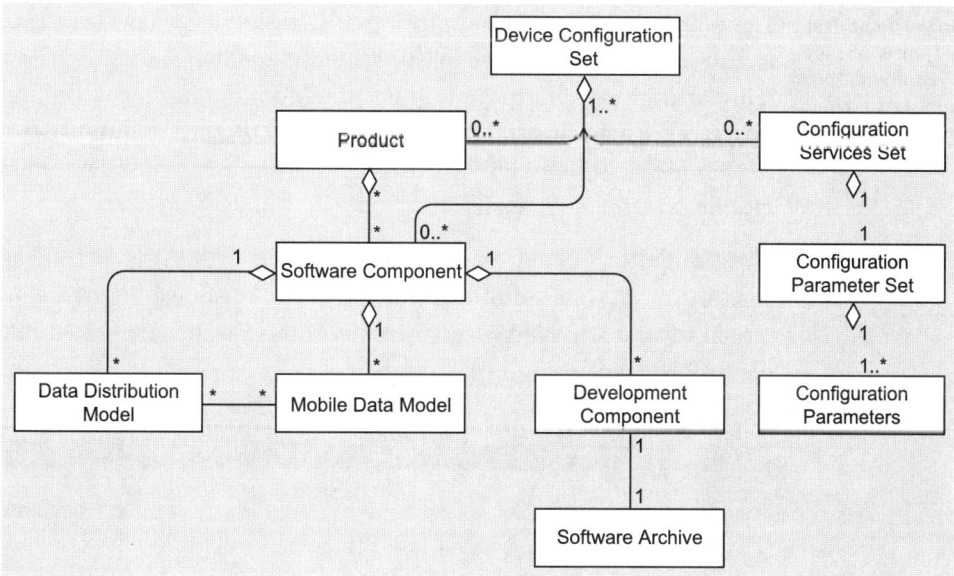

Figure 6.12 Device Configuration Set (Device Template)

In summary, the mass device administration capability of the DOE provides a mechanism to avoid any repetition of human activity for each device, thereby drastically reducing the cost involved in rolling out large numbers of mobile devices.

> Avoid any repetition of human activity

The concepts described so far also help in managing large mobile deployments because the administration and monitoring tools we'll look at next also use these concepts.

6.4 Administration and Monitoring Tools

Because the number of mobile devices supported via the SAP NetWeaver Mobile Application Platform is quite large, the effort required to manage them is significant. Thus, the purpose of the SAP NetWeaver Mobile Administrator is to ensure smooth management of the entire landscape, starting with setting up of the devices by distributing applications, then configuring data distribution, managing the daily processes, and monitoring them, and finally tracking and handling errors. SAP NetWeaver Mobile Administrator is the single-point user interface for configuration, administration, and monitoring of the mobile system landscape and makes it possible to manage large numbers of mobile devices.

Single-point user interface for configuration, administration and monitoring

The administration and monitoring of the mobile system landscape is also an extension of the existing lifecycle management of IT systems within an enterprise. Thus, the Mobile Administrator user interfaces are an integral part of the SAP NetWeaver Administrator to provide a unified view to customers of their in-house as well as mobile system landscape.

The Computing Center Management System (CCMS) is also leveraged in the Mobile Administrator. Figure 6.13 shows the overview screen for the SAP NetWeaver Mobile Administrator integrated into the SAP NetWeaver Administrator.

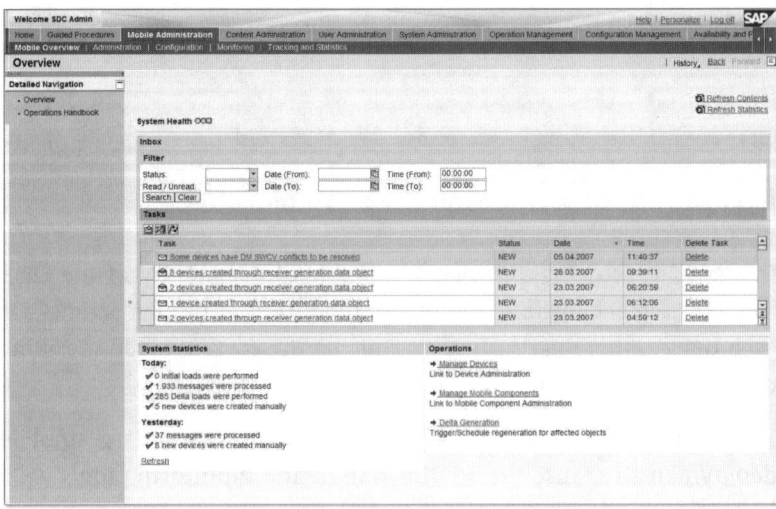

Figure 6.13 SAP NetWeaver Mobile Administration Overview Screen

Administration and Monitoring Tools | 6.4

In a productive landscape, it is of the outmost importance to continuously monitor the health of the applications and systems to ensure that no business disruptions occur. This is especially important in a mobile deployment, which has some unique challenges in this space, including the following:

▶ **Size of the landscape**

The number of systems in a production mobile landscape is an order of magnitude higher than a conventional SAP deployment due to the usage of small mobile devices for running business processes. It is possible that the number of devices could be in the range of tens of thousands. All of these devices need to be monitored centrally. Figure 6.13, Figure 6.14, and Figure 6.15 show snapshots of samples of these centralized monitoring capabilities. It is possible to create alerts that page the administrator in case of specific situations that need attention. Device synchronization monitoring (see Figure 6.14 and Figure 6.15) can also be used to alert end users if they are not synchronizing regularly.

▶ **Disconnected systems**

These devices are not connected to the corporate network most of the time. Furthermore, it is highly unlikely that they are all connected together, even for a short period of time. Therefore, the monitoring systems are designed to collect information on the devices when they are operating but then disconnect and upload the data to the server.

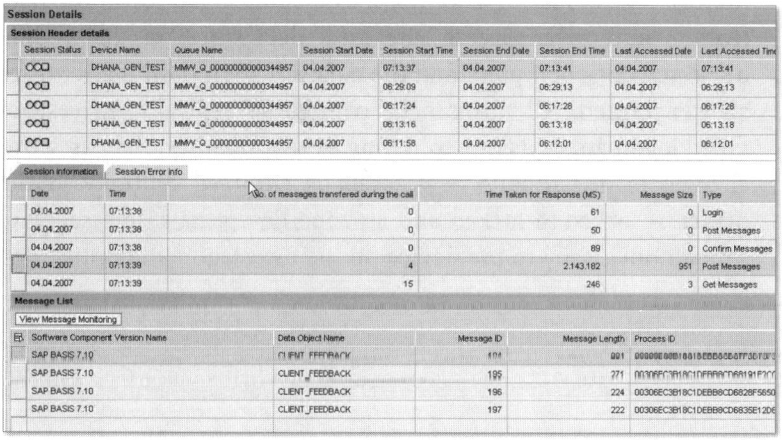

Figure 6.14 Device Synchronization Monitoring

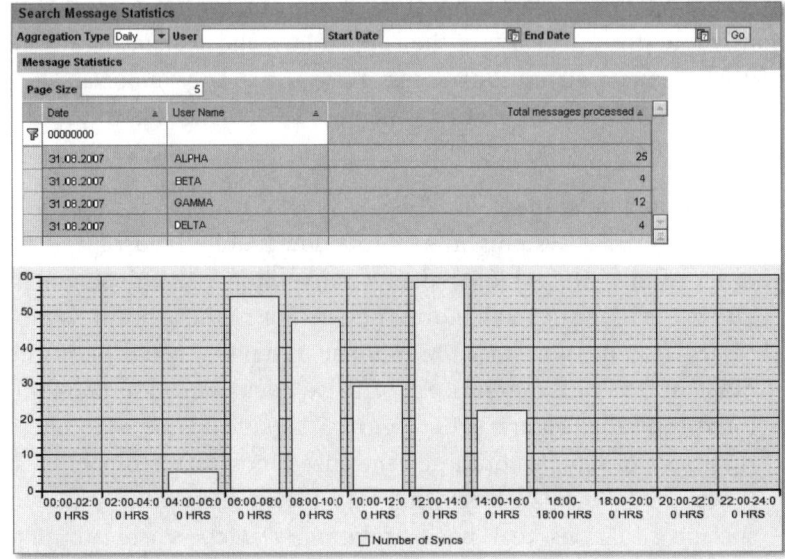

Figure 6.15 Device Synchronization Statistics

- **Security**

    Ensuring the security of corporate data in a mobile deployment requires extra attention because the mobile devices containing corporate information are constantly outside of company premises, and mobile devices are frequently disconnected from the corporate network. It is possible to centrally monitor security-related incidents and take corrective action. Figure 6.16 and Figure 6.17 show snapshots of these capabilities. To protect the data from unauthorized access, the local data store on the mobile device can be encrypted, and the data transferred on the wire are also encrypted. All this can be configured centrally. In case of failed logon attempts due to wrong password entry, the password changes on the mobile device can be enforced centrally. If the device is locked, a locked and a "wipe device data" message are sent automatically to the device on the next logon attempt.

Administration and Monitoring Tools | 6.4

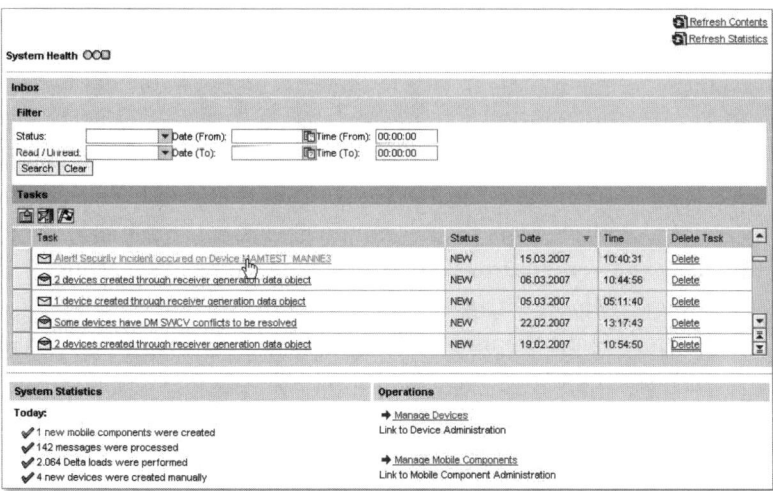

Figure 6.16 Centralized Monitoring of Security-Related Incidents

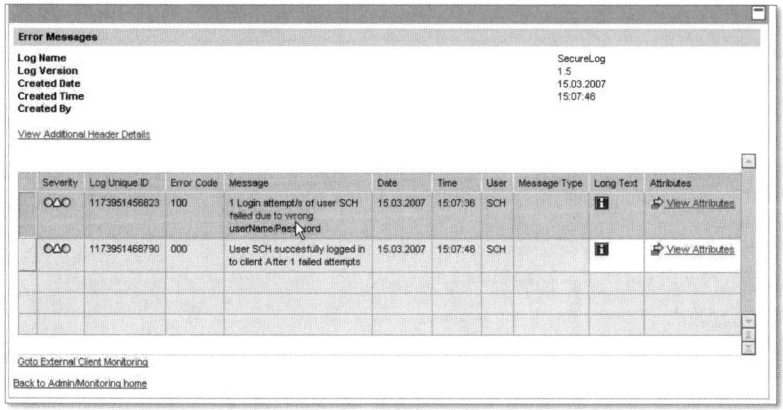

Figure 6.17 Centralized Tool to View Security Incident Details

▶ **Central error handling**

It is natural for business and technical errors to occur during the operation of any enterprise application. The chances that these errors will occur are much higher in an offline mobile application because of the usage of offline mobile applications with their own databases. Because these work in disconnected mode, they might not have access to information updated since the last synchronization, leading to the data modifications being rejected on the server. A simple example is two of the users of the mobile applica-

Distributed transactions

6 | Mobile Application Lifecycle Management

tions modifying the same instance of a data object, resulting in a conflict that needs to be resolved. Another example is rejection of changes on the mobile device by the backend system due to technical or business errors. Figure 6.18 shows the centralized business transaction monitoring. It is also possible to edit the failure message centrally and resubmit it for processing to the server. In case of technical errors on the mobile device, it is quite difficult to identify the error, as the device is not always online. Thus, it is possible to remotely trigger logs and traces of the mobile applications running on the mobile devices. These are then uploaded to the server on the next synchronization and can be viewed centralized on the server as shown in Figure 6.19.

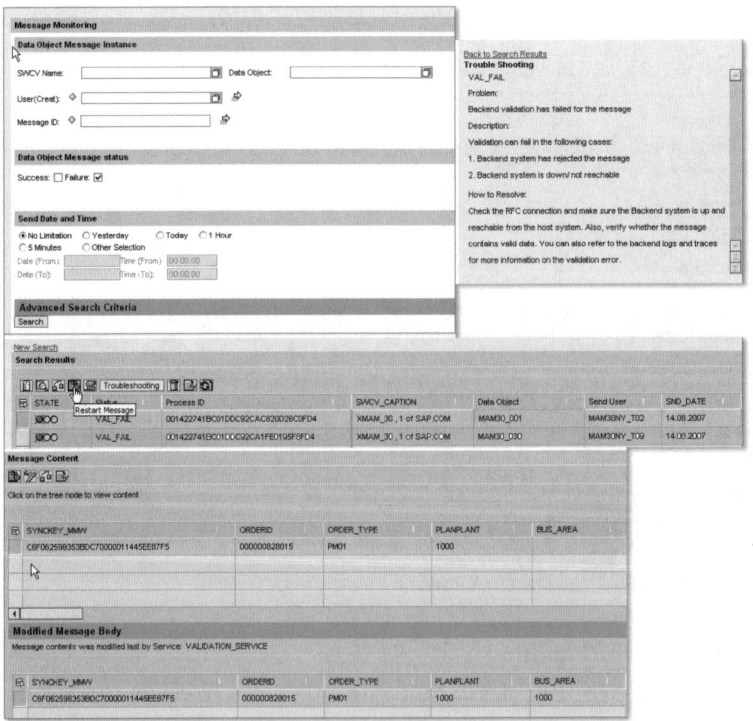

Figure 6.18 End-to-End Business Transaction Monitoring for a Mobile Application Deployment

Open architecture　An open architecture that allows the integration of tools of other software providers was a design goal of the SAP NetWeaver Mobile 7.1 platform. In the following section, we will show how this can be applied to the integration of device management tools.

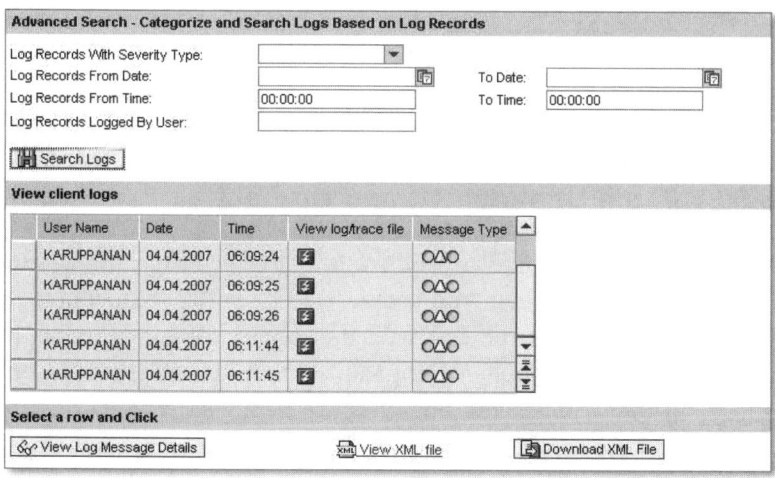

Figure 6.19 Central Visualization of Device Logs and Traces

6.5 Third-Party Device Management Integration

SAP integration with a third-party device management (DM) system can benefit organizations that want to leverage their investment in an existing DM system, resulting in a lower TCO. Organizations with an existing DM tool can use the existing functionality provided by those tools for deploying SAP mobile components.

Because an SAP mobile component does not install itself, an intermediary component is required. The integration framework acts as such an intermediary between a DM system and an SAP NetWeaver Mobile client and enables SAP integration with a third-party DM system. Organizations with an existing DM system can use the deployment tools offered by the DM system and take advantage of the benefits provided by the SAP NetWeaver Mobile client.

SAP third-party DM system integration is separated into different levels. The first level, L01, is available with this release. L01 refers to a minimum type of integration in which only the Integration Framework is provided to enable SAP mobile component deployment by an external DM system. L01 allows you to use any DM system for deploying SAP mobile components. Currently, SAP ships integration with Microsoft Systems Management Server (SMS) out of the box.

Systems Management Server (SMS)

In the next section, we will focus on how patches and newer versions of the mobile application components can be deployed to the mobile devices.

6.6 Patch Deployment and Upgrade

Involvement of data objects

Mobile applications, like any software once it is installed and running, need to be updated with patches and newer version upgrades. This is to ensure that the bug fixes and ongoing improvements to existing features are deployed onto a productive landscape. It is very important that patches and upgrades are deployed without disruption to business operations. In SAP NetWeaver Mobile 7.1, the process to be followed for the deployment of patches and rolling out the upgrades is same. The process only depends on the involvement of data objects. The reason for this is that the deployment of the mobile application patch or a version upgrade with data object changes necessitates updating the data store on the mobile device, so the process includes initiating data extraction on the SAP NetWeaver Mobile 7.1 DOE and synchronization on the mobile device.

An overview of the process is shown in Figure 6.20. It can be seen that the process is analogous to the process followed for initial rollout. However, steps such as the backend download and data object configurations and triggering the initial download again are not needed unless the patch or upgrade contains changes to the data objects or has new data objects.

In the absence of data object changes, it is sufficient to deploy new executables on the mobile devices. If there are changes to the data objects, and these changes are incompatible changes such as deletion of a data object node or attribute or change of the data type of an attribute, then it is necessary to have the two differing versions of the data models in different Software Component Versions (SWCV).

Different versions of mobile applications

The DOE allows coexistence of multiple SWCVs in the same server. Figure 6.21 and Figure 6.22 show the possible landscapes and versions in an upgrade scenario with data model changes.

6.6 Patch Deployment and Upgrade

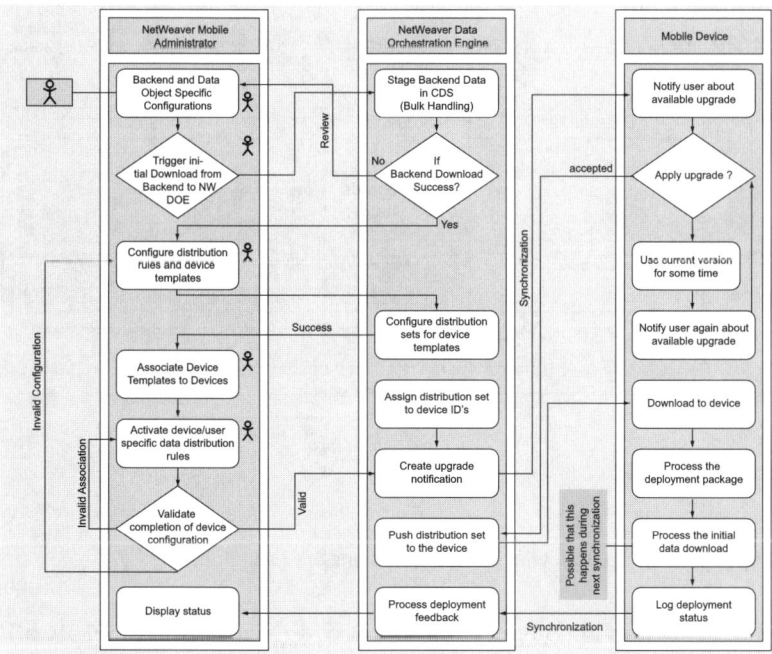

Figure 6.20 Process Overview for Patch and Upgrade of Mobile Applications

> **Note**
>
> This approach allows mobile devices with different versions of mobile applications to coexist in the landscape. These devices can be then upgraded in a phased manner to the newer version, thereby providing the phased upgrade feature. This capability is extremely important to the ability to upgrade an offline mobile application deployment.

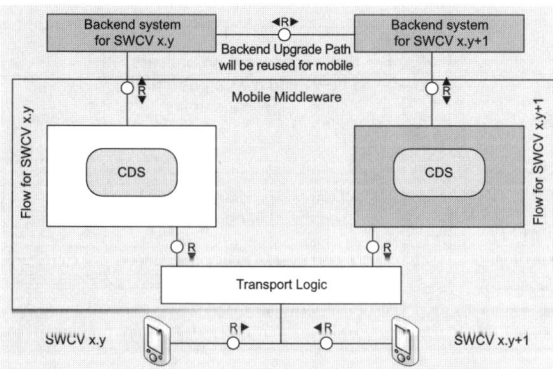

Figure 6.21 Integration with Different Versions of Backend and Client Entities

6 | Mobile Application Lifecycle Management

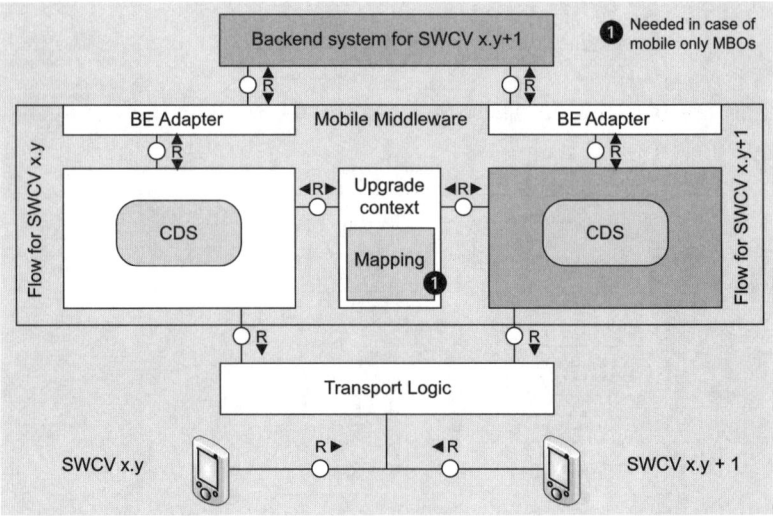

Figure 6.22 Integration with Different Versions of Client Entities

If a mobile deployment running on SAP NetWeaver 2004 or SAP NetWeaver 2004s needs to migrate to SAP NetWeaver Mobile 7.1, then a two-box upgrade process needs to be followed, and the approach described in this section is not valid. Figure 6.23 shows a high-level process overview for this situation.

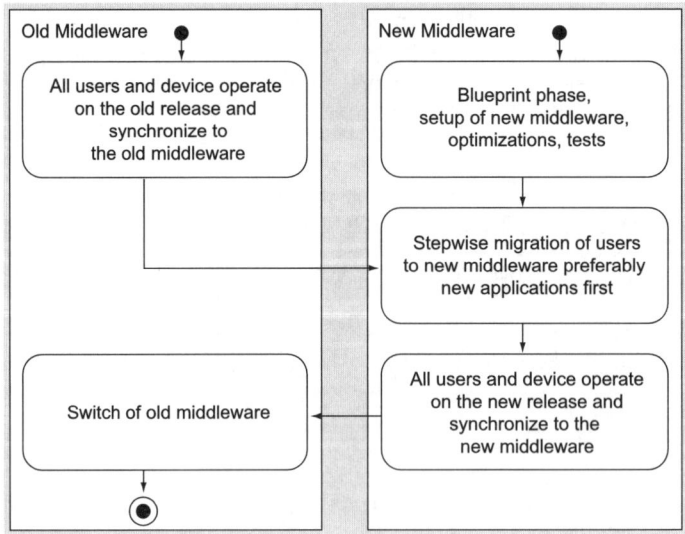

Figure 6.23 High-Level Process Overview of Migration from NW04 or NW04s to SAP NetWeaver Mobile 7.1

6.7 Lifecycle Management of Mobile Web Dynpro Online Applications

The lifecycle management of the online mobile applications developed via Mobile Web Dynpro Online follows the standard Web Dynpro lifecycle management. Please refer to the appropriate documentation of Web Dynpro lifecycle management, which can be found on the SAP service marketplace (*http://service.sap.com*).

6.8 Summary

As you learned in this chapter, the SAP NetWeaver Mobile 7.1 development platform comes with extensive capabilities for managing the lifecycle of the mobile application and managing large mobile deployments. The investments made in this area should help customers reduce the TCO of mobile applications. This chapter also explained the process overview of the development and deployment of mobile applications. Chapter 7 explains the usage of the design time tools for building mobile applications.

Having explained the architectural foundations of the Data Orchestration Engine in the previous chapters, we will in this chapter present a tutorial that describes all necessary steps to build an occasionally connected mobile application.

7 Design Study of an Occasionally Connected Mobile Application using Mobile Applications for Laptop

The following tutorial provides you with step-by-step instructions for creating an occasionally connected mobile application using the Mobile Applications for Laptop design time. The aim of this tutorial is to provide an overview of all the tasks required to create a mobile application from an end-to-end point of view. Apart from the design of the mobile application, this example also covers the modeling of the data objects and data distribution schema on the data orchestration engine (DOE) and provides sample code to integrate the application with a backend system.

Aim of the tutorial

> **Note**
>
> Please note that the application we will create in this chapter is not suitable for use in a production scenario. The aim is to show some capabilities of the design time rather than to create a fully fledged business application with an optimized UI and data object model.

7.1 Scenario Description

The following fictional case describes the scenario we will implement in this chapter. Mr. John is a service person who services customer equipment. The company receives service requests in the call center and enters them in the backend system. Since Mr. John works at the customer site and is disconnected from the backend system, he

Use case description

needs to have all required data on his laptop to perform the service request. After he finishes his work, he updates the data on his laptop. Back in his hotel, he connects to the backend systems, uploads the changed data to the server, and receives new service requests.

Mr. John works in a service team, which has representatives in many regions. It is expected that each service person receives only the service orders for the customers assigned to his work center and that the service persons only receive service orders for the equipment they are qualified to service.

7.2 Development Process

The steps of the development process

The diagram shown in Figure 7.1 depicts the required steps and their logical relationships for creating the service-order application for this sample project.

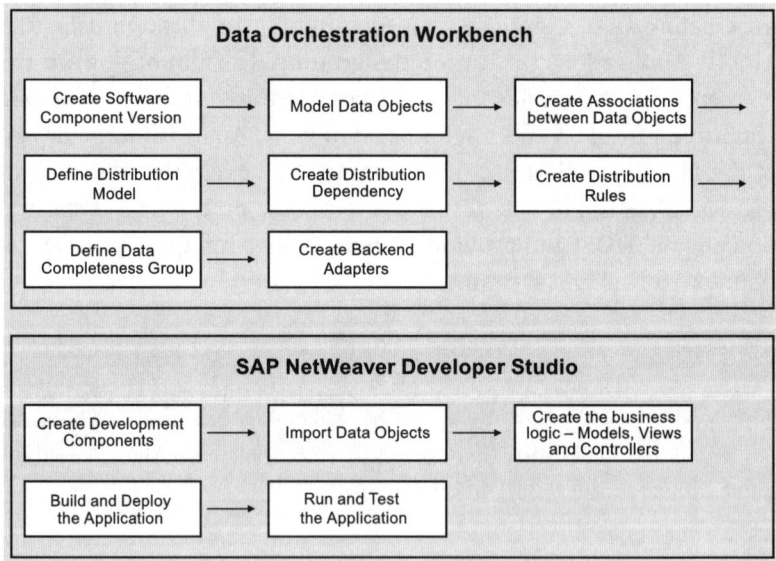

Figure 7.1 Development Process for the Service Order Application

To create an occasionally connected mobile application, you need to do the following:

- Model the data objects on the DOE, create the associations between them, and define the distribution model
- Import the data objects into the SAP NetWeaver Developer Studio; create and build the model, the views, and the controllers; and deploy the application
- In a development project for an occasionally connected mobile application, you make use of existing services, which are already implemented in the backend system. In this tutorial, however, we provide the code for the service of the backend system to make the tutorial independent from your specific backend system release.

7.3 User Interface

For the sample application, two views need to be designed. The templates for the UIs are described in this chapter. The first view we require is the CustomerDetails view. This view displays the details of the customers that have registered a service request. You should be able to select a particular customer and navigate to the second view, where the orders of the selected customer are displayed. The template for the first view is shown in Figure 7.2.

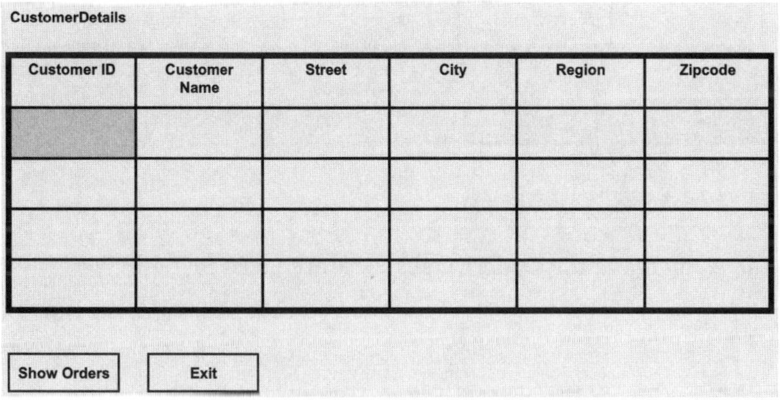

CustomerDetails view

Customer ID	Customer Name	Street	City	Region	Zipcode

[Show Orders]   [Exit]

Figure 7.2 UI of the CustomerDetails View

The elements of this view are listed in Table 7.1.

UI Element	Action
Table	Displays all customer information, including Customer ID, Customer Name, Street, City, Region, and Zipcode for each customer. You can select the customer whose orders you want to see.
Button 1: Show Orders	Displays the orders of the selected customer in the OrderDetails view.
Button 2: Exit	The application exits and returns to the SAP NetWeaver Mobile Client home page.

Table 7.1 UI Elements of CustomerDetails View

OrderDetails view — The second view we require is the OrderDetails view. This view displays the orders of the selected customer. You can also update the data in this view. The template for this view is as shown in Figure 7.3.

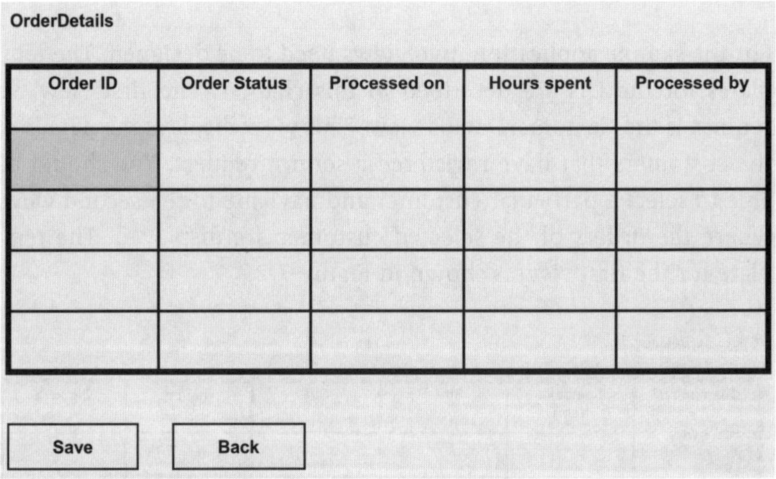

Figure 7.3 UI of the OrderDetails View

The elements of the OrderDetails view are listed in Table 7.2.

UI Element	Action
Table	Displays information about all orders of the selected customer, including the Order ID, Description, Material, Equipment Type, Hours Spent, and Percentage for each order.
Button 1: Save	Saves the changes that the user enters.
Button 2: Back	Displays the previous view — the CustomerDetails view

Table 7.2 UI Elements of OrderDetails View

7.4 Defining Data Objects and Distribution Model

Next, you need to define the data objects and the distribution model for the tutorial application on the DOE. You perform these activities on the DOE Workbench.

7.4.1 Creating a Software Component Version

This procedure allows you to create a software component version (SWCV), which is a shipment unit for design time objects in the DOE repository. SWCVs are part of the software catalog in the System Landscape Directory. You must create an SWCV before you can create data objects. Data objects from one SWCV are transported and shipped together. It is possible to join multiple SWCVs for the version of a product and ship them together. For the sake of simplicity, all repository objects in the ABAP stack are created as local objects ($TMP).

Create a SWCV

Procedure to Create a SWCV

Follows these steps to create a SWCV:

1. Log on to the SAP NetWeaver AS and choose **Data Orchestration Engine • Development • Data Orchestration Workbench**.

2. Choose **Create SWCV**. The fields in the **SWCV Creation** dialog box are activated.

3. Enter the details for the SWCV as shown in Table 7.3.

Field Name	Value
Name	SERVICEORDERAPP
Vendor	SAP
Version	1.0
Element ID	1234
Destination	QPT(*)
Data Object Package	$TMP

Table 7.3 Details for the SWCV

> **Note**
> The destination needs to be substituted according to your system landscape. Enter the RFC destination of your test backend system.

4. Choose **Save**.

5. On the **Create Object Directory Entry** view, click **Local Object**.

You have now created the SWCV SERVICEORDERAPP.

7.4.2 Modeling the Data Objects

For the sample project, you need to create the following data objects:

- Service Order
- Customer
- Equipment
- Employee
- Work Center

Standard data objects You create the data objects Service Order, Customer, and, Equipment as standard data objects. The information contained in them must be distributed to the service technicians' devices, as it is required for completing the service orders. The Service Order data object must contain all the attributes relevant for its distribution, that is, the equipment and the region information. This must be provided by the corresponding business objects in the backend system.

▶ To have the devices created for the employees, you define an Employee data object as a *Receiver Generation* (RecGen) data object. In the sample project, this data object contains the information about the employee who is registered as the user of the device including his qualifications and the work center this employee is assigned to.

Receiver Generation data object

▶ The data object Work Center is required to subscribe to the service orders for customers in the region for which the employee's work center is responsible. Therefore, you create the Work Center data object as a *Subscription Generation* (SubGen) data object containing the information about the work center region assignment.

Subscription Generation data object

Figure 7.4 provides an overview of the data objects to be created, the basic information contained in them, and the associations between them. An association is defined between the Service Order and the Customer data objects using the field CUSTOMER_ID, and between the Service Order and Equipment data objects using the field SERIAL_NO.

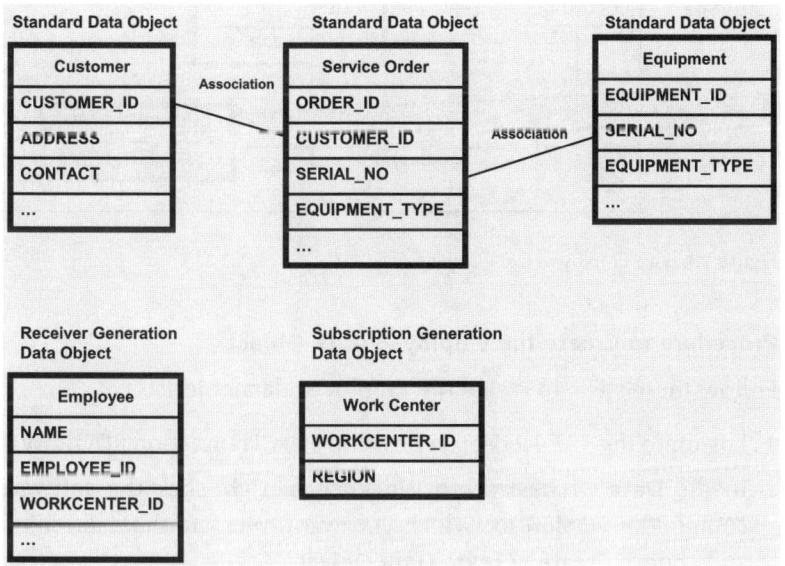

Figure 7.4 Data Object Model of the Service Order Application

7.4.3 Creating the Employee Data Object

The Employee data object

Model the Employee data object as a Receiver Generation data object. It contains the information required for generating the devices. The devices will be generated based on this data object and the customized Receiver Meta Model (RMM). The sample Receiver Generation data object contains information about the employee who uses the device (the employee ID, the work center to which the employee is assigned, and his qualifications). It has the structure shown in Figure 7.5. It contains a root node with the attributes EMPLOYEE_ID, NAME, and WORKCENTER_ID and a child node QUALIFICATIONS with the attributes EQUIPMENT_TYPE and EQUIPMENT_BRAND. The child node contains all the equipment the employee is qualified for.

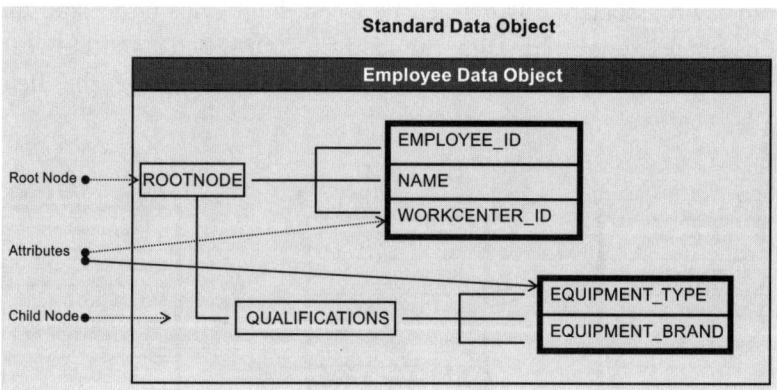

Figure 7.5 The Employee Data Object

Procedure to Create the Employee Data Object

Follow these steps to create the Employee data object:

1. Log on to the SAP NetWeaver AS and start Transaction SDOE_WB.
2. In the **Data Orchestration Workbench**, right-click the software component version for which you want to create the data object and choose **Create • Create Data Object**.
3. Under **Data Object Category**, select **Receiver Generation** from the drop-down list.
4. Choose **Continue**.

5. On the **Data Object Overview** tab, under **Data Object Details**, enter the details shown in Table 7.4.

Field	Value	Comment
Name	EMPLOYEE	
Client Specific	Enabled	Default: This indicator is set.
Switch On Automatic Key Mapping	Disabled	Default: This indicator is not set.
Direction	Download Only	For a Receiver Generation data object, this field is automatically set to the default value **Download Only**. Receiver Generation data objects are used for generating devices, and therefore no information is uploaded to the backend.

Table 7.4 Details for the Employee Data Object

6. Select **Save**

You have now created a data object and can proceed to create the root node for the data object and the child nodes.

Procedure to Create the Root Node for the Data Object and the Child Nodes

Follow these steps to create the root node for the data object and the child nodes:

The root node of the Employee data object

1. Log on to the SAP NetWeaver AS and start Transaction SDOE_WB.
2. In the **Data Orchestration Engine Workbench**, right-click the **EMPLOYEE** and select **Add Node**.
3. On the **Node Overview** tab, in the **Node Details** area, enter the details shown in Table 7.5.

Field	Value	Comment
Node Name	ROOTNODE	
Description	Root node	Short text

Table 7.5 Details for the Root Node of the Employee Data Object

4. On the **Node Attributes** tab, enter the details shown in Table 7.6.

7 | Design Study of Application using Mobile Applications for Laptop

Field Name	Data Element	Data Type	Length	BE Field	BE Key Field	Comment
NAME	CHAR32	CHAR	32	X		This field is used to retrieve from the backend the name of the user and to write it to the device inventory.
EMPLOYEE_ID	CHAR10	CHAR	10	X	X	This field is used to retrieve from the backend the employee ID of the user and to write it to the device inventory. This field holds the backend key, that is, the key under which the backend stores the employee record.
WORKCENTER_ID	CHAR5	CHAR	5	X		This field is used to retrieve from the backend the work center to which the employee is assigned.

Table 7.6 Attributes of the Root Node

> **Note**
>
> The synchronization key field SYNCKEY_MMW is generated automatically for all nodes in all data object categories.

5. Select **Save**.

You have now created the root node and can continue by creating the child node.

Procedure to Create the Child Node

Follow these steps to create the child node:

The child node of the Employee data object

1. Log on to the SAP NetWeaver AS and start Transaction SDOE_WB.
2. In the **Data Orchestration Engine Workbench**, right-click the root node **ROOTNODE** and select **Add a Child Node**.
3. On the **Node Overview** tab, in the **Node Details** area, enter the details shown in Table 7.7.

Field	Value	Comment
Node Name	EQUIPMENT	
Description	Equipment	Short text

Table 7.7 Details for the Child Node of the Employee Data Object

4. On the **Node Attributes** tab, enter the details shown in Table 7.8.

Field Name	Data Element	Data Type	Length	BE Field	BE Key Field	Comment
EQUIPMENT_TYPE	CHAR5	CHAR	5	X		This field is used to retrieve from the backend the type of equipment the employee is qualified to service and to write it to the device inventory.
EQUIPMENT_BRAND	CHAR5	CHAR	5	X		This field is used to retrieve from the backend the equipment brands the employee is qualified to service and to write it to the device inventory.

Table 7.8 Attributes of the Child Node

The attributes defined in the root node of a Receiver Generation data object are mapped to single-value attributes in the RMM customizing group. The attributes defined in a child node are mapped to multivalue attributes in the RMM customizing group (a Receiver Generation data object can have one child node). Since the employee can be qualified to service several types and brands of equipment, these attributes are defined in a child node.

The synchronization key field PSYNCKEY_MMW is always generated automatically in all child nodes of all data object categories and holds the synchronization key of its parent node.

5. Click **Activate**.

You have now created the child node. You are ready to create the Equipment data object.

7.4.4 Creating the Equipment Data Object

The *Equipment* data object contains all the information the service staff requires for servicing the equipment, that is, the exact location of the equipment and servicing instructions (for instance, a PDF file). It has the hierarchical structure shown in Figure 7.6.

The Equipment data object

7 | Design Study of Application using Mobile Applications for Laptop

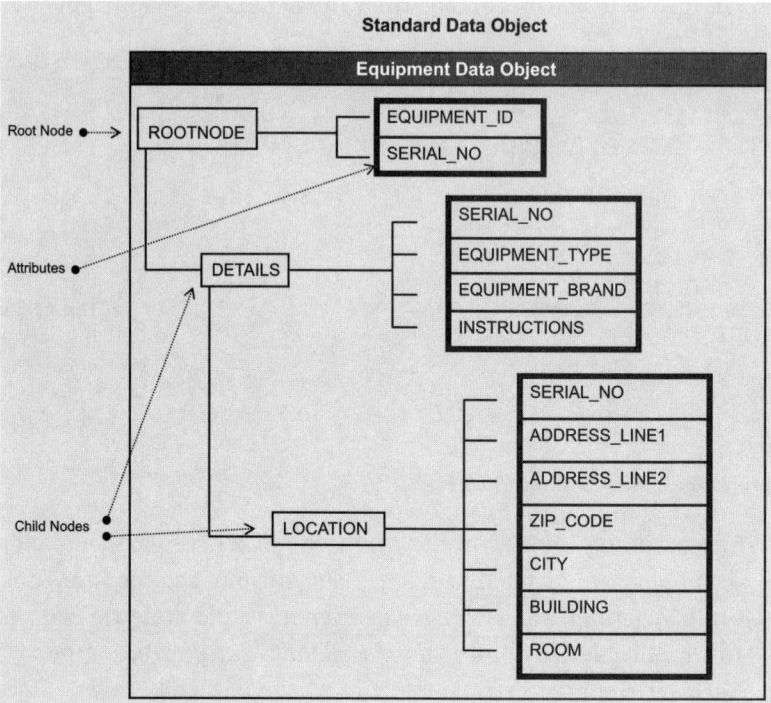

Figure 7.6 The Equipment Data Object

Procedure to Create the Equipment Data Object

The procedure to create the Equipment data object is very similar to the procedure to create the Employee data object. Thus, we only provide the data that need to be entered:

1. Create the Equipment data object as a Standard data object using the values in Table 7.9:

Field	Value	Comment
Name	EQUIPMENT	
Direction	Download Only	Equipment information is to be sent from the backend application to the service technician's device only; service staff does not change equipment data in the client application to send it to the backend

Table 7.9 Details of the Equipment Data Object

Field	Value	Comment
Conflict Detection Scheme	Last One Wins	This field is not relevant for direction Download Only, as there is no incoming data.
Switch On Automatic Key Mapping	Enabled	You can set this indicator here as the ROOTNODE, and the DETAILS and LOCATION child nodes contain the same backend key field.

Table 7.9 Details of the Equipment Data Object (cont.)

2. Create the root node ROOTNODE for the data object with the fields shown in Table 7.10.

The root node

Field Name	Data Element	Data Type	Length	BE Field	BE Key Field	Comment
EQUIPMENT_ID	CHAR10	CHAR	10	X		The device's equipment ID defined in the backend
SERIAL_NO	CHAR15	CHAR	15	X	X	The device's serial number assigned by the manufacturer

Table 7.10 Attributes of the Root Node

3. Create the child node DETAILS with the fields shown in Table 7.11.

The Details child node

Field Name	Data Element	Data Type	Length	BE Field	BE Key Field	Comment
SERIAL_NO	CHAR15	CHAR	15	X	X	Each node requires at least one backend key field, so we add this field here.
TYPE	CHAR5	CHAR	5	X		For example, PRINT for a printer, SCAN for a scanner (values defined in the backend system) Manufacturer.
BRAND	CHAR5	CHAR	5	X		Brand values defined in the backend system
INSTRUCTIONS	RAW-STRING			X	X	Instructions for servicing this equipment (PDF file).

Table 7.11 Attributes of the Child Node DETAILS

Now you can proceed to creating the LOCATION child node as a sub-node of the DETAILS child node.

The Location child node

4. Create the LOCATION child node to the DETAILS child node with the fields shown in Table 7.12.

Field Name	Data Element	Data Type	Length	BE Field	BE Key Field	Comment
SERIAL_NO	CHAR15	CHAR	15	X	X	Each node requires at least one backend key field, so we add this field here.
ADDRESS_LINE1	CHAR32	CHAR	32	X		Address of the device location.
ADDRESS_LINE2	CHAR32	CHAR	32	X		
ZIP_CODE		NUMC	5	X		
CITY	CHAR32	CHAR	32	X		
BUILDING	CHAR32	CHAR	32	X		Building where the device is located.
ROOM	CHAR32	CHAR	32	X		Room where the device is located.

Table 7.12 Attributes of the Child Node LOCATION

5. Activate the data object.

You have now created the Equipment data object along with the root node and child nodes. Next, you will create the Customer data object.

7.4.5 Creating the Customer Data Object

The Customer data object

The sample Customer data object contains all the information the service staff requires to find and contact the customer. It has the hierarchical structure shown in Figure 7.7.

7.4 Defining Data Objects and Distribution Model

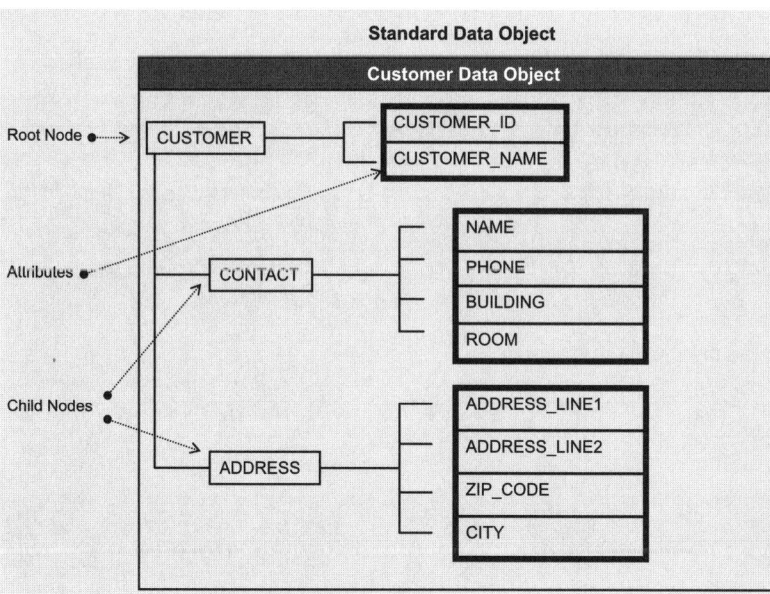

Figure 7.7 The Customer Data Object

Procedure to Create the Customer Data Object

Follow these steps to create the Customer data object:

1. Create the Customer data object as a Standard data object using the values shown in Table 7.13.

Field	Value	Comment
Name	CUSTOMER	
Direction	Download Only	Service staff does not change customer data in the client application.
Conflict Detection Scheme	Last One Wins	This field is not relevant for direction Download Only, as there is no incoming data.

Table 7.13 Details of the Customer Data Object

> **Note**
>
> The Switch On Automatic Key Mapping indicator is disabled for this and all the following data objects, so it is not mentioned again here or in the following descriptions.

207

7 | Design Study of Application using Mobile Applications for Laptop

The root node   2. Create the root node CUSTOMER with the fields shown in Table 7.14.

Field Name	Data Element	Data Type	Length	BE Field	BE Key Field	Comment
CUSTOMER_NAME	CHAR32	CHAR	32	X		Customer name as defined in the backend
CUSTOMER_ID	CHAR10	CHAR	10	X	X	Customer ID as defined in the backend

Table 7.14 Attributes of the Root Node CUSTOMER

The Contact child node   3. Create the child node CONTACT with the fields shown in Table 7.15.

Field Name	Data Element	Data Type	Length	BE Field	BE Key Field	Comment
NAME	CHAR32	CHAR	32	X		Name of the contact person for the equipment to be serviced
PHONE		NUMC	15	X	X	Phone number of the contact person
BUILDING	CHAR32	CHAR	32	X		Building where the contact person works
ROOM	CHAR32	CHAR	32	X		Room where the contact person works

Table 7.15 Attributes of the Child Node CONTACT

The Address child node   4. Create the child node ADDRESS with the fields shown in Table 7.16.

Field Name	Data Element	Data Type	Length	BE Field	BE Key Field	Comment
ADDRESS_LINE1	CHAR32	CHAR	32	X		Customer Address
ADDRESS_LINE2	CHAR32	CHAR	32	X		
ZIP_CODE		NUMC	5	X	X	
CITY	CHAR32	CHAR	32	X		

Table 7.16 Attributes of the Child Node ADDRESS

5. Activate the data object.

You have now created the Customer data object along with the root node and the child nodes. You are ready to create the *ServiceOrder* data object.

7.4.6 Creating the ServiceOrder Data Object

The ServiceOrder data object contains all the basic information the service staff requires about the order, that is, the name of the customer and the equipment that is involved. It has the hierarchical structure shown in Figure 7.8.

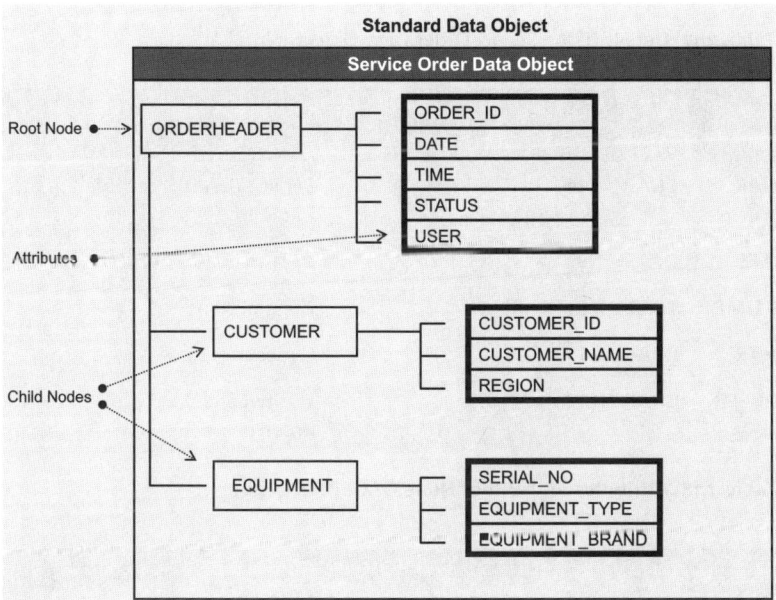

Figure 7.8 The ServiceOrder Data Object

Procedure to Create the ServiceOrder Data Object

Follow these steps to create the ServiceOrder data object:

1. Create the ServiceOrder data object as a Standard data object using the values shown in Table 7.17.

    The ServiceOrder data object

2. Create the root node ORDERHEADER with the fields shown in Table 7.18.

    The root node

3. Create the child node CUSTOMER with the fields shown in Table 7.19.

    The Customer child node

7 | Design Study of Application using Mobile Applications for Laptop

Field	Value	Comment
Name	SERVICEORDER	
Direction	Bi-Direction	Service order information is to be sent from the backend application to the service technician's device and back, for example, to indicate that the job has been completed.
Conflict Detection Scheme	Last One Wins	To indicate that, in the case of a conflict of incoming data, the last device that sends data "wins," meaning the last device's data is saved in the backend.

Table 7.17 Details of the ServiceOrder Data Object

Field Name	Data Element	Data Type	Length	BE Field	BE Key Field	Comment
ORDER_ID	CHAR	CHAR	10	X	X	Service order ID recorded in the backend
DATE	DATS	DATS	8	X		Creation date
TIME	CRTIME	TIMS	6	X		Creation time
STATUS	CHAR	CHAR	1	X		Order status
USER	CRUSER	CHAR	12	X		User who created the service order

Table 7.18 Attributes of the Root Node ORDERHEADER

Field Name	Data Element	Data Type	Length	BE Field	BE Key Field	Comment
CUSTOMER_NAME	CHAR32	CHAR	32	X		Customer name as defined in the backend
CUSTOMER_ID	CHAR10	CHAR	10	X	X	Customer ID as defined in the backend
REGION	CHAR5	CHAR	5	X		Region the customer belongs to by his zip code (this is used to identify the work center responsible for the customer)
CUS_SYNCKEY_MMW	CHAR32	CHAR	32			Optional; association synchronization key (see above

Table 7.19 Attributes of the Child Node CUSTOMER

Note

When you define an association or a dependency later, you have to identify a field in the specified Link data object that is to contain the synchronization key for this association or dependency. In the sample project, you create a dependency between the Customer data object and the ServiceOrder data object. In this dependency, you choose the ServiceOrder data object as the Link data object, that is, the data object containing the link information. Therefore, you require a field in the ServiceOrder data object to contain the synchronization key for this dependency. You can create this field here (for example, as the above-listed CUS_SYNCKEY field) or have it created by the system when you define an association. The system automatically creates this key field in the node where the association is defined (here the CUSTOMER child node).

4. Create the child node EQUIPMENT with the fields shown in Table 7.20.

The Equipment child node

Field Name	Data Element	Data Type	Length	BE Field	BE Key Field	Comment
EQUIPMENT_TYPE	CHAR5	CHAR	5	X		For example, PRINT for a printer, SCAN for a scanner (values defined in the backend)
EQUIPMENT_BRAND	CHAR5	CHAR	5	X		Brand values defined in the backend
SERIAL_NO	CHAR15	CHAR	15	X	X	The device's serial number assigned by the manufacture

Table 7.20 Attributes of the Child Node EQUIPMENT

5. Activate the data object.

You have now created the ServiceOrder data object along with the root node and the child nodes. You are ready to create the WorkCenter data object.

7.4.7 Creating the WorkCenter Data Object

Model the sample WorkCenter data object as a Subscription Generation data object to allow for a rule that only retrieves the service orders that apply to a specific work center. The information contained in the Subscription Generation data objects is only used for retrieving the relevant information and is not transferred to the devices. The WorkCenter Subscription Generation data object has the fields shown in Figure 7.9.

7 | Design Study of Application using Mobile Applications for Laptop

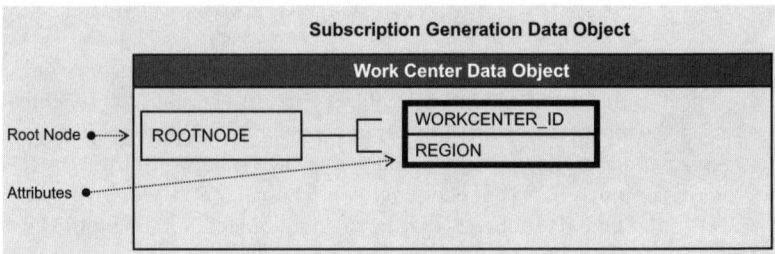

Figure 7.9 The WorkCenter Data Object

The WorkCenter data object

Procedure to Create the WorkCenter Data Object

Follow these steps to create the WorkCenter data object:

1. Create the WorkCenter data object as a Subscription Generation data object using the values shown in Table 7.21.

Field	Value	Comment
Name	WORKCENTER	
Direction	Download Only	Only possible option for Subscription Generation data objects

Table 7.21 Details of the WorkCenter Data Object

2. Create the root node ROOTNODE with the fields shown in Table 7.22.

Field Name	Data Element	Data Type	Length	BE Field	BE Key Field	Comment
WORKCENTER_ID	CHAR5	CHAR	5	X	X	The data type and length must be the same as for the WORKCENTER_ID field in the Employee data object.
REGION	CHAR5	CHAR	5	X		The data type and length must be the same as for the REGION field in the ServiceOrder data object

Table 7.22 The root node ROOTNODE

3. Activate the data object.

You have now created the WorkCenter data object along with the root node and the child nodes. You are ready to create the associations between the data objects.

7.4.8 Create the Associations Between the Data Objects

In this sample project, the CUSTOMER_ID attribute of the ServiceOrder data object is associated with the CUSTOMER_ID attribute of the Customer data object, and the SERIAL_NO attribute of the ServiceOrder data object is associated with the SERIAL_NO attribute of the Equipment data object. Define the association in the ServiceOrder data object, as the referred field must be the backend key field in the root node of the referred data object. In the sample project, the associations are therefore defined in the ServiceOrder data object. The associations are illustrated in Figure 7.10.

Associations between the data objects

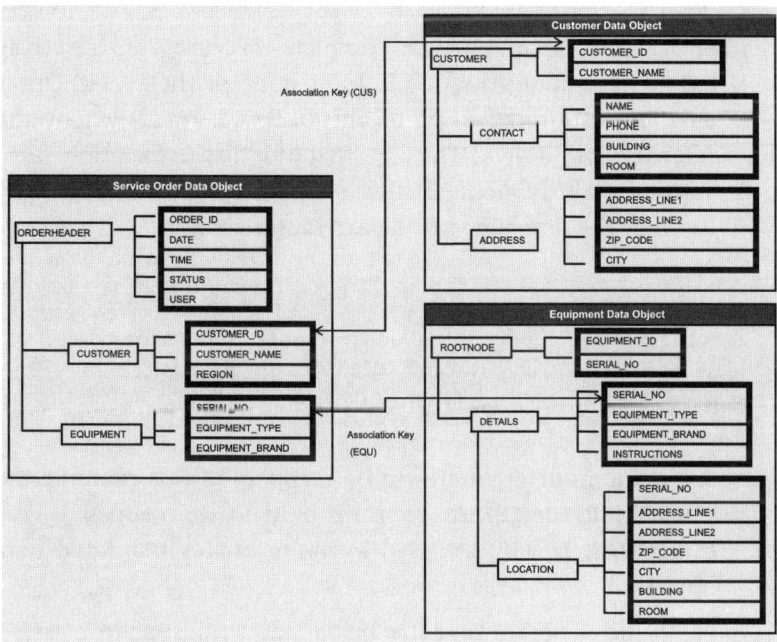

Figure 7.10 Associations Between the Data Objects

Procedure to Define an Association Between the ServiceOrder and Customer Data Objects

The following procedure describes how to define the association between the ServiceOrder data object and the Customer data object (the equivalent values for the Equipment data object are specified in brackets):

1. Locate and right-click the **CUSTOMER (EQUIPMENT)** node of the ServiceOrder data object and select **Change**.
2. Select the **Node Association** tab.
3. Select **Add Association**. The **Association Wizard** starts.
4. Follow the steps in the **Association Wizard**:
    - Enter the association name. This is a three-character key identifying the association, for example, "CUS" ("EQU").
    - Enter the description for the association (optional).
    - Select the **CUSTOMER** data object (**EQUIPMENT** data object) as the data object with which you want to establish the association.
    - Select the association type **Complete**, because your referring data object node (the CUSTOMER node of the ServiceOrder data object) contains all of the backend key fields of the referred data object. The **Key Mapping for Association** table appears with the node attributes of the associated data object listed in the **Associated Node Attributes** column.

> **Note**
> Select the association type **Partial** only if a subset of the backend keys of the referred data object is available in the referring data object node. Partial associations are only used in special cases.

   - Select the node attributes to be mapped, in this example the **CUSTOMER_ID (SERIAL_NO)** attribute to be mapped to the **CUSTOMER_ID (SERIAL_NO)** attribute of the associated data object.
   - Select the **Generate Sync Key** button to have a synchronization key generated to be mapped to the synchronization key of the associated Customer data object (Equipment data object). The generated synchronization key attribute is added to the attributes of the CUSTOMER (EQUIPMENT) node of the ServiceOrder data object. The generated attribute is named CUS_SYNCKEY_MMW (EQU_SYNCKEY_MMW).

> **Note**
> If you have created a synchronization key field (for example, ASSOCIATION_KEY) in the referring node of the ServiceOrder data object, you can also select this here instead of having one generated.

- Leave all link fields and values empty, as these are not required in the sample project.
- Complete the association and save your entries.

5. Activate the data object.

You have now created the associations between the ServiceOrder data object and the Customer data object and between the ServiceOrder data object and the Equipment data object. You can proceed to define the distribution logic. When you create a dependency between these data objects, you can use the association you have defined here as a basis.

7.4.9 Customizing the RMM

To be able to define the distribution logic, you must first customize the RMM to reflect the criteria fields you want to use in the rule definitions. Only then can you map the fields of the Standard or Subscription Generation data objects to the RMM fields (device attribute mapping) when you define rules for the distribution logic.

Receiver Meta Model

Procedure to Customize the RMM

Follow these steps to customize the RMM:

1. Log on to the DOE and start Transaction SDOE_RMM01.
2. Under **Receiver Meta Model**, select the RMM you want customize. At present, you can create devices by using the Mobile RMM only. However, if you want to customize this RMM based on your requirements, you must create a customizing group. This is required because you cannot modify the RMM directly, as it is part of the SAP package. In addition, when you create a customizing group, you can transport the changes independently without transporting the entire RMM.
3. Select **Customize**.
4. Select **New**.
5. Enter "TUTORIAL" as name for the **Customizing Group**, and select **Continue**.
6. Under the **Configuration** tab, add the attributes shown in Table 7.23.

Customizing group

Attribute Name	Read-Only	Multi-Value	Admin UI	Data Element
EMPLOYEE_ID	X		X	CHAR10
WORKCENTER_ID			X	CHAR5
EQUIPMENT_TYPE		X	X	CHAR5
EQUIPMENT_BRAND		X	X	CHAR5

Table 7.23 Attributes of the Customizing Group

Also follow these considerations:

- In the sample project, define the **EMPLOYEE_ID** attribute as read-only because it should be changed in the backend system only, not in the DOE.
- Do not define the **WORKCENTER_ID**, **EQUIPMENT_TYPE**, or **EQUIPMENT_BRAND** attributes as read-only because the administrator needs to change the value easily in the SAP NetWeaver Mobile Administrator. For example, when a service technician is assigned to another work center as a vacation replacement or gains an additional qualification, the administrator needs to make these changes quickly.
- Define the **EMPLOYEE_ID** and **WORKCENTER_ID** attributes as single-value attributes because each device is assigned to one user only.
- Define the **EQUIPMENT_TYPE** and **EQUIPMENT_BRAND** attributes as multivalue attributes because the employee can be qualified to service several equipment types and brands.
- Activate the **Admin UI Display** indicator for all attributes because all this information is of interest to the administrator.

7. Save and generate the customizing group.

7.4.10 Define the Distribution Logic

The next step is building the distribution logic. This involves defining a distribution model with dependencies and distribution rules and defining a data completeness group. The following logic must be established for the sample project:

- Service technicians must only receive the service orders for the customers assigned to their work center based on their region (the region depends on the zip code and is recorded in the Service Order data object).

- Service technicians must only receive the service orders for the equipment they are qualified to service.

This requires a distribution rule for the service orders that maps the following attributes:

- The REGION attribute in the WorkCenter data object to the REGION attribute of the ServiceOrder data object (SubGen mapping) and the WORKCENTER_ID attribute in the WorkCenter data object to the WORKCENTER_ID attribute defined in the RMM customizing group.
- The EQUIPMENT_TYPE and EQUIPMENT_BRAND attributes in the ServiceOrder data object to the EQUIPMENT_TYPE and EQUIPMENT_BRAND attributes in the RMM customizing group (device attribute mapping).

Together with the service orders, service staff must receive the following information:

- Customer information such as customer address and contacts.
- Equipment information such as equipment location and servicing instructions.

This requires a dependency between the ServiceOrder data object and the Customer data object and between the ServiceOrder data object and the Equipment data object (these can be based on associations defined at the data object level). The service orders are only to be distributed if the equipment and customer information is complete and available for distribution. This requires a data completeness group including the dependencies mentioned above.

Dependencies between data objects

Figure 7.11 illustrates the associations, dependencies, distribution rules, and data completeness group for the sample project.

Data completeness group

7.4.11 Defining the Distribution Model

Next, create the distribution model SERVICEORDER. Create the distribution model for the ServiceOrder data object, as it is the basic object to be distributed and must be the leading data object in the dependencies you define.

Distribution model

7 | Design Study of Application using Mobile Applications for Laptop

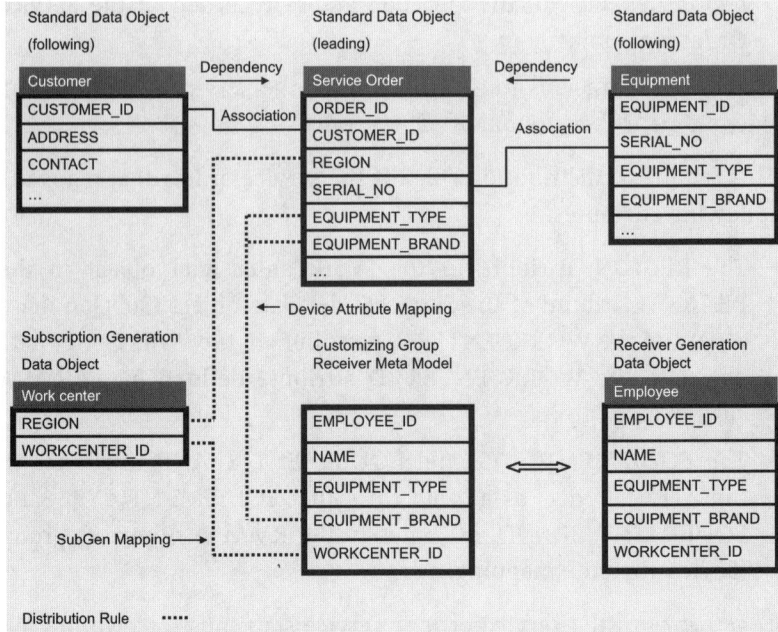

Figure 7.11 Data Distribution Model for the Service Order Application

Procedure to Define the Distribution Model

Follow these steps to define the distribution model:

1. Log on to the SAP NetWeaver AS and start Transaction SDOE_WB. The **Data Orchestration Workbench** screen appears.

2. Right-click the **SERVICEORDER** data object and select **Create • Distribution Model**. The **Distribution Model** screen appears.

3. In the **Distribution Model Name** field, enter "SERVICEORDER."

4. In the **Distribution Model Description** field, enter a description of the distribution model and then choose **Save**. The **Rules and Dependencies** tabs appear on the screen. You can now add a rule to the distribution model or create a distribution dependency.

You have now successfully created a distribution model. You are ready to create a distribution dependency.

7.4.12 Creating a Distribution Dependency

Add two dependencies to the SERVICEORDER distribution model using the associations defined between the Customer data object and the ServiceOrder data object and between the Equipment data object and the ServiceOrder data object. This ensures that the Customer and Equipment data object data is distributed together with the ServiceOrder data object data.

Distribution dependencies based on associations

You have to set the **Selectable for Completeness** indicator for these dependencies to include them in the data completeness group. When you define these dependencies, the ServiceOrder data object is defaulted as the leading data object. You can choose the **Use Association** button to fill in the fields automatically. Static filters and conditional dependencies are not used in the sample project.

Procedure to Create a Distribution Dependency

Follow these steps to create a distribution dependence:

1. Log on to the SAP NetWeaver AS and start Transaction SDOE_WB.
2. In the **Data Orchestration Engine Workbench**, select the SWCV **SERVICEORDERAPP**. To display all projects, type "*" in the instance list field and press **Enter**.
3. Locate and right-click the distribution model **SERVICEORDER** and select **Add • Dependency**. The **Distribution Dependency Wizard** starts.
4. Select **Continue** to start creating a distribution dependency.
5. Follow the steps as indicated by the wizard:
    - In the **Dependency Name** field, enter "DEP1" and, if required, add a description in the **Description** field.
    - Select the **Enabled** field.
    - Select the **Selectable for Completeness** field to include them in the data completeness group and then select **Continue**.
    - On the MBO information screen, in the **Leading Data Object** field, select **SERVICEORDER**, click **Use Association**, and select **CUSTOMER (EQUIPMENT)** as **Following DO Name**, and then choose **Continue**.
    - On the **Static Filters** screen, click **Continue**.

▶ On the **Verification** screen, click **Continue**.

▶ Click **Complete**.

6. Repeat this procedure to create a dependency called "DEP2" between the EQUIPMENT data object and the ServiceOrder data object.

You have now created two dependencies, DEP1 and DEP2, for the distribution model. Next, you will add a rule to the distribution model.

7.4.13 Adding a Rule to the Distribution Model

Distribution rules Add a rule to the SERVICEORDER distribution model to ensure that only service orders for customers that belong to the region serviced by the employee's work center and that match the employee's qualifications are distributed to the device.

Procedure to Add a Rule to the Distribution Model

Follow these steps to add a rule to the distribution model:

1. Log on to the SAP NetWeaver AS and start Transaction SDOE_WB.

2. From the **Data Orchestration Engine Workbench**, select the project in which you want to work. To display all projects, type "*" in the instance list field and press **Enter**.

3. Navigate to the distribution model **SERVICEORDER**, right-click it, and choose **Add • Rule**. The **Distribution Rule Wizard** starts.

4. Select **Continue**.

5. Under **Rule Details**, enter "R1" as the **Rule Name** and optionally a description for the rule.

6. Select **Continue**.

7. In the **Rule Fields** section, perform the following steps:

    a. Select the **CUSTOMER** node, the **REGION** attribute of this node, and **EQ** as the operator.

    b. Select the **EQUIPMENT** node, the **EQUIPMENT_TYPE,** and the **EQUIPMENT_BRAND** attributes of this node and **EQ** as the operator for both.

8. Select **Continue**.

9. In the **Logic Selection** section, perform the following steps:
   - Select **SubGen Mapping** as the mapping option and **MOBILE** as the receiver category type (RMM).
   - Select **WORKCENTER** as the Subscription Generation data object. The root node is entered automatically in the **SubGen Node** field.
   - Click **Device Attribute Mapping**, navigate to the receiver attribute **WORKCENTER_ID** of your customizing group in the list, and select the **EQ** operator and **WORKCENTER_ID** in the **Attribute Low** column. This associates the receiver attribute with the corresponding Subscription Generation data object attribute.
10. Click **Save** and then choose **Continue**.
11. In the **Logic Details** section, perform the following steps:
    - Select the **REGION** attribute of the **CUSTOMER** node and click **SubGen Data Object** (because the value for the region is to be taken from the Subscription Generation data object).
    - In the **Distribution Rule** screen, choose **REGION** in the **Attribute Low** column to map the **REGION** attribute of the Subscription Generation data object to the **REGION** attribute of the ServiceOrder data object.
    - Click **Save**.
    - Select the **EQUIPMENT_TYPE** and **EQUIPMENT_BRAND** attributes and click **Device Attribute**.
    - In the **Distribution Rule** screen, in the **Attribute Low** column, choose **EQUIPMENT_TYPE** and **EQUIPMENT_BRAND**, respectively, to map the EQUIPMENT_TYPE and EQUIPMENT_TYPE attributes of the ServiceOrder data object to the corresponding device attributes.
    - Click **Save** and then **Continue**.
12. The Execution Plan lists the events that trigger rule evaluation. You can add a custom job here that triggers rule evaluation every day at 1 a.m., as the service staff retrieves their jobs first thing in the morning. This makes sure they receive all orders currently assigned to them. **Execution Plan**
13. Complete the rule.
14. Activate the distribution model.

You have now added a rule to the SERVICEORDER distribution model.

7.4.14 Defining a Data Completeness Group

Define a data completeness group to ensure that the service orders are only distributed if the equipment and customer information is complete and available for distribution.

Procedure to Define a Data Completeness Group

Follow these steps to define a data completeness group:

Data completeness group

1. Log on to the SAP NetWeaver AS and start Transaction SDOE_WB.
2. In the **Data Orchestration Engine Workbench** browser, locate and right-click the software component version **SERVICEORDERAPP** and select **Create • Completeness Group**.
3. Enter "DCG" as the name, and optionally a description for the data completeness group.
4. In the **Data Object Name** field, select **SERVICEORDER**.

> **Note**
> The data object must be a leading data object. All the dependencies that are related to this data object and marked as **Selectable for Completeness** appear in a table.

5. Select both dependencies for inclusion in the data completeness group and click **Save**.
6. Activate the data completeness group.

You have now created a data completeness group. Next, define backend adapters.

7.5 Defining Backend Adapters

Connecting to a backend system

You are now ready to define the required backend adapters for all the data objects used in the sample project. These must be defined as follows:

▶ **ServiceOrder data object**
The ServiceOrder data object is defined as a bidirectional data object because the service staff can update the status of the service order. However, the service staff cannot create new service orders or delete existing service orders. Therefore, the backend adapter must include BAPI wrappers for the GetList, GetDetail, and Modify functions. This backend adapter should be defined as backend-triggered, as new service orders are added frequently and must be made available to the service technicians immediately.

Backend-triggered adapters

▶ **Customer data object**
The Customer data object is defined as download only, as the service staff cannot modify or delete or create new instances of the Customer data object. Therefore, the backend adapter must include BAPI wrappers for the GetList and GetDetail functions only. This backend adapter should be defined as middleware-triggered, as new customer data are not added frequently, and it is sufficient to schedule the loading of new or modified instances from the backend system once a day.

Middleware-triggered adapters

▶ **Equipment Data Object**
The Equipment data object is defined as download only, as the service staff cannot modify or delete or create new instances of the Customer data object. It includes an attachment of a PDF file with servicing instructions for the equipment. Therefore, the backend adapter must include a BAPI wrapper for the GetList function, a special BAPI wrapper for the GetDetail function that allows for the distribution of attachments, and a function module for the retrieval of the attachment from the backend. This backend adapter should be defined as middleware-triggered, as new equipment data are not added frequently, and it is sufficient to schedule the loading of new or modified instances from the backend system once a day.

Download only data objects

▶ **WorkCenter data object**
As a Subscription Generation data object, the WorkCenter data object is download only. Therefore, the backend adapter must include BAPI wrappers for the GetList and GetDetail functions only. This backend adapter should be defined as middleware-triggered, as an assignment of a work center to a specific region does not change frequently.

7 | Design Study of Application using Mobile Applications for Laptop

> ► **Employee data object**
> As a Subscription Generation data object, the Employee data object is download only. Therefore, the backend adapter must include BAPI wrappers for the GetList and GetDetail functions only. This backend adapter should be defined as middleware-triggered, as employee data do not change frequently.

Procedure to Create a Backend Adapter for a Customer Data Object

The procedure of creating the backend adapter is described using the Customer data object of the sample project as an example.

Backend adapter for the Customer data object

Follow these steps to create a backend adapter for the Customer data object:

1. Log on to the SAP NetWeaver AS and start Transaction SDOE_WB.

2. In the **Data Orchestration Engine Workbench** browser, navigate to the **CUSTOMER** data object, right-click, and select **Create • Back-end Adapter**.

3. Navigate to the data object for which you want to create the backend adapter, in our example the Customer data object, right-click, and choose **Create Back-End Adapter**.

4. Choose **BAPI WRAPPER ADAPTER** as the adapter type. The **Adapter Details** tab for data object **CUSTOMER** appears.

5. In the **Adapter Name** section, enter "CUSTOMER."

6. Select **MIDDLEWARE TRIGGERED** as the **Synchronization Type**, as the customer data do not change frequently and do not have to be loaded into the consolidated data store frequently but, for example, only once a night. The synchronization must then be scheduled in the DOE at the required intervals.

7. Select the **Default Adapter** indicator. The sample project does not use any BAdI exits.

8. In the **BAPI Wrappers** group box, enter the BAPI wrappers used for retrieving the data object data from the backend, as shown in Table 7.24:

> **Note**
>
> If you select **BACKEND TRIGGERED** as the **Synchronization Type**, the synchronization is triggered by the corresponding business object in the backend system. In this case you would have to enter the name of the backend business object that triggers the synchronization. In the sample project, this is the CUSTOMER business object.

Field	Value
Get list	ZINF_CUSTOMER_GETLIST
Get detail	ZINF_CUSTOMER_GETDETAIL
Create	Not required for this data object, as it is download only and new instances cannot be created in the client application
Modify	Not required for this data object, as it is download only and the data object instances cannot be modified in the client application.
Delete	Not required for this data object, as it is download only, and existing customer records cannot be deleted in the client application
Instance Push Function	Not available for this data object
Corr Cleanup Function	Not required for this data object, as new instances cannot be created in the client application.
Use Mass Data	Not required for this data object.
Use Bulk	Not required for this data object.

Table 7.24 BAPI Wrappers for Retrieving the Data Object Data from the Backend

> **Note**
>
> The BAPI wrappers must have been defined beforehand.

9. Leave the **Get Attachments** group checkbox empty (because the Customer data object does not use any attachments).
10. In the **Mapping Tool** screen, select the tables for the individual data object nodes and map the fields to the corresponding fields in the GetDetail BAPI wrapper.
11. Save your entries.
12. Activate the backend adapter.

7 | Design Study of Application using Mobile Applications for Laptop

> **Tip**
> For your convenience, you can download the ABAP source of ZINF_CUSTOMER_GETLIST and ZINF_CUSTOMER_GETDETAIL from the SAP PRESS websites at *www.sap-press.com* and *www.sap-press.de/1481*, as well as the coding for the remaining backend adapters.

You have now created the backend adapter for the Customer data object. The remaining backend adapters can be created in a similar way. Once you have created and activated the backend adapters for each data object, you will have finished modeling your project with the Data Orchestration Workbench. The data objects can now be imported into the SAP NetWeaver Developer Studio for further use in the development project.

Before you start creating the application with the SAP NetWeaver Developer Studio, we will briefly discuss the necessary configuration settings.

7.6 Configuring SAP NetWeaver Developer Studio

Configuration settings

As a prerequisite for procedures later in this chapter (as well as the next chapter, Chapter 8), please ensure that the SAP NetWeaver Mobile Client for Laptops and the SAP NetWeaver Developer Studio 7.1 are installed on your developer workstation and that SAP NetWeaver Developer Studio is configured the right way. To check this, choose **Windows • Preferences** in SAP NetWeaver Developer Studio and expand the node **Mobile**. Then check the following settings:

- In the **Client** configuration setting, you can enter the installation directory for the Mobile Client for Laptop and the settings for the Java Virtual Machine (JVM). This is needed if you want to run the application.

- In the **Middleware** configuration setting, you can enter the logon data for the MMW server. These settings are needed to import the data objects as model classes into your project. An example is shown in Figure 7.12.

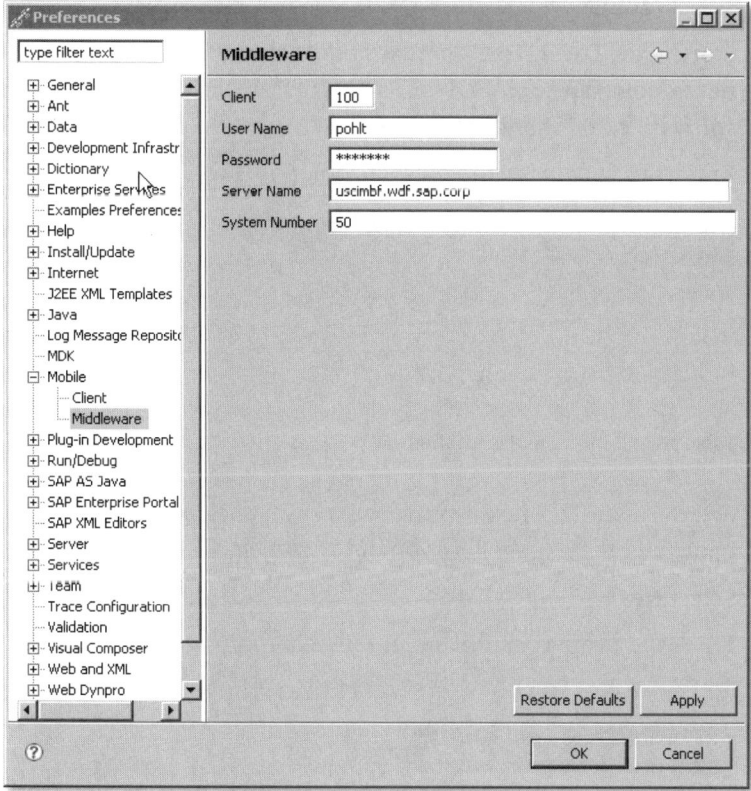

Figure 7.12 Configuration of Middleware Settings

7.7 Creating Development Components

In your application, create two development components (DCs) — one for the models and the other for the application logic (views and controllers).

Procedure to Create Development Components

Follow these steps to create development components:

1. In the SAP NetWeaver Developer Studio, choose **File · New · Project**.

    Creating a DC for the application's model

2. Expand the **Development Infrastructure** node, select **Development Component**, and select **Next**. The **New Development Component (Project) Wizard** starts.

7 | Design Study of Application using Mobile Applications for Laptop

3. Select **Mobile Web Dynpro Offline** type and then **Next**.
4. Expand the **Local Development** node. Select the software component **demo.sap.com**, and select **Next**. The DC is assigned to the software component you selected.
5. Enter the details for the project shown in Table 7.25.

Field Name	Value
Vendor	sap.com.app.model
Name	models
Caption	ServOrd

Table 7.25 Project Details for the DC

6. Select **Next**. The next wizard window appears, displaying the name and the storage location of the project.
7. Select **Next**.
8. Enter the properties for the mobile component shown in Table 7.26.

Field Name	Value
Name	ServiceOrd
Version	1
Description	It stores the models

Table 7.26 Mobile Component Details for the DC

9. Select **Finish**.

Creating a DC for the application logic

10. Similarly, create a DC for the application logic with the project and mobile component details shown in Table 7.27 and Table 7.28, respectively.

Field Name	Value
Vendor	sap.com.app.logic
Name	servapp
Caption	Service Order

Table 7.27 Project Details for the DC

Field Name	Value
Name	Serviceapp
Version	1
Description	It is the logic for the application

Table 7.28 Mobile Component Details for the DC

You have now created the development components for the models and for the application logic. Next, import data objects from the DOE.

7.8 Importing Data Objects from the DOE

In this procedure, you import data objects as model classes in your project. Import the data objects into the model's DC. Use these model classes for context binding. After you import the data objects as model classes for the application, you must make them public so that they can be used in the servapp DC.

Procedure to Import Data Objects from the DOE

Follow these steps to import data objects from the DOE.

1. In the **Mobile Applications for Laptop** explorer, expand the **models** DC.
   Create the model of the application
2. Expand the **Web Dynpro** node. Right-click the **Models** node and select **Create Model**.
3. Select **Data Object Model**, and choose **Next**.
4. Enter the details as specified in Table 7.29:

Field Name	Description
Model Name	ServiceModels
Model Package	com.sap.models

Table 7.29 Details for Import

5. With **Business Model** as the type of model selected, select **Next**.

6. In the **Software Component** section, select **SERVICEORDERAPP**. The IDE displays all data objects of the selected software component.

7. In the **Data Object** section, select the data objects **CUSTOMER** and **SERVICEORDER**.

8. Select **Finish**.

You have now imported data objects from the DOE and next need to define the model classes as public.

7.9 Defining the Model Classes as Public

Add the model classes to the Public Part

You can use the models defined in the models DC in the servapp DC. To do this, you must define the imported model classes as public.

Procedure to Define the Model Classes as Public

Follow these steps to define the model classes as public:

1. Right-click the model that you imported (**ServiceModels**) and select **Add to Public Part**. The **Add Entities to Public Part** window appears.
2. Select **New**.
3. In the **Name** field, enter "Modelspublic."
4. Select **Finish**.
5. Select **Modelspublic** and **Next**.
6. Select **Finish**.
7. Select **Window • Open Perspective • Other…**
8. Select **Development Infrastructure** and select **OK**.
9. From the **Component Browser**, expand **Local Development • MyComponents** and select **servapp**.
10. In **ComponentProperties**, select the **Dependencies** tab.
11. In **Required DCs**, select **Add**. The **Adding Dependencies Wizard** starts.
12. Expand **Local Development • MyComponents** and select **models**.
13. Select **Next**.

14. In the **Required New DCs** screen, select the node **Modelspublic** and select **Finish**.
15. Select **Window • Open Perspective • Other…**
16. Select **Mobile Web Dynpro Offline** and select **OK**.

You have now defined the model classes as public and are ready to define queries.

7.10 Defining the Queries

Create queries in the application using the query editor of Mobile Applications for Laptop. In the query editor, define the input and output classes, aliases, and conditions for the query. According to the logic of the tutorial application, a user selects a particular customer in the first view and clicks the **Show Orders** button. Then the second view, which contains the service orders of the selected customer, appears. To make this particular logic happen, you have to define queries.

Creating a query class

In the application, the query parameter used for comparison is the Customer ID since this is common to both customer details and service orders. In the application, you must define two classes:

▸ A composite class, which obtains the value for the Customer ID.
▸ A query class, which compares the value of Customer ID in the two data objects (customer details and service orders) and stores the result of the comparison.

Procedure to Define Queries

Follow these steps to define queries:

1. In the **Mobile Applications for Laptop Explorer**, expand the development component models.
2. Expand **ServiceModels**. Right-click **Model Classes** and select **Create Query / Composite Model Class**.
3. Enter "QueryComp" as the query name, and select **Finish**.
4. On the **Properties** tab, select **Add**.

5. In the attributes list, select **ServiceModels • CUSTOMER_CUSTOMER • CUSTOMER_ID**.
6. Select **Next** and then select **Finish**.
7. In the **Mobile Applications for Laptop Explorer**, right-click **Model Classes** and select **Create Query / Composite Model Class**.
8. Enter "ServiceQuery" as the query name and select **Finish**.
9. Select the **Query** tab and enter the details shown in Table 7.30.

Field Name	Value
Input Model Class	QueryComp
Result Model Class	SERVICEORDER_ORDERHEADER
Conditions	SERVICEORDER_CUSTOMER.CUSTOMER_ID LIKE :CUSTOMER_ID

Table 7.30 Details of the ServiceQuery

10. Select **Save**.

You have now defined queries and are ready to create the application.

7.11 Creating the Application

Next, create the application along with a new component and add the two views. The application represents the point of entry to the functions provided by the WebDynpro component.

Procedure to Create the Application

Follow these steps to create the application:

1. In the **Mobile Applications for Laptop Explorer**, expand the DC **servapp**.
2. Expand the node **Web Dynpro**. Right-click the **Applications** node and select **Create Application**.
3. Enter the details shown in Table 7.31.

Field	Value
Name	CustomerService
Package	com.sap.app.customerservice

Table 7.31 Details of the Application

4. Select **Next**.
5. The option **Create New Component** is selected by default. Select **Next**.
6. In the **Component Properties** window, replace the default values with the values shown in Table 7.32.

Field	Value
Component Name	CustomerComp
Component Package	com.sap.app.customercomp

Table 7.32 Properties of the Component

7. Select **Next**.
8. To create the OrderDetails view, select **Add**. *The OrderDetails view*
9. Enter "OrderDetails" as the name for the view.
10. Select **Finish**.
11. In the **Mobile Applications for Laptop Explorer**, right-click the view **CustomerCompView** and select **Refactor • Rename**.
12. Enter "CustomerDetails" as the new name.
13. In the **Mobile Applications for Laptop Explorer**, right-click the development component **servapp** and select **Development Component • Build**.

The build ensures that Java files of the project recognize the newly created classes. Next, you will define context binding.

7.12 Defining Context Binding

The data objects imported from the DOE are available in the models that you defined. For the data to be available in the views, however, you must define a context binding (or context mapping) from the

Context mapping

views to the models via the component controller. For mapping the context of the models to the views, perform the following steps:

1. Embed the models in the component controller.
2. Define context binding from the component controller to the models.
3. Define context binding from the views to the component controller.

Procedure to Define Context Binding

Follow these steps to define context binding:

1. Expand the node **CustomerComp**. Right-click **Used Models** and select **Add**.
2. Select **ServiceModels** and then **OK**. This ensures that the model classes you defined in the DC **models** can be used in the current development component (**servapp**).
3. Right-click **CustomerComp** and select **Open Data Modeler**.
4. In the toolbar that appears on the left-hand side, select **Embed Model** and click inside the **Data Modeler** view.
5. From the list, select the model **ServiceModels** and select **OK**. On the toolbar that appears on the left-hand side, select **Create Data Link**.
6. In the **Data Modeler** view, from the **Component Controller** click and drag the mouse pointer to the **ServiceModels**.
7. In the **ServiceModels** context (in the right pane of the window), click and drag all the node elements to the **CustomerComp** context (in the left pane of the window).
8. Select all the node attributes as shown in Figure 7.13 and select **Finish**.

Embed the model in the component controller

You have now mapped the data from the model classes to the component controller. In a similar way, you must map the data from the component controller to the views as listed in Figure 7.14 and Figure 7.15. To do this, you have to click the corresponding view and drag the mouse to the component controller and then proceed as follows:

▸ For the CustomerDetails view, map the Customer node attributes and the QueryResults attributes of the Service node from the component controller as shown in Figure 7.14.

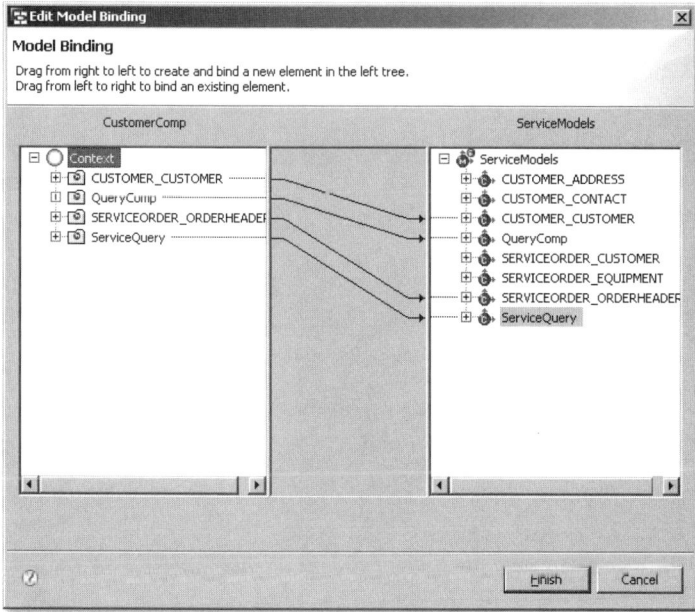

Figure 7.13 Context Mapping from the ServiceModels Context to the CustomerComp Context

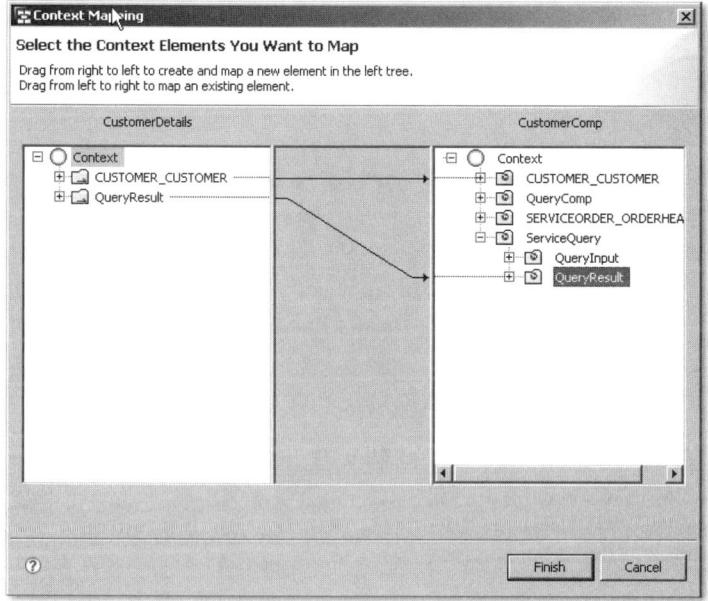

Figure 7.14 Context Mapping from the CustomerComp Context to the CustomerDetails View Context

▶ For the OrderDetails view, map the QueryResult attributes of the Service node from the component controller as shown in Figure 7.15.

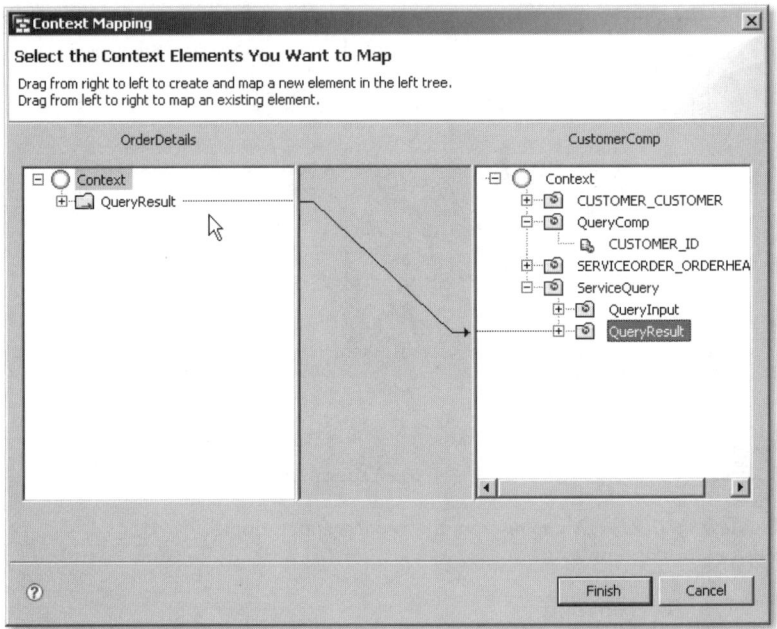

Figure 7.15 Context Mapping from the CustomerComp to the OrderDetails View Context

7.13 Defining Supply Functions for the Node Elements

When the SAP NetWeaver Mobile Client synchronizes with the DOE, the data are stored in the local database. Thus, an application running on the client has to read data from the local database (MaxDB is the default database for the client).

Supply function   The data the application has to read are the attribute values. For each node element, you need to define a supply function. In the application, when a particular node element is instantiated, its supply function populates the node attributes with values that are present in the database.

Procedure to Define Supply Functions for the Node Elements

Follow these steps to define supply functions for the node elements:

1. In the **Mobile Applications for Laptop Explorer**, expand the DC **scrvapp** and then expand the **CustomerComp** node. Right-click **Component Controller** and select **Open • Controller Editor**.
2. Choose the **Context** tab.
3. Select the context node **CUSTOMER_CUSTOMER** and on the **Properties** tab, select **Supply Function**.
4. To create the supply function, select **Create**.
5. With the default name for the supply function selected, click **OK**.
6. Click **Save**.
7. In the same way, create a supply function for the context node **ServiceQuery**.
8. In the **CustomerComp** node, right-click on **Component Controller** and select **Open • Java Editor**.
9. Perform the following steps by entering the code shown in Listings 7.1, 7.2, and 7.3 in the file CustomerComp.java: To remove syntax errors caused by unknown data types, right-click on the editor and choose **Source • Organize Imports**. This will add the necessary import statements at the beginning of your code and remove the syntax errors.

```
/*
 * The following code section can be used for any Java code
 * that is
 * not to be visible to other controllers/views or that
 * contains constructs
 * currently not supported directly by Web Dynpro (such as
 * inner classes or
 * member variables etc.). <p>
 *
 * Note. The content of this section is in no way managed/
 * controlled
 * by the Web Dynpro Designtime or the Web Dynpro Runtime.
 */
//@@begin others
ServiceModels model = ServiceModels.getInstance();
ServiceQuery SQ = model.createServiceQuery();
```

```
  String Qid;
//@@end
```

Listing 7.1 Variable Declaration and Initialization

```
public void supplyCUSTOMER_CUSTOMER(
  IPrivateCustomerComp.ICUSTOMER_CUSTOMERNode node,
  IPrivateCustomerComp.IContextElement parentElement) {
  // @@begin supplyCUSTOMER_CUSTOMER(IWDNode,IWDNodeElement)
  Collection col = model.getCUSTOMER_CUSTOMERs();
           if (col == null) {
               CUSTOMER_CUSTOMER inst =
                      model.createCUSTOMER_CUSTOMER();
                  model.addToCUSTOMER_CUSTOMERs(inst);
                  col = model.getCUSTOMER_CUSTOMERs();
           }
           node.bind(col);
           // @@end
    }
```

Listing 7.2 Supply Function for the Customer Node

```
// @@begin javadoc:supplyServiceQuery(IWDNode,IWDNodeElement
)
/**
 * Declared supply function for
 * IPrivateCustomerComp.IServiceQueryNode.
 * <p>
 *
 * This method is called when the node is invalid and the
 * collection
 * is requested. This may occur during any phase, even at the
 * beginning to initialize the node. The method is expected
 * to fill
 * the node collection using IWDNode.bind(Collection) or
 * IWDNode.addElement(IWDNodeElement).
 * <p>
 *
 * @param node
 *      the node that is to be filled
 * @param parentElement
 *      The element that this node is a child of. May be
 *      <code>null</code> if there is none.
 * @see com.sap.tc.webdynpro.progmodel.api.
 * IWDNode#bind(Collection)
 * @see com.sap.tc.webdynpro.progmodel.api.
 * IWDNode#bind(IWDNodeElement)
```

```
*/
// @@end
public void supplyServiceQuery(IPrivateCustomerComp.IService
QueryNode node,
        IPrivateCustomerComp.IContextElement parentElement) {
        // @@begin supplyServiceQuery(IWDNode,IWDNodeElement)
        wdContext.nodeServiceQuery().bind(SQ);
        // @@end
}
```

Listing 7.3 Supply Function for the ServiceQuery node

You have now implemented the supply function for the Service-Query method and are ready to define the method for calling the query.

7.14 Defining the Method for Calling the Query

In the tutorial application, you have to define a method that calls the query. In this method, you have to obtain the ID of the selected customer and provide this value to the composite class. You then have to call the query class.

Procedure to Define the Method for Calling the Query

Follow these steps to define the method for calling the query:

Implementation of the fireQuery method

1. In the **Mobile Applications for Laptop Explorer**, expand the development component **servapp**.

2. Expand the nodes **Web Dynpro • Components • CustomerComp**.

3. Double-click **Component Controller**.

4. Select the **Methods** tab.

5. Select New.

6. The **New Method Wizard** starts. Create a method with the name "fireQuery".

7. Click **Save**.

8. On the **Methods** tab, right-click **fireQuery** and choose **Navigate to • Implementation**.

9. Enter the code shown in Listing 7.4.

```
public void fireQuery( ) {
    //@@begin fireQuery()
        int Sel =
            wdContext.nodeCUSTOMER_CUSTOMER().getLeadSelection();
                if (Sel > -1) {
                    Qid = wdContext.nodeCUSTOMER_CUSTOMER()
                            .getCUSTOMER_CUSTOMERElementAt(Sel).
                            getCUSTOMER_ID();
                    SQ.getQueryInput().setCUSTOMER_ID(Qid);
                }
                try {
                        SQ.execute();

                } catch (CMIException e) {
                        e.printStackTrace();
                }
                wdContext.nodeQueryResult().invalidate();
    //@@end
}
```

Listing 7.4 The fireQuery method

You have now implemented the fireQuery method and are ready to specify the navigation schema.

7.15 Specifying the Navigation Schema

You will now define navigation plugs to navigate from one view to another. After creating the plugs, create the navigational links between the plugs. Then assign the plugs to actions of the specific buttons created in the two views. The navigational schema is specified in the default window (**CustomerCompWindow**) of the DC servapp. When you created the application, you embedded both the views in the default window.

Procedure to Specify the Navigation Schema

Follow these steps to specify the navigation schema:

1. In the **Mobile Applications for Laptop Explorer**, expand the DC **servapp**.
2. Expand the nodes **Web Dynpro** • **Components** • **CustomerComp** • **Windows**.

Specifying the Navigation Schema | 7.15

3. Right-click **CustomerCompWindow** and select **Open • Window Editor**. In the **Window Editor**, you can see the two views you already created. Please note that the views overlap and need to be rearranged on the screen.

4. For the CustomerDetails view, create the plugs shown in Table 7.33.

Type of Plug	Name of the Plug
Inbound	FromOrderDetails
Outbound	ToOrderDetails

Creating navigation plugs for the CustomerDetails view

Table 7.33 Plugs for the CustomerDetails View

To create a plug, in the **Navigational Modeler** right-click the required view and select the type of plug.

5. For the OrderDetails view, create the plugs shown in Table 7.34.

Type of Plug	Name of the Plug
Inbound	FromCustomerDetails
Outbound	ToCustomerDetails

Creating navigation plugs for the OrderDetails view

Table 7.34 Plugs for the OrderDetails View

6. Create the navigational links shown in Table 7.35.

From Outbound plug	To Input plug
ToOrderDetails	FromCustomerDetails
ToCustomerDetails	FromOrderDetails

Table 7.35 Navigational Links Between the Plugs

To create a navigational link, right click the outbound plug element that you created and select **Create Link**.

7. From the list, select the required inbound plug and select **OK**.
8. Select **Save**.

Creating navigational links

In Figure 7.16, you can see the Navigation Modeler of the CustomerCompWindow with the navigational plugs and links.

241

7 | Design Study of Application using Mobile Applications for Laptop

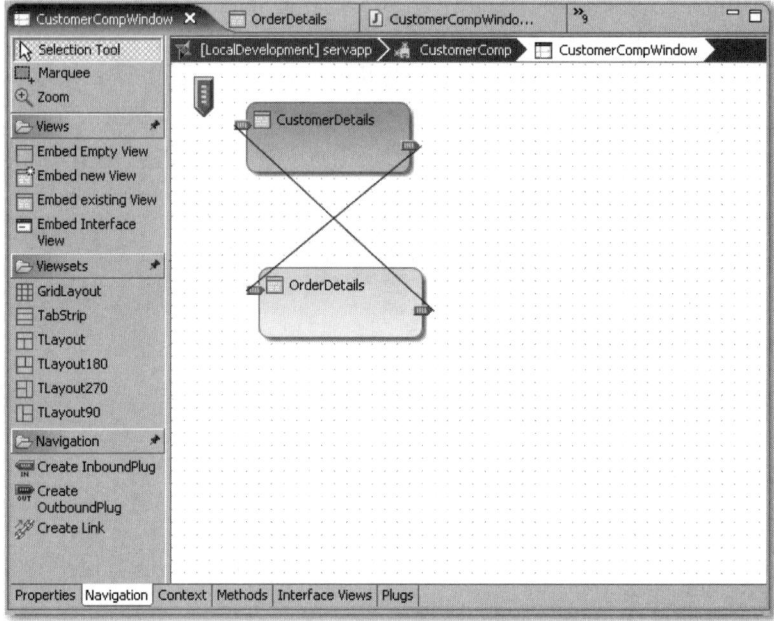

Figure 7.16 Navigation Modeler with Navigational Plugs and Links

You have now defined the navigation schema for the two views queries and are ready to create the navigation schema for the **Exit** button.

7.16 Specifying the Navigation Schema for the Exit Button

Exiting the application

In the CustomerDetails view, you can specify the **Exit** button, which closes the application when the button is clicked. To exit the application, you must exit the view and then you can exit from the application window.

Procedure to Specify the Navigation Schema for the Exit Button

Follow these steps to specify the navigation schema for the Exit button:

1. In the **Mobile Applications for Laptop Explorer**, expand the DC **servapp**.

2. Expand the nodes **Web Dynpro · Components · CustomerComp · Windows**.
3. Right-click **CustomerCompWindow** and select **Open · Window Editor**.
4. Select the **Navigation** tab.
5. In the toolbar that appears on the left-hand side, select **Create Outbound Plug** and click inside the **Navigational Modeler** area.
6. Enter "Exit" as the name of the plug.
7. Select **Exit** as the type and select **Finish**.
8. In the **Mobile Applications for Laptop Explorer**, expand the **Views** node and double-click the **OrderDetails** view.
9. Select the **Properties** tab and then select **Add**
10. Select **CustomerCompWindow** as the required controller and select **OK**.
11. In the **Mobile Applications for Laptop Explorer**, expand the nodes **Local Component Interface · Interface Views**.
12. Right-click the **CustomerCompInterfaceView** node and select **Open · Controller Editor**.
13. In the **Outbound Plugs** section, select **New**.
14. Enter "Exit" as the name of the plug.
15. Select **Exit** as the type of the plug and select **Finish**.

You have now defined the navigation schema and are ready to customize the CustomerDetails view.

7.17 Customizing the CustomerDetails View

The CustomerDetails view is the default view of the application. When the application is accessed from the SAP NetWeaver Mobile Client, this is the first view that is displayed. The view should have the following UI elements:

Default view

▸ **DefaultTextView text view**
  Contains the screen's title.
▸ **Customer table**
  Should display all the attribute values of the Customer data object.

UI elements for CustomerDetails view

7 | Design Study of Application using Mobile Applications for Laptop

▶ **Show Orders button**

On activation, the application should call the fireQuery method and navigate to the OrderDetails view.

▶ **Exit button**

On activation, the application should exit from the window. For this, you have to call the exit method you defined in the CustomerCompWindow.

Procedure to Customize the CustomerDetails View

Follow these steps to customize the CustomerDetails view:

1. In the **Mobile Applications for Laptop Explorer**, expand the **servapp** DC.
2. Expand the nodes **Web Dynpro • Components • CustomerComp • Views**.
3. Double-click the **CustomerDetails** view.
4. Select the **Properties** tab.
5. Select **Add** and select **CustomerCompWindow** as the required controller.
6. Select **Save** and then select the **Layout** tab.

Adding a DefaultTextView

7. In the **Outline** view of the SAP NetWeaver Developer Studio, right-click **DefaultTextView**. Enter "Customer Details" in the **text** property on the **Properties** tab.
8. In the **Outline** view, right-click **RootElement** and select **ApplyTemplate**.

Adding a Table Element

9. Select the **Table** template, and enter "Customer" as the table name. Then click **Next**.
10. Select the attributes **CUSTOMER_ID** and **CUSTOMER_NAME** of the **Customer** node and select **Finish**.

> **Note**
> When you apply a table template, you can only select attributes that belong to the same node. Therefore, you have to add the remaining table columns manually.

11. In the **Outline** view, click the node **CUSTOMER_0_header** (**CUSTOMER_0_0_header**) and enter "Customer ID" ("Customer name") in the text property on the **Properties** tab.

12. In the **Outline** view, right-click the table you just created and select **Insert GroupedColumn**. Then select **TableColumn**, and enter "CUSTOMER_1" as **ID**. — Add a table column

13. In the **Outline** view, right-click the table column **CUSTOMER_1** and select **Insert • Header**. In the text property on the **Properties** tab, enter "Street." — Add a table header

14. In the **Outline** view, right-click the table column **CUSTOMER_1** and select **Insert TableCellEditor**. Select **Textview** as the **UI Element**. In the text property on the **Properties** tab, click **Bind** and select the context node **ADDRESS_LINE1**. — Add a TableCellEditor

15. Repeat the steps 12 to 14 to create the remaining three table columns. Enter the data shown in Table 7.36.

TableColumn ID	TableHeader text	Context node bound to TableCellEditor
CUSTOMER_2	City	CITY
CUSTOMER_3	Region	ADDRESS_LINE2
CUSTOMER4	Zipcode	ZIP_CODE

Table 7.36 Columns of the Customer table

16. In the **Outline** view, right-click **RootElement** and select **Insert Child**.

17. Select **Button** and enter **ShowOrders** for the button ID. — Add the ShowOrders button

18. On the **Properties** tab for the button, perform the actions described in Table 7.37.

Property	Actions
Text	**Show Orders**
OnAction	a. Choose **Create** and enter the following details: Name: ShowOrders Fire Plug: ToOrderDetails b. Choose *Finish*

Table 7.37 Button Properties

19. Select **Save**.
20. In the **Outline** view, double-click the **Show Orders** button.
21. On the **Properties** tab, select the **OnAction** property and select **Go**.
22. Enter the code shown in Listing 7.5.

```
public void onActionShowOrders(com.sap.tc.webdyn-
pro.progmodel.api.IWDCustomEvent
        wdEvent) {
    // @@begin onActionShowOrders(ServerEvent)
    wdThis.wdGetCustomerCompController().fireQuery();
    wdThis.wdFirePlugToOrderDetails();
    // @@end
    }
```

Listing 7.5 Implementation of onActionShowOrders

23. Right-click the **CustomerDetails** view and select **Open • View Editor**. In the **Outline** view, right-click **RootElement** and choose **Insert Child**.

Add the Exit button

24. Choose **Button** and enter "Exit" for the button ID.
25. On the **Properties** tab for the button, perform the actions described in Table 7.38:

Property	Actions
Text	Enter "Exit"
OnAction	a. Select **Create** and enter "ExitApp" in the field **Name**. b. Select **Finish**.

Table 7.38 Button Properties

26. Select **Save**.
27. In the **Outline** view, double-click the **Exit** button.
28. On the **Properties** tab, select the **OnAction** property and select **Go**.
29. Enter the code shown in Listing 7.6:

```
public void onActionExitApp(com.sap.tc.webdynpro.prog-
model.api.IWDCustomEvent wdEvent )
    {
```

```
    //@@begin onActionExitApp(ServerEvent)
            wdThis.wdGetCustomerCompWindowController().
            wdFirePlugExit();
    //@@end
}
```
Listing 7.6 Implementation of OnActionExit

Now that you have customized the CustomerDetails view, you are ready to customize the OrderDetails view.

7.18 Customizing the OrderDetails View

The OrderDetails view displays the orders for the selected customer. Users select the customer in the CustomerDetails view. The view should have the following UI elements:

▶ **DefaultTextView text view**
It contains the screen's title.

▶ **Orders table**
This should display the attribute values of the Service data object. It should display only the orders of the selected customer and should allow the user to enter and update specific values in the table.

▶ **Save button**
On activation, the application should save the values entered in the Orders table to the local database.

▶ **Back button**
On activation, the application should navigate to the CustomerDetails view.

UI elements for the OrderDetails view

Procedure to Customize the OrderDetails View

Follow these steps to customize the OrderDetails view:

1. In the **Mobile Applications for Laptop Explorer**, expand the DC **servapp**.
2. Expand the nodes **Web Dynpro • Components • CustomerComp • Views**.

7 | Design Study of Application using Mobile Applications for Laptop

3. Double-click the **OrderDetails** view, and select the **Layout** tab.
4. In the **Outline** view of the SAP NetWeaver Developer Studio, right-click **DefaultTextView**. Enter "Order Details" in the text property on the **Properties** tab.
5. In the **Outline** view, right-click **RootElement** and select **ApplyTemplate**.

Add the Orders Table

6. Select the **Table** template, and enter "Orders" as the table name.
7. Select the attributes **DATE**, **ORDER_ID**, **STATUS**, **TIME**, and **USER** of the **QueryResult** node and select **Next**. On the **Specify Table Properties** screen, you can define the order of the columns in the table. Use the following order: ORDER, STATUS, DATE, TIME, USER.
8. Enter the name for the column headers. Each table attribute has a header attribute and an editor attribute. Enter the name in the **text** property of the **header** attribute as shown in Table 7.39.

Name	Column Header
ORDER	Order ID
STATUS	Order Status
DATE	Processed on
TIME	Hours spent
USER	Processed by

Table 7.39 Field and Column Header Names

9. In the **Outline** view of the NetWeaver Developer Studio, right-click **RootElement** and select **Insert Child**.

Add the Save Button

10. Select **Button**, and enter "Save" for the button ID.
11. On the **Properties** tab for the for the **Save** button, perform the actions described in Table 7.40.

Property	Actions
text	Enter "Save"
OnAction	a. Select **Create** and enter "Save" in the field **Name**. b. Select **Finish**.

Table 7.40 Button Properties

12. Select **Save**.
13. In the **Outline** view, double-click the **Save** button.
14. On the **Properties** tab, select the **OnAction** property and select **Go**. *Implement the OnAction event*
15. Enter the code shown in Listing 7.7 and Listing 7.8.

```
//@@begin others
        ServiceModels model = ServiceModels.getInstance();
//@@end
```

Listing 7.7 Variable Declaration for onActionSave

```
public void onActionSave(com.sap.tc.webdynpro.
progmodel.api.IWDCustomEvent wdEvent )
  {
  //@@begin onActionSave(ServerEvent)
            model.commit();
  //@@end
  }
```

Listing 7.8 Implementation of onActionSave

16. In the same way, create a button with button ID Back.
17. On the **Properties** tab for the **Back** button, perform the actions described in Table 7.41. *Add the Back button*

Property	Actions
Text	Enter "Back"
OnAction	a. Select **Create**. b. Enter "Back" in the field **Name** and **ToCustomerDetails** in the field **Fire Plug**. c. Select **Finish**.

Table 7.41 Button Properties

You have now created the application and are ready to build, deploy, and run the application.

7.19 Building, Deploying, and Running the Application

After you create the application, you build the application to create the binaries. You then create the archive format of the file (.sda). This is the format that your SAP NetWeaver Mobile Client recognizes. You can deploy and run the application from the SAP NetWeaver Developer Studio. Before you deploy and run the application locally, make sure you have installed SAP NetWeaver Mobile Client for Laptops, and that you have entered the path of your installation directory (for instance, *C:\Program Files\SAP\SAP Netweaver Mobile Client*) in **Window • Preferences • Mobile • Client**.

Procedure to Build, Deploy, and Run the Application

Follow these steps to build, deploy and run the application:

Build the application
1. In the **Mobile Applications for Laptop Explorer**, right-click the **servapp** DC and select **Development Component • Build**.

2. In the **Mobile Applications for Laptop Explorer**, right-click the **servapp** DC and select **Create Archive**.

Deploy the application
3. In the **Mobile Applications for Laptop Explorer**, right-click the **CustomerService** application and choose **Deploy**. This will deploy the application locally on the installed client runtime.

4. Select **Run • Run** to create a run configuration of the project.

Create a launch configuration
5. Click on **Mobile Web Dynpro configuration** and click **New launch configuration**.

6. Enter "ServiceApp" as the name for the run configuration.

7. Browse and select **servapp** as the project and **CustomerService** as the **Mobile Web Dynpro Offline** application.

Run the application
8. Select **Run**.

9. The login screen of the SAP NetWeaver Mobile Client appears. Enter your user and password and then click on the link **CustomerService** (see Figure 7.17).

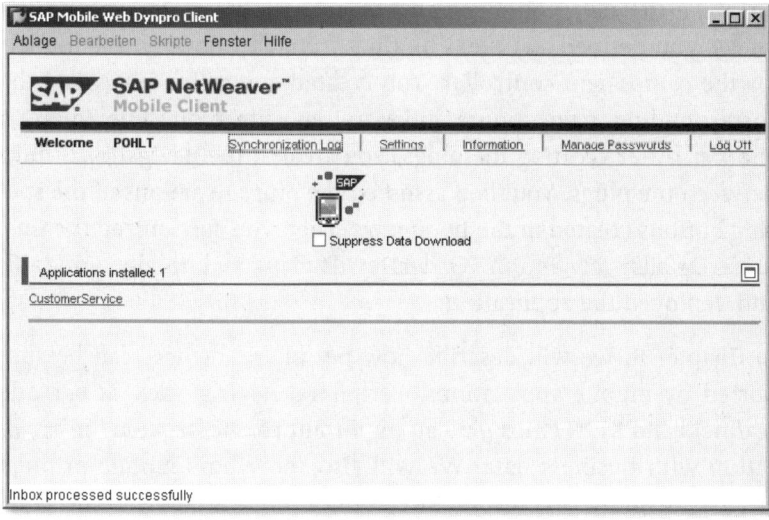

Figure 7.17 Start Screen of the SAP NetWeaver Mobile Client

You have now successfully built, deployed, and run the application. Now you are able to create your own occasionally connected mobile application according to the specific requirements. Because SAP NetWeaver Mobile can be installed as a separate unit, you are able to mobilize your business processes, regardless of the specific backend system and release.

7.20 Summary

In this chapter, you created an occasionally connected mobile application. Based on a use case that is typical for a service scenario, you designed the data object model and the distribution logic. To ensure that the orders are distributed only if the equipment and customer information is available for distribution, you created a data completeness group. You created a SubGen data object that contains the information about the assignment of the work centers to the regions. This enabled you to create subscriptions to the service orders in the region for which the employee's work center is responsible. After that, you imported the data objects as model classes in your mobile application project, which you created in the SAP NetWeaver Developer Studio.

To make the data contained in the model classes available in the views, you defined a context binding from the views to the models via the component controller. You created navigation plugs and the corresponding navigational links to navigate from one view to another. After creating the plugs, you created the navigational links between the plugs. You then assigned the plugs to actions of the specific buttons created in the two views. Then you customized the CustomerDetails view and the OrderDetails view, and, finally, you built and deployed the application.

In Chapter 8, we will describe how peripheral devices can be supported by mobile applications. Peripheral devices such as barcode scanners and RFID chips play an important role to provide the application with business data. We will also show how mobile printers can be integrated in the mobile application and show some code examples, which can be used as templates for your application.

Peripheral devices can supplement the capabilities of mobile devices. Barcode scanners, RFID tags, and mobile printers are examples of peripherals, which are supported by a common architectural framework.

8 Support of Peripheral Devices

In many business scenarios the efficiency of a mobile worker can be significantly increased by using peripheral devices such as barcode scanners, mobile printers, or radio frequency identification (RFID) readers. For instance, mobile printers allow a delivery driver to create invoices on the spot, and barcode scanners or RFID readers can automatically transfer information about a technical object into an application. This accelerates the data entry process and avoids the errors that often occur if the data are entered manually.

Technically, peripheral devices are accessed by the application via native drivers that are installed on the mobile device. Peripheral devices are supported by the client runtime using *Java Native Interface (JNI)*. JNI is a standard programming interface for writing Java native methods and embedding the Java virtual machine into native applications. Using JNI, it is possible for a Java application to call methods, which are implemented in a *Dynamic Link Library (DLL)* on Windows or a shared library on Linux. A popular example of this approach is the *Standard Widget Toolkit (SWT)* library, which facilitates the usage of native user interface controls of the underlying operating system. JNI also enables a native application to call a Java application. JNI is included in JDK1.1 and thus can be used on PDAs as well.

Java Native Interface

SAP provides in cooperation with the ABACO (see *www.abacomobile.com*) a bundle of native drivers for various peripheral devices, along with a *Peripheral Input/Output Services Infrastructure (PIOS)*, which acts as an abstraction layer between the application and the peripheral. A developer using PIOS does not have to be concerned

Support of native drivers

8 | Support of Peripheral Devices

about the implementation details for each supported peripheral device. Instead, the developer can call abstracted functionality provided by the peripheral and required by the application.

This chapter outlines the PIOS key capabilities. Due to the extensive functionality of PIOS, it is not possible to describe each part of it in detail.

> **Note**
> For further reading, we recommend the "How to... Configure Peripheral Drivers with Mobile Infrastructures" document, which is available on the SAP Developer Network (SDN).

8.1 Peripheral Input/Output Services Infrastructure

Peripheral Input/Output Services Infrastructure (PIOS) provides a common framework to access peripheral devices. In this chapter, we will discuss the PIOS architecture and the PIOS design time and runtime components. To enable developers to access peripheral devices in the application, we provide code examples, which can serve as templates in a development project.

8.1.1 PIOS Architecture

PIOS integration

PIOS provides services to enable mobile applications accessing peripheral devices. To facilitate this, PIOS is integrated into the client runtime, the SAP NetWeaver Developer Studio, and the administrative part of SAP NetWeaver Mobile. This integration supports developers in creating mobile applications for various target platforms and peripheral devices, and administrators to deploy the application components to the mobile device. An overview of the PIOS architecture is shown in Figure 8.1.

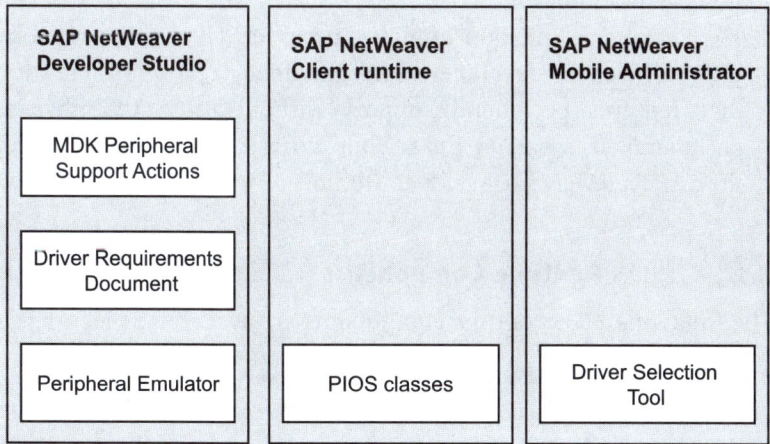

Figure 8.1 The PIOS Architecture

8.1.2 PIOS Design Time Components

The PIOS design time components are split into the following two parts.

- **MDK Peripheral Support Actions Toolbar**
  This component is integrated into the SAP NetWeaver Developer Studio and is used to define and emulate the peripheral features required by a mobile application. It provides the following functionality:

  - **Create or modify driver requirement documents (DRMs)**
    This launches a wizard to specify the mobile application's peripheral requirements and resources, such as bitmapped or scalable fonts. It is important to select all peripheral attributes and options required by the application for the Driver Selection Tool (see Section 8.1.4) to accurately select peripheral model drivers that match those requirements.

    Driver requirement documents

  - **Set MDK Peripheral Emulation Mode**
    This configures the SAP NetWeaver Developer Studio to run the application's peripheral actions in emulation mode.

  - **Launch the Peripheral I/O Emulator**
    This launches the Peripheral I/O Emulator.

8 | Support of Peripheral Devices

Emulating peripheral devices

- **Peripheral Emulator**
  The Peripheral Emulator emulates peripheral types supported by PIOS. It helps the developer to test and debug a mobile application that requires peripheral support without using the physical peripheral. It is part of the Mobile Infrastructure perspective of the SAP NetWeaver Developer Studio.

8.1.3 PIOS Runtime Components

The following PIOS runtime components are available.

- **PIOS classes in SAP client runtime**
  The developer can use these classes to discover, connect, and use the functionality available in supported peripheral devices. They are described in more detail in Section 8.2.

- **Driver Add-On**
  This is the component that contains the software packages required use a specific peripheral model on a client device.

8.1.4 Driver Selection Tool

Administration of peripheral drivers

Using the Driver Selection tool, the administrator can identify available peripheral drivers that match the peripheral requirements of a mobile application, as specified in the DRD. This selection process also considers the operating system of the mobile device, processor, and Java Virtual Machine.

You now have an understanding of the PIOS design time and runtime components. In the next section, we describe the Java APIs, which can be used to access the peripheral device, in more detail.

8.2 PIOS API Core

Abstraction layer for native drivers

The PIOS API Core contains all the classes used to discover, connect, and use the functionality available across different peripheral device types. A developer using PIOS can use this abstracted functionality provided by the peripheral and required by the application and is shielded from the native peripheral device driver. The PIOS API Core is part of the SAP NetWeaver Mobile 7.1 client runtime. It contains common functionality available across peripheral device types, such as:

- Methods to discover peripheral drivers installed on a mobile device
- Methods to open a connection to a peripheral
- Methods to configure the driver

8.2.1 Printer API

The Printer API provides an abstraction layer between the intricacies of different printer drivers and the application.

Printer API Feature Description

The PIOS Printer API provides support for various printer features. These features vary depending on the printer model. Table 8.1 provides an overview of the printable objects. Table 8.2, Table 8.3, Table 8.4, and Table 8.5 provide an overview of the supported printer features, graphical and line modes, and supported symbologies, respectively.

Printable Object	Description
Bitmap image	Images in bitmap format
PCX image	Images in PCX format
Scalable fonts	Fonts based on vector graphic
Bitmap fonts	Fonts made of character images
Barcode	Barcode printing

Printing fonts, bitmaps and barcodes

Table 8.1 Overview of the Printable Objects

Printer Features	Description
Clear Error	Clear error condition from the printer
Advance Forward	Advance the paper forward
Advance Backward	Retract the paper
Dispose	Dispose of the commands sent to the printer

Table 8.2 Overview of the Printer Features

Printer Features	Description
Get Status	Query the printer status
Page Measurements	Page length and width given in points
Printer Head Width	Obtain the printer head width (in points)
Text Metrics	Obtain the text dimension (in points) based on the font
Barcode Metrics	Obtain the barcode dimension (in points)
Image Metrics	Obtain the image dimension (in points)
Load Image	Upload an image into the printer's memory
Delete Image	Delete an image from the printer's memory
Get DPI	Returns the printer's resolution
Transport Configuration	Modify and set the default transport options (i.e., serial, Bluetooth)
Font Configuration	Configure (add, delete, change) font information
Send Raw Data	Send raw bytes to the printer

Table 8.2 Overview of the Printer Features (cont.)

Graphic Mode Feature	Description
Barcode Rotation	Barcode rotations in 90° increments
Image Rotation	Image rotation in 90° increments
Text Rotation	Text rotation in 90° increments
Line Thickness	Set the line thickness (in points)
Draw Text	Print text
Page Measurements	Page length and width given in points
Draw Barcode	Print barcode
Draw line	Print lines
Draw rectangle	Print rectangle
Draw image	Print images

Table 8.3 Overview of the Graphical Modes

Line Mode Feature	Description
Barcode Alignment	Align a barcode in a line (center, right, left)
Image Alignment	Align an image in a line (center, right, left)
Text Alignment	Align text in a line (center, right, left)
Print Text	Print text in a line
Print Barcode	Print barcode in a line
Print Image	Print image in a line
Set Line Spacing	Define the space in points between two lines

Table 8.4 Overview of the Line Modes

Symbology	Description
Codabar	Support for Codabar barcode symbology
Code 39	Support for Code 39 symbology
Code 128	Support for Code 128 barcode symbology
EAN-8	Support for EAN-8 barcode symbology
EAN-13	Support for EAN-13 barcode symbology
Interleaved 2 of 5	Support for Interleaved 2 of 5 barcode symbology
PDF417	Support for PDF-417 2D barcode symbology
UCC/EAN-128	Support for UCC/EAN barcode symbology
UPC-A	Support for UPC barcode symbology

Table 8.5 Overview of the Supported Symbologies

Printer API Usage Example

In the following code snippet, the printer is set in line mode, and a line is printed with left alignment. In addition, the following steps are performed:

- Opening connection to the printer (1)
- Printing the sample text with left alignment (2)
- Closing the connection to the printer (3)

```
package test;
import com.sap.ip.me.api.pios.connection.*;
```

8 | Support of Peripheral Devices

```
import com.sap.ip.me.api.pios.printer.*;
public class TextLeftLineMode {
    public static void main(String[] args) {
    LinePrinter lP = null;
    try{
        Connector conn = Connector.getInstance();
        DriverInfo[] driverInfo =
            conn.listDrivers(ConnectionType.PRINTER);
        PrinterParameters params = new
        PrinterParameters(driverInfo[0]);
        params.setPrinterMode(PrinterParameters.LINE_
            MODE);
//----------------------(1)--------------------
        lP = (LinePrinter) conn.open(params);
        String[] sFonts = lP.getFontConfigurationManag
er().listFontNames();
        PrinterFont pF = lP.getFont(sFonts[0]);
        lP.printText(pF, "", LinePrinter.NO_ALIGN-
MENT);
//----------------------(2)--------------------
        lP.printText(pF,"Left side of the line.",
            LinePrinter.ALIGN_LEFT);
        lP.doPrint(1);
    }
    catch (Throwable error){
        error.printStackTrace();
    }
    finally {
//----------------------(3)--------------------
        try {
            lP.close();
        }
        catch (Exception ex) {}
    }
    return;
    }
}
```

Listing 8.1 Code snippet for printing text

8.2.2 Scanner API

The Scanner API is an abstraction layer between the intricacies of different scanner drivers and the application.

Scanner API Feature Description

The PIOS scanner API provides support for several features. Due to the large diversity of scanners, it may happen that scanner models offer additional features not supported by this API. Table 8.6 provides an overview of the scannable objects, Table 8.7 provides an overview of the supported scanner features, and Table 8.8 provides an overview of the supported symbologies and options.

Reading barcodes

Scannable Object	Description
Linear Barcode	An automatic identification technology that encodes information into a linear array of adjacent parallel rectangular bars and spaces of varying width
Two-Dimensional Barcode	An automatic identification technology that encodes information in a two-dimensional array of adjacent bars and spaces of varying width and height

Table 8.6 Overview of Scannable Objects

Scanner Feature	Description
Soft Trigger	Allows the scan engine laser beam to be triggered from the software; it is a one shot mode, meaning the laser turns off when a barcode is scanned
Beep on Fail	Hardware beeps on failed scanning
Beep on Read	Hardware beeps on successful scan
Beep Off	Turns off the scanner's hardware beep
Scan Aware Mode	The application handles the scanned data through events; the scanning process generates events on data received or on error
Wedge Mode	When using this mode, scanned data is sent as if it was typed from the keyboard; it is sent to the window that has the focus

Table 8.7 Overview of Scanner Features

Symbology/Option	Description
Codabar	Enables the Codabar symbology
CLSI Optional	If a CLSI barcode is scanned, the CLSI formatting is applied to the returned data
CLSI Required	Scanned barcode must be CLSI compliant

Table 8.8 Overview of Supported Symbologies and Options

Symbology/Option	Description
NOTIS	NOTIS formatting is applied to the scanned data
Check Digit MOD 16	Enables check digit validation in the scanner engine
Check Digit Transmit	Sends the check digit in a barcode as part of the data; requires Check Digit MOD 16 to be enabled
Code 39	Enables the Code 39 barcode symbology
Standard	The scanner engine interprets the barcode as standard data; this is the default character set if no character set is specified
Full ASCII	Support for the whole ASCII character set
Check Digit MOD43	Support for Module 43 check
Check Digit French CIP	Support for French CIP (Club Inter Pharmaceutique) check digit
Check Digit Transmit	Sends the check digit in a barcode as part of the data
Code 128	Enables the Code 128 barcode symbology
EAN-8	Enables the EAN-8 barcode symbology
Check Digit Transmit	Sends the check digit in a barcode as part of the data
EAN-13	Enables the EAN-13 barcode symbology
Check Digit Transmit	Sends the check digit in a barcode as part of the data
Interleaved 2 of 5	Enables the interleaved 2 of 5 barcode symbology
Check Digit MOD 10 USS	Support for Module 10 USS (Uniform Symbology Specification) check digit
Check Digit MOD 10 OPCC	Support for Module 10 OPCC (Optical Product Code Council) check digit
PDF417	Enables the PDF-417 (Portable Data Format) barcode symbology
UCC / EAN-128	Enables the UCC / EAN barcode symbology
UPC-A	Enables the Universal Product Code (UPC) barcode symbology
Check Digit Transmit	Sends the check digit as part of the data
UPC/EAN Five Digit Add-On	Transmits the two digit add-on as part of the data if the add-on is present in the barcode
UPC/EAN Two Digit Add-On	Transmits the five digit add-on as part of the data if the add-on is present in the barcode
UPC/EAN Add-On Digits	Forces the add-on digits to be present in the barcode

Table 8.8 Overview of Supported Symbologies and Options (cont.)

PIOS Scanner API Usage Example

In this example, the scanner uses Scanner Aware Mode, and three barcodes are scanned after Code 39, Code 128, and Codabar symbologies are added to the scanner. It is assumed that a driver has been installed that supports all the attributes that are being used. In the code snippet shown in Listing 8.2, the following steps are performed:

1. Calling the constructor, opening a connection to the scanner in scan aware mode, and setting an event listener.
2. Implementing the onError method from Scanner Listener.
3. Implementing the onDataReceived method from Scanner Listener.
4. Declaring and implementing a method called scanBarcode to start the scanning engine, waiting for the application to read the barcode, and stopping the scanning.
5. Declaring and implementing the openScanAwareConnection method.
6. Declaring and implementing the activateSymbologies method. This method adds Code 39, Code 128, and Codabar symbologies to the scanner.
7. Declaring and implementing the deactivateSymbologies method to remove the Code 39, Code 128, and Codabar symbologies from the scanner.
8. Declaring and implementing the close method to close the connection to the scanner.
9. Creating an instance of the class and calling the activateSymbologies method.
10. Scanning three barcodes; the scanned barcodes must have their symbologies activated.
11. Calling the deactivateSymbologies method, scanning one barcode, and closing the connection to the scanner.

```
package scanner_api_examples;
import com.sap.ip.me.api.pios.PIOSException;
import com.sap.ip.me.api.pios.connection.*;
import com.sap.ip.me.api.pios.scanner.*;
import com.sap.ip.me.api.pios.symbology.*;
```

```java
public class AddingSymbologies implements ScannerListener {
        private ScannerConnection scannerConnection = null;
        private boolean barcodeScanned = false;
        private Exception lastException = null;
//----------------------(1)----------------------
        public AddingSymbologies() throws PIOSException {
        openScanAwareConnection();
        scannerConnection.setEventListener(this);
}
//----------------------(2)----------------------
public void onError(ScannerException e) {
        lastException = e;
        barcodeScanned = true;
}
//----------------------(3)----------------------
public void onDataReceived(ScannerData scannerData) {
        try {
            System.out.println(
            "Data = " + new String(scannerData.toByteArray(),
                "ASCII"));
        }
        catch (Exception ex) {
        lastException = ex;
        }
        barcodeScanned = true;
}
//----------------------(4)----------------------
public void scanBarcode() throws Exception {
        scannerConnection.startRead();
        while (!barcodeScanned) {
                Thread.sleep(500);
        }
        if (lastException != null) {
                throw lastException;
        }
        scannerConnection.endRead();
        barcodeScanned = false;
}
//----------------------(5)----------------------
private void openScanAwareConnection() throws PIOSException
{
        Connector connector = Connector.getInstance();
        DriverInfo[] scanners =
            connector.listDrivers(ConnectionType.SCANNER);
```

```
        ScannerParameters parameters =
            new ScannerParameters(scanners[0]);
        parameters.setMode(ScannerParameters.SCAN_AWARE);
        scannerConnection =
            (ScannerConnection) connector.open(parameters);
}
//-----------------------(6)-----------------------
public void activateSymbologies() throws PIOSException {
        scannerConnection.addSymbology(new Code39(Code39.FULL
            ASCII));
        scannerConnection.addSymbology(new Code128());
        scannerConnection.addSymbology( new Codabar(
         Codabar.CHECK_DIGIT_MOD16 |
         Codabar.CHECK_DIGIT_TRANSMIT));
}
//-----------------------(7)-----------------------
public void deactivateSymbologies() throws PIOSException {
        scannerConnection.removeSymbology(SymbologyType.CODE128);
        scannerConnection.removeSymbology(SymbologyType.CODE39);
}
//--------------------   (8)  -----------------
public void close() {
        try {
                scannerConnection.close();
        }
        catch (Exception ex) { ex.printStackTrace(); }
}
public static void main(String[] args) {
        AddingSymbologies addSymbologiesExample = null;
        try { //-----------------------(9)-----------------
            addSymbologiesExample = new AddingSymbologies();

        addSymbologiesExample.activateSymbologies();
//-----------------------(10)-----------------------
                for (int i = 0; i < 3; i++)
                    {addSymbologiesExample.scanBarcode();}
//-----------------------(11)-----------------------
        addSymbologiesExample.deactivateSymbologies();
        addSymbologiesExample.scanBarcode();
        }
        catch (Exception ex) {
                ex.printStackTrace();
        }
        finally {
```

```
            addSymbologiesExample.close();
        }
    }
}
```

Listing 8.2 Code example of Scanner API usage

8.2.3 RFID API

PIOS offers services to support RFID. The RFID API provides an abstraction layer between the intricacies of different RFID readers' drivers and the application.

RFID API Feature Description

Reading and writing RFID tags

PIOS RFID API provides support for several features. These features vary depending on the RFID reader model. Table 8.9 provides a description of these features.

RFID Reader Feature	Description
Program Tag ID	Assigns a new Tag ID to all the tags inside the RFID range
Identify All	Returns all the tags available within its area of coverage; the tag must have been previously defined in the tag configuration file
Identify by Tag Type	Returns all the tags available within its area of coverage; the tag type must be defined in the tag configuration file and supported by the RFID reader hardware
Read a Single Tag	Reads bytes from a specific tag
Write a Single Tag	Writes bytes to a specific tag
Lock Tag ID with Password	Locks a tag ID with password so it cannot be changed; once locked, the tag must be reset to be reprogrammed with a new tag ID
Reset Tag ID with Password	Resets a locked tag ID, making it programmable again; unlocks and erases the tag ID

Table 8.9 Overview of RFID Reader Features

RFID API Example

In this example, the RFID reader identifies all the tags, independently of the tag type, in the reader's range. In the code snippet shown in Listing 8.3, the following steps are performed:

1. Getting the RFID parameter s from the first driver and opening a connection to the RFID reader
2. Checking if the driver supports the IDENTIFY_ALL attribute and displays how many tags are in range
3. Displaying the tag ID and tag type for each of the detected RFID tags

```
import com.sap.ip.me.api.pios.PIOSException;
import com.sap.ip.me.api.pios.connection.*;
import com.sap.ip.me.api.pios.rfid.*;

public class ExampleIdentifyAll {
   public static void main(String[] args) {
      RfidConnection rfidConnection = null;
      try {
         Connector connector = Connector.getInstance();
//---------------------(1)--------------------
         DriverInfo[] rfidDrivers =
            connector.listDrivers(ConnectionType.RFID);
         if (rfidDrivers.length > 0) {
            RfidParameters rfidParams =
               new RfidParameters(rfidDrivers[0]);
            rfidConnection =
               (RfidConnection) connector.open(rfidParams);
//---------------------(2)--------------------
            if (rfidDrivers[0].isAttributeSupported
               (RfidConnection.Attributes.IDENTIFY_ALL)) {
               RfidTag[] tagList =
                  rfidConnection.identify();
               if (tagList.length <= 0) {
                  System.out.println("There are no tags in
                                    range.");
               } else {
                  System.out.println(
                  "Total tags: " + tagList.length + ".");
               }
//---------------------(3)--------------------
               for (int i = 0; i < tagList.length; i++) {
```

```
                    System.out.print("TagID: ");
                    for (int j = 0;
                    j < tagList[i].getTagID().length;
                    j++) {
              System.out.print(tagList[i].getTagID()[j] + " ");
                    }
                  System.out.println(
                      "\t tag type: "
                      + tagList[i].getTagType().getName());
                  }
                } else {
                  System.out.println("Required driver
                            attribute is not supported.");
                }
              } else {
                System.out.println("There are no RFID
                            drivers.");
              }
          } catch (Exception ex) {
            ex.printStackTrace();
          } finally {
            try {
                rfidConnection.close();
            } catch (PIOSException pex) {
                pex.printStackTrace();
            }
          }
        }
      }
    }
```

Listing 8.3 Code example of RFID API usage

In this section, we described the PIOS Printer API, the Scanner API, and the RFID API in detail. For each API, we provided a feature overview and a usage example with a code snippet, which shows how the peripheral devices can be accessed from your application.

8.3 Summary

Many business scenarios require the use of peripheral devices. For example, a mobile printer enables a sales person to print invoices at the customer site, barcode scanners allow fast and reliable data entry, and RFID tags have the capability to store data. Support of the appropriate peripheral devices can increase the usability of your mobile application tremendously. By using the code examples as templates for your application, you can integrate peripheral devices in your mobile solution.

In Chapter 9, we will continue the discussion of introducing a mobile environment in your company and provide you with hints to consider when you implement a mobile solution.

In this chapter we will explain Best Practices based on the experiences of SAP's support team for mobile applications. They can help you avoid pitfalls when you introduce a mobile solution in your company.

9 Tips for a Successful Implementation of Mobile Projects

The success of introducing a mobile solution in your company depends on many factors. In this chapter, we present some key success factors that need to be considered before you start implementing a mobile project. They include the following:

- Selecting the appropriate mobile devices
- Selecting the appropriate (wireless) network protocol and (wireless) service provider
- Selecting the appropriate peripheral devices
- Sizing the system landscape
- Selecting the appropriate security technology

9.1 Selecting the Appropriate Devices

Before introducing a mobile solution in your company, it is worthwhile to spend some time selecting the most appropriate devices. Due to the fragmentation of the mobile device market, the selection of an appropriate device is not a trivial task. We will discuss some of the criteria that should be taken into consideration before you purchase devices, including device form factor, processor and memory capacity, data entry method, network support, peripheral device support, and other consideration.

Fragmentation of the mobile device market

9 | Tips for a Successful Implementation of Mobile Projects

9.1.1 Device Form Factor

Screen format

The device form factor describes the screen format of the device, which can vary considerably. It depends mostly on the user interface of the application: if, for instance, a laptop or a PDA is better suited to run the application. To find the device with the optimal form factor for your application, we recommend that you install the application on a test device to check if you feel comfortable with it. Small devices like PDAs have the advantage that they can be carried in a pocket and are up and running almost immediately. Laptops allow the user to run other business-related programs but need some time to boot and log in.

9.1.2 Device Processor and Memory Capacity

Processor performance and adressable memory

PDAs can't compete with laptops in terms of processor performance and addressable memory. Thus, if your business scenario requires you to process many data (over 8 to 10MB), then a laptop might be the better option. On the SAP Service Marketplace (*http://service.sap.com*), data calculators are available for xMAM, xMAM for Utilities, and xMSA, which enable you to calculate the expected data volume. Currently, the Windows Mobile operating system doesn't allow allocating more than 32MB per process, but also across PDAs, there are significant differences with regard to performance. It is recommended that you first deploy the application on a couple of test devices from different vendors and to compare the response time.

9.1.3 Data Entry Method

Virtual keyboards

There are two main methods to enter data on a PDA. One method is to use a touch screen and enter characters via the virtual keyboard. The other method is to use a built-in physical keyboard and hardware buttons to enter data. Again, the most appropriate device depends on the business scenario.

9.1.4 Network Support

Network support is a very important feature and requires careful consideration. For the acceptance of the end users, the response time and synchronization time is crucial. Unless users are synchronizing in a LAN/WAN environment, the synchronization time heavily depends on the bandwidth of the wireless network. To select the best-suited network provider, you should first estimate the average amount of data that is exchanged between the mobile device and the backend system based on your business scenario.

Using the transfer rates given by your network provider, you can easily calculate the average time needed to transfer the data. Keep in mind that the transfer rates are often theoretical values and cannot be reached in reality. In addition, there is some protocol overhead, which will reduce the data transfer rate as well. To minimize the costs of data transfer, we recommend comparing the various pricing models of the network providers. The location of the SAP NetWeaver AS that runs the mobile middleware can also have an impact on the costs of the data traffic. For wireless connections, the distance between the mobile devices and the SAP NetWeaver AS should be minimized.

Transfer rates and network bandwidth

9.1.5 Peripheral Device Support

Using mobile peripheral devices can significantly increase the efficiency of a mobile solution. In many scenarios peripheral devices are needed or helpful, including the following:

Interfaces for peripheral devices

- Manual data entry can be replaced by barcode scanners or RFID readers. Figure 9.1 shows an example of a commercial RFID reader by Symbol, and Figure 9.2 shows an RFID tag by Texas Instruments.

Figure 9.1 Symbol MC9090-G Handheld RFID Reader

Figure 9.2 RFID Tag (Texas Instruments)

- Bills can be printed on a mobile printer and handed out to the customer.
- Built-in cameras can be used to document damage to equipment.
- GPS receivers can be used to provide navigation support.
- Thus, it is important to select a mobile device that provides the required interfaces for peripherals or already contains the functionality in a built-in component.

9.1.6 Other Considerations

We also recommend carefully reading the device data sheet, which contains important device-specific information about physical characteristics, performance characteristics, peripherals and accessories, support of wireless networks, battery power and lifespan, and display characteristics such as resolution, contrast and brightness, operating system version, and user environment. Depending on the working conditions, it might be advisable to use ruggedized devices, which are able to withstand drops and are protected against water and dust.

9.1.7 Conclusion

The purchase of mobile devices is a significant cost factor of an entire project. A wrong decision can have a strongly negative impact on user acceptance, performance, security, and the overall success of a project.

The selection of the device that best fits your requirements is a complex task. It is advisable to create a decision matrix containing the characteristic device properties and technical requirements, assign weights to those criteria, and determine to what extent the requirements are fulfilled for each device under consideration.

Finally, you can relate those results to the estimated costs for purchase, installation and integration into your system landscape, and operation. This will give you a sound basis to make your decision.

9.2 Performance and Sizing

Performance and sizing is another critical factor for a successful Go Live. The data synchronization of the mobile devices with the backend system has an impact on the overall system performance, and therefore it is necessary to check if the available hardware can handle it. To support customers to buy the required hardware, SAP defined a performance benchmark, which is briefly described in the next section.

9.2.1 SAP Standard Application Benchmark (SAPS)

The *SAP standard application benchmark* (SAPS) is the basis for all performance-related considerations. It defines a performance benchmark unit, which is independent of the underlying hardware. The reason to take this approach is obvious. Physical reference machines will be outdated very quickly, and the impact of different hardware architectures doesn't have to be considered.

The SAPS is defined in business application terms and not in technical terms. One hundred SAPS are equivalent to 2,000 fully processed order line items per hour. The performance benchmark is defined by throughput (n [objects/h]). It does not provide an estimation how long a specific operation will take. This is not possible, because the actual duration depends on multiple factors, such as availability of resources such as CPU, memory, or network bandwidth.

Throughput

9.3 Sizing of Mobile Applications

During the lifecycle of a mobile installation, many operations occur that have an impact on system performance. Two we will look at include initial replication and delta synchronization. In addition, client sizing and network sizing also affect performance.

9.3.1 Initial Replication

Parallelization of the initial replication
Before data can be exchanged between the mobile devices and the backend system, it is necessary to replicate all required data from the backend system to the *data orchestration engine* (DOE). The data volume clearly depends on the business scenario and can be more than 100 million records. To support customers in their planning phase, SAP provides throughput measurements for the various applications, which can be found on the SAP Service Marketplace. Initial replication generally happens only once. Nevertheless, it can take some time to transfer all the objects to the mobile middleware. Thus, it is recommended that you consider the replication phase in the overall project planning. For the replication of huge data amounts, a parallelization of the replication is possible.

9.3.2 Delta Synchronization

By delta synchronization we mean the daily business of the device users. They create new objects, or change objects such as sales orders, on their devices and download new objects that have been assigned to them in the backend system to their devices. The mobile infrastructure calculates the difference of the data and transfers only the delta result to minimize the network traffic.

Upload and download requests
During the delta synchronization, the device sends an upload and download request to the middleware. The upload request puts the uploaded data in an inbound queue for further processing by the middleware, and the download request retrieves the data, either from the device outbound queue or by a BAPI call from the backend.

The way data are downloaded to the device is important for performance-related considerations and requires further explanation, as follows:

▶ **Retrieval via service calls into the backend (pull scenario)**

Data pull
In this case, the data are "pulled" from the backend system during synchronization. This approach is not recommended, because it does not scale for a large number of synchronization requests.

▶ **Pushing data from the backend into device queues on middleware (push scenario)**

In this case, the backend application triggers an event as soon as a business object has been changed or created in the backend, and an event handler "pushes" the object to the mobile middleware. The middleware flow in turn consolidates the data, evaluates the distribution rules, and puts them in the right device queues. This all happens timely decoupled from the synchronization. During synchronization, all data are already prepared in the device queues and can be easily transferred to the devices. CPU-intensive calculations during synchronization do not occur in this approach. SAP NetWeaver Mobile 7.1 fully supports the push scenario.

Data push

9.3.3 Client Sizing

PDAs from different manufacturers vary significantly with regard to performance. To better support customers in comparing PDA performance, SAP provides the Mobile Client Benchmarking Tool. Using this tool, the customer is able to generate benchmarks for the various devices that take the specific requirements of mobile applications into consideration without having to install an entire system landscape. The client component of the tool executes a script. After executing the script, the measured benchmark is displayed on the screen that compares the performance with the performance of a reference device. An example of this benchmark tool is shown in Figure 9.3.

Mobile Client Benchmarking Tool

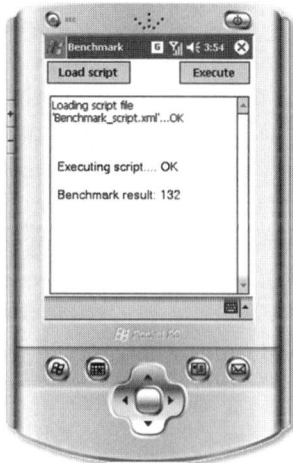

Figure 9.3 Screenshot of the Benchmark Tool

9.3.4 Network Sizing

Network bandwidth

Another important factor that has an impact on performance is network bandwidth. In a campus scenario, where access to the corporate network via LAN is available, the impact is negligible. Modern LANs have a bandwidth of 1GBit/s, and a typical delta sync of a mobile device should be transferred over the wire within seconds.

The situation changes when device users are working in the field and connect to the corporate network via a wireless connection. In this case, the network bandwidth requires close attention.

> **Example**
>
> General Packet Radio Service (GPRS) provides a theoretical transfer rate of 21.4kBit/s per GSM channel, and by bundling 8 channels, the maximum rate is 171.2 kBit/s. In reality, those transmission rates can not be reached. The real transmission rate is about 50kBit/s, but this depends on the configuration of the mobile phone, the data volume that is being transferred simultaneously by different users in the same cell, and the capabilities of the GPRS infrastructure.

To better estimate the impact of network bandwidth, SAP provides a Network Sizing Document that can be found on the SAP Service Marketplace (*http://service.sap.com*) and contains information about the data volume that is sent over the (wireless) network for some typical scenarios. The results can be used to find the most appropriate network provider.

9.4 Security

A mobile device is much more vulnerable than a server because it is used on the road. It might get lost or stolen or misused by an unauthorized person. Its vulnerability is increased when it is used by multiple users. Vulnerability also occurs during data transmission over an insecure network such as the Internet. Different techniques can be used to tackle these security issues, and we will show you how the SAP infrastructure helps you set up a secure system landscape.

9.4.1 User Management

User management is available on the SAP client runtime and on the SAP NetWeaver AS. On the server, the SAP user administration of SAP NetWeaver AS is used. Before logging on the server, a user must be created on the server with the necessary authorizations. On the client, local users are administered as well. There are two passwords for local users. The local password allows access of the client application, and a dedicated synchronization password is used when logging into the server. Depending on the security policy at the customer site, the security level can be configured appropriately. Three options are available:

SAP authorizations

- **atSync**
  The synchronization password does not correspond to the local password and must be entered for each synchronization.

- **Local**
  The synchronization password corresponds to the local password and need not be entered at synchronization.

- **Once**
  The synchronization password does not correspond to the local password and must be entered once for each logon.

Due to the sensitive nature of the synchronization password that enables access to the server, it is only stored on the server. The local client passwords are case sensitive and are locally stored in an encrypted form. For the various operations, SAP provides different types of users on the backend system and SAP NetWeaver AS, as outlined in the following list:

- Technical users, which can be used as RFC user for data replication from the backend system to the SAP NetWeaver AS.

- Individual users that correspond to the users on the mobile devices. On the SAP NetWeaver AS, they need to be equipped with the appropriate authorizations for synchronization. For further processing of the synchronization request in the backend system, you can assign a technical user to the RFC connection, or you can use the same user in the backend system by establishing a trusted relationship between the SAP NetWeaver AS and the backend system.

9.4.2 Communication Channel Security

HTTPS — Sensitive data that are transferred over an insecure connection face a security risk. The SAP client runtime uses the HTTP protocol to exchange data between the device and the server. Transferring sensitive business data across insecure public networks may not meet your security requirements, because the data are transferred as a plain data stream readable by everyone who has access to the network. To close this security gap, SAP supports the HTTPS protocol to encrypt and authenticate the communication between the device and the server. HTTPS uses SSL, which is located in the OSI model layers between the Transport layer and Application layer. In the SSL handshake protocol that happens before data are exchanged, the communication partners are identified. Then a symmetric session key is exchanged between them that is used for data encryption. To enable SSL, a server certificate is required for the server authentication.

> **Further Information**
>
> The SAP how-to guide "Enable Secure Synchronization with the ABAP Synchronization Service," available from the SAP Service Marketplace, describes in more detail how to generate a server certificate and import a server certificate into the client device's trust store file.

9.4.3 Single Sign-On

SAP logon tickets — *Single sign-on* (SSO) provides secure and easy-to-use access to systems. It allows users to authenticate themselves once and then log on to all the systems operating in the SSO environment. Using SSO simplifies the implementation of the company's authentication policy and provides increased usability for the end users, who are no longer required to deal with different users and passwords. The SSO support provided by the mobile client is based on SAP logon tickets issued, for instance, by SAP NetWeaver Portal.

Figure 9.4 shows the components involved in an SSO scenario. It assumes that the SAP NetWeaver Portal acts as the authentication component that issues SAP logon tickets, and that a trusted relationship between the SAP NetWeaver Portal and the SAP NetWeaver AS is established.

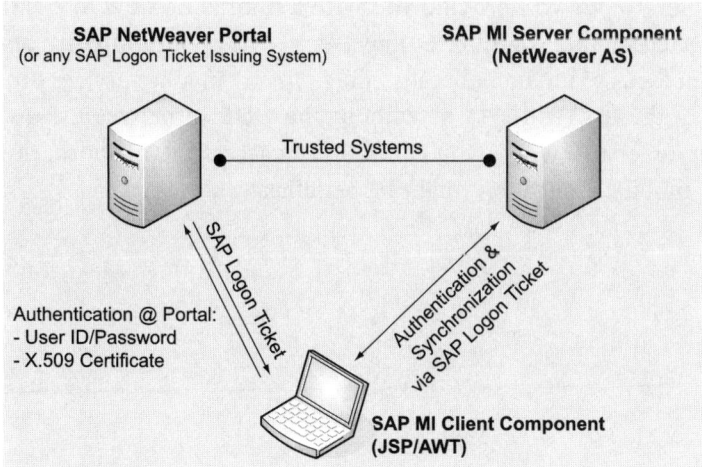

Figure 9.4 System Landscape for an SSO Scenario

To get the logon ticket, the user logs on to the SAP NetWeaver Portal, which selects the appropriate authentication scheme based on the mobile device type. For devices running Windows Mobile, it uses a basic authentication via user/password, and for laptops it uses X.509 certificates installed on the laptop. Then the SAP logon ticket is sent back to the device. During synchronization, the device passes the logon ticket to the SAP NetWeaver AS, where it is used for the authentication of the client.

> **Further Reading**
>
> On the SAP Service Marketplace you can find the how-to guide "How to Configure Single Sign-On Support of SAP Mobile Infrastructure," which contains additional information on this subject.

9.5 Summary

In this chapter, we described some common pitfalls that might occur during a mobile implementation project. These pitfalls can have a significant negative impact on overall project costs and end users project acceptance. The tips contained in this chapter should help you avoid these pitfalls.

In Chapter 10, we will provide you with a tutorial on how to create a connected mobile solution. Connected mobile applications are not the main focus of the book because they directly invoke services provided by the backend system without the DOE in between. However, in a scenario where you continuously access the network, this type of mobile application might be beneficial.

Connected mobile applications need to have a permanent network connection to the backend system. These can be created easily. In this chapter we show an approach to create connected mobile applications by importing an adaptive RFC model from the backend system.

10 Design Study of a Connected Mobile Application Using Mobile Web Dynpro Online

The following tutorial provides step-by-step instructions for creating a connected, or synonymously online, mobile application that runs on a mobile device such as a PDA or a Nokia320. The tutorial can be used as a template to create online applications for specific purposes. In the tutorial, we show you how to design, implement, deploy, and run a basic Web Dynpro application that accesses persistent data from a remote SAP system. The application runs on the SAP J2EE engine.

To access data from a remote SAP backend system, we will use an adaptive RFC model. This approach allows use of existing RFC-enabled function modules. For each function module you need, the system generates a corresponding Java proxy class. All the generated proxy classes are bundled together in the RFC model and treated as part of the Web Dynpro project.

Adaptive RFC model

10.1 Scenario Description

In this tutorial, we will design a simple web application, which will display flight connections between a given departure and destination port. The user interface for this web application will consist of only two views, as shown in Figure 10.1. In the first view, the user should

10   Design Study of a Connected Mobile Application Using Mobile Web Dynpro Online

be able to enter the departure and destination airports, and with the click of a **Search** button, all of the available flight data will be displayed as a table in the next view.

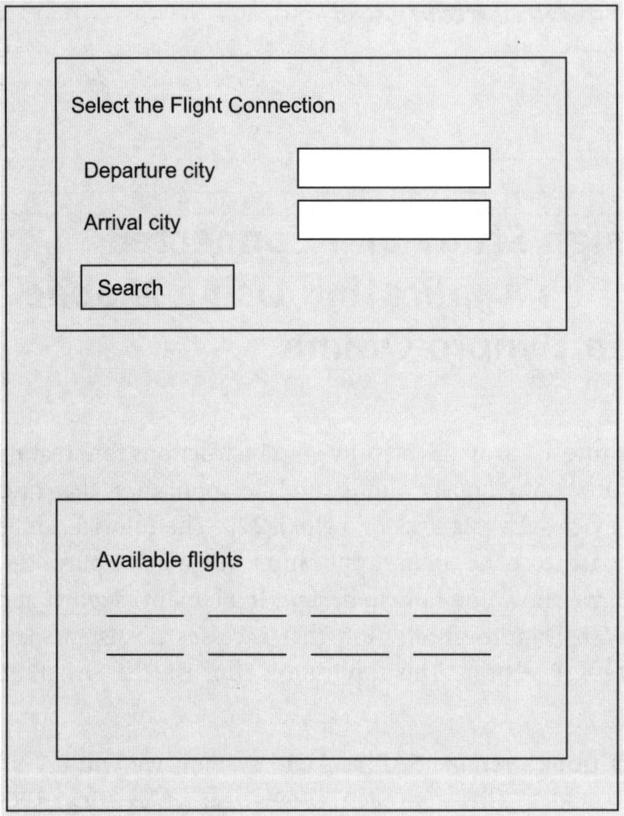

Figure 10.1 The UI for the Tutorial Application

10.2   Development Process

The diagram shown in Figure 10.2 shows the required steps and their logical relationship for creating the flight connection application in this sample project.

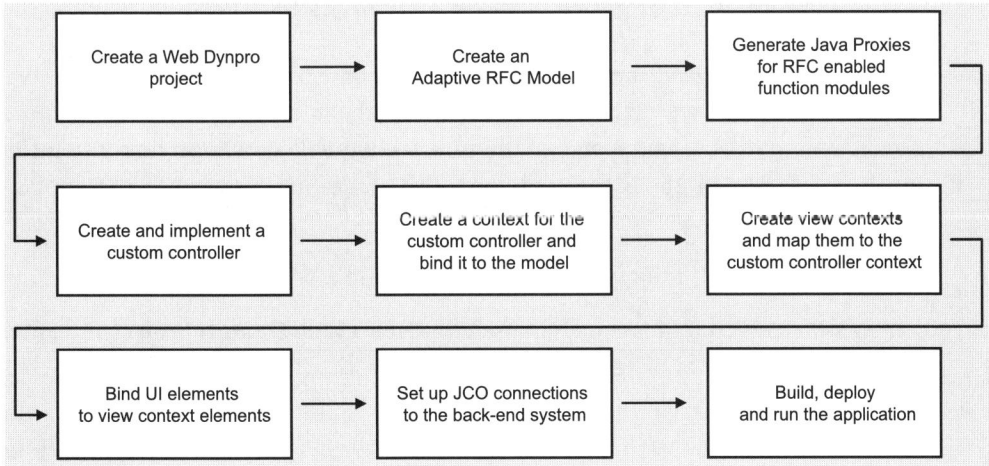

Figure 10.2 Development Process for the Flight Connection Applicationn

10.3 Prerequisites

Before you proceed, please ensure that the following prerequisites are met:

Hardware and software requirements

- The SAP NetWeaver Developer Studio is installed on your computer. You use it to create the mobile application.
- You have access to the SAP J2EE Engine. It is required to run the application.
- You have access to a remote SAP backend system. The backend system should contain the function module BAPI_FLIGHT_GETLIST.
- The *System Landscape Directory* (SLD) and the SLD bridge are configured and running. The SLD contains component information about all SAP software modules, and the SLD bridge is used to transform the system data to the SLD server format.

System Landscape Directory

- A connection between the J2EE engine and the SLD is configured in the J2EE engine administrator.

The Java Connector (JCo) connections to the remote SAP backend system are configured in the Web Dynpro Content Administrator. In Section 10.11, we provide you with the necessary steps to create and configure the JCo connections.

JCo connection

10.4 Creating a Web Dynpro Project

Connected mobile applications are based on Web Dynpro for Java. Thus, we start the tutorial with the creation of a Web Dynpro Project. At the end of the tutorial, we will show you how the information about the mobile device can be propagated to the application.

Use the following procedure to create a Web Dynpro Project:

Using SAP NetWeaver Developer Studio

1. From the menu, choose **File** • **New** • **Web Dynpro Project** and enter "MobileFlightConnection" in the field **Project name**. Then click **Finish**.

2. In the **Web Dynpro Explorer**, right-click on the node **Applications** and select **Create application**.

3. On the **New Application** screen, enter "FlightConnapp" in the field **Name** and "com.sap.tut.app" in the field **Package**. Then click **Next**.

4. On the next screen, select **Create a new component** and then click **Next** and confirm the settings for the new application by clicking **Finish**. As a result, the new application is generated along with a new Web Dynpro component FlightConnApp, a default view, and a default window.

5. In the **Web Dynpro Explorer**, right-click on the view **FlightConnAppView** and select **Rename**. Enter "SearchView" as the new name for the view. Then click **Finish**.

6. In the **Web Dynpro Explorer**, right-click on **Views** and select **Create View**. Enter "ResultView" in the field **View Name**. Then click **Finish**.

7. In the **Web Dynpro Explorer**, expand the node **Windows**, right-click on the subnode **FlightConnApp**, and select **Embed View**. On the next screen, select **Embed existing View** and click **Next**. Select the **ResultView** and then click **Finish**.

Custom Controller

8. In the **Web Dynpro Explorer**, right-click on **Custom Controllers** and select **Create Custom Controller**. Enter "FlightConnCust" as the **Name** of the custom controller and then click **Finish**.

10.5 Import an Adaptive RFC Model and Generate the Java Proxies

You are now ready to import an adaptive RFC model and generate the Java proxies. The procedure is as follows:

1. In the **Web Dynpro Explorer**, expand the node **Web Dynpro Models**.

   Importing an adaptive RFC model

2. From the context menu, select **Create Model**. The appropriate wizard appears.
3. Select the **Import Adaptive RFC Model** option, followed by **Next**.
4. Enter the model name "FlightModel" and the package name "com.sap.tut.model". In the next two fields, enter the values as shown in Table 10.1 and then click **Next**.

Field Name	Field Value
Default logical system name for model instances	WD_FLIGHTLIST_MODELDATA_DEST
Default logical system name for RFC metadata	WD_FLIGHTLIST_RFC_METADATA_DEST

Table 10.1 RFC Connection Data

5. On the **SAP Logon Information** screen, enter the appropriate data for logging on to the SAP backend system and then click **Next**. An example is shown in Figure 10.3.
6. On the **Select RFC modules** screen, enter "BAPI_FLIGHT_GETLIST" in the field **Function Name** and then click **Search**.
7. Select the function module **BAPI_FLIGHT_GETLIST** from the list that appears.
8. Select **Next**. This will automatically trigger the generation process. The import process is triggered by a detailed description, which you can see in the next dialog.
9. Select **Finish**. If you expand the model node, you can see the model classes as shown in Figure 10.4.

10 | Design Study of a Connected Mobile Application Using Mobile Web Dynpro Online

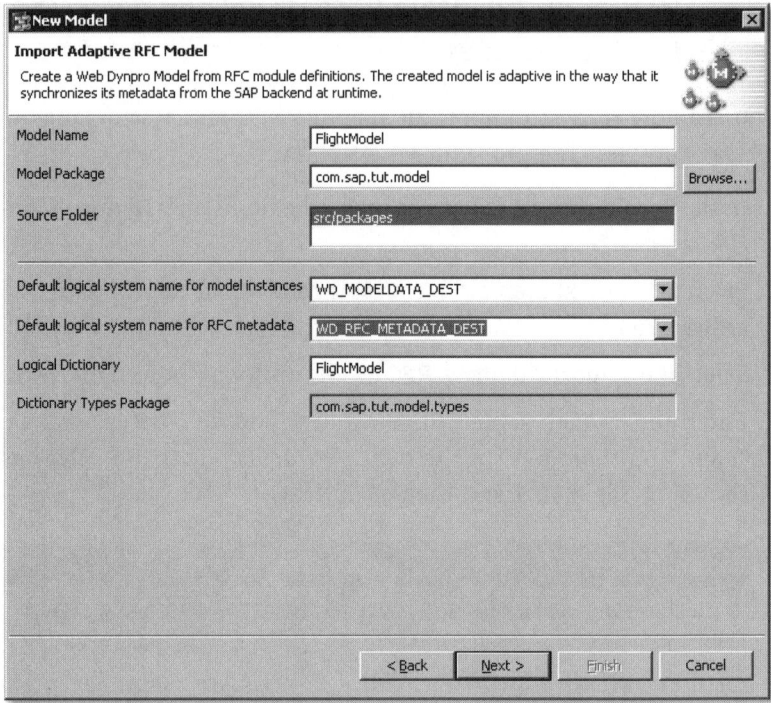

Figure 10.3 Data Entry Screen to Import an Adaptive RFC Model

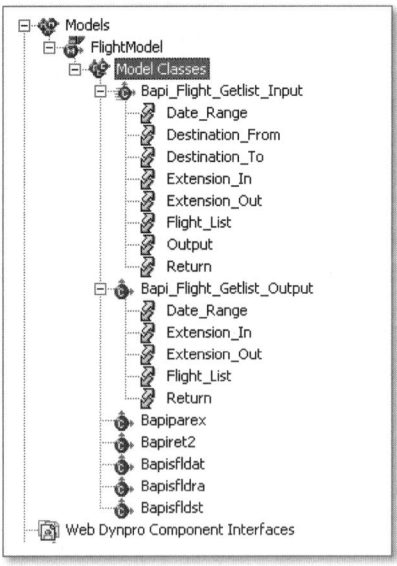

Figure 10.4 The Generated Model Classes for the Flight Connections Application

You have now imported the adaptive RFC model. A new node Flight-Model has been created, which contains all of the generated model classes, that is, the Java proxies.

10.6 Creating a Custom Controller Context and Binding it to the Model

In this section, you will create the context for the custom controller FlightConnCust. The custom controller is responsible for retrieving flight data from the SAP backend system. In addition, you will create an appropriate controller context and then bind the context nodes to the model structure. This ensures that the model data are stored and manipulated in a central location.

Custom controller

As a first step, add the model to the Web Dynpro component, as shown in the following step-by-step list. This ensures that all views and controllers in the Web Dynpro component have a dependency relationship with the model FlightModel.

Adding the model to the Web Dynpro component

1. In the **Web Dynpro Explorer**, navigate to the node **Web Dynpro • Web Dynpro Components • FlightConnApp**.
2. Right-click on the subnode **Used Models** and select **Add**. In the list that appears on the next screen, select the **FlightModel** model. Confirm by clicking **OK**.

In the second step, you will create a context for the custom controller.

1. In the **Web Dynpro Explorer**, double-click on the **FlightConnCust** custom controller.
2. Select the **Context** tab.
3. Right-click the **Context** root node and select **New • Model Node**.
4. Enter the name "Bapi_Flight_Getlist_Input" for the model node and select **Finish**.
5. Right-click on the node you just created and select **Edit Model Binding**.
6. On the **Model Binding** screen, select the node **Bapi_Flight_Getlist_Input** and click **Next**.
7. Select the entries as shown in Figure 10.5 and click **Finish**.

Creating the custom controller context

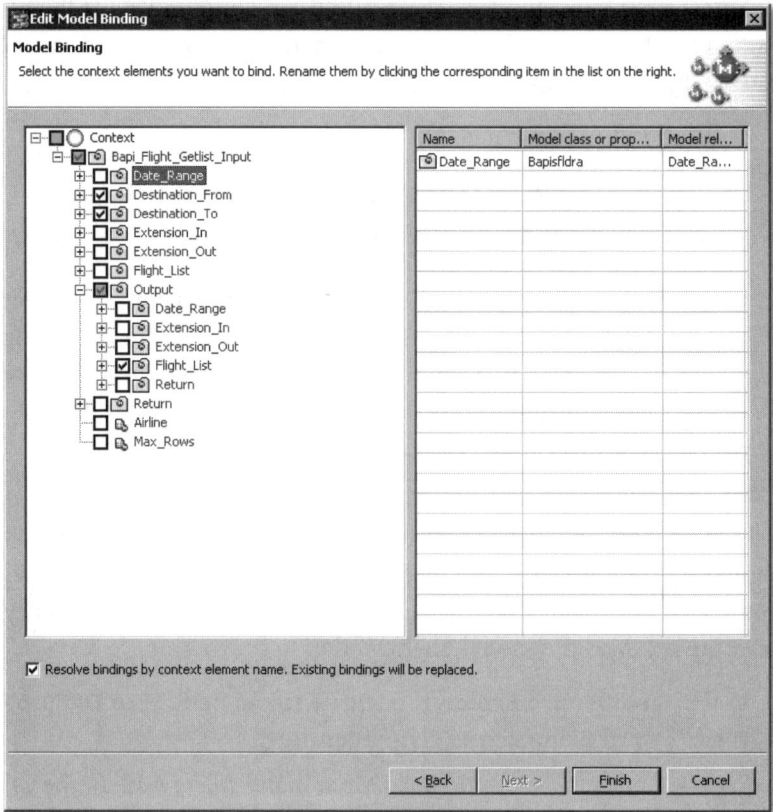

Figure 10.5 Model Binding of the Custom Controller Context

10.7 Mapping Custom Controller Context Elements to View Context Elements

Context mapping In this step, you will map the context elements of the custom controller FlightConnCust to the appropriate context elements of the views SearchView and ResultView. As a first step, add the dependency on the custom controller to the views, as follows:

1. In the **Web Dynpro Explorer**, double-click the **SearchView** node. The **View Designer** for the **SearchView** appears.

2. Select the **Properties** tab, and under **Required Controllers**, select **Add**.

3. In the list that appears, select the **FlightConnCust** controller and confirm by clicking **OK**.

4. In the same way, add the custom controller as required controller to the **ResultView**.

Next, you need to create a context for the views, as follows:

1. In the **Web Dynpro Explorer**, double-click the **SearchView** node and select the **Context** tab.

    Creating the view contexts

2. Right-click the **Context** root node and select **New • Model Node**.
3. Enter the name "Bapi_Flight_Getlist_Input" for the model node and click **Finish**.
4. Right-click the node you just created and select **Edit Context Mapping**.
5. Select the custom context node **Bapi_Flight_Getlist_Input**, and then click **Next**.
6. Select only the elements **Destination_From** and **Destination_To** and then click **Finish**.
7. In the same way, create a context for the **ResultView**. For the model node, enter the name "FlightList", choose the custom context node **Bapi_Flight_Getlist_Input • Output**, and select the context node **Flight_List**.

10.8 Creating Actions and Declaring Methods

In this step, you will create an action that triggers the display of the flight data from the SAP system. Then you will bind the action to a UI element, in this case, to a button. In addition, you will declare a method of the custom controller. This method will be called to get the data from the backend system. Proceed as follows:

Actions and controller methods

1. In the **Web Dynpro Explorer**, double-click the **SearchView** view.
2. In the **View Designer**, select the **Actions** tab.
3. Click the **New** button.
4. In the wizard that appears, enter the name "Search" for this new action and then click **Finish**. An event handler, **onActionSearch**, is automatically created for this new action.
5. In the **Web Dynpro Explorer**, double-click on the **FlightConnCust** custom controller.

6. In the editor, select the **Methods** tab.
7. Select **New**.
8. Select the **Method** option and then **Next**.
9. In the wizard screen that appears, enter the name "executeBapi_Flight_Getlist_Input" for this new method and select **void** as the return type.
10. Choose **Finish** and save the new metadata by clicking the **Save all metadata** icon on the toolbar.

10.9 Defining the View Layouts

View layouts

In this step, you will add the appropriate UI elements to the views and configure their properties. Proceed as follows:

1. In the **Web Dynpro Explorer**, double-click the **SearchView** view, and select **Layout**. Add and arrange the UI elements as shown in Figure 10.6. You can add the UI elements by drag and drop, or by right-clicking the **RootUIElementContainer** and selecting **Insert child**.

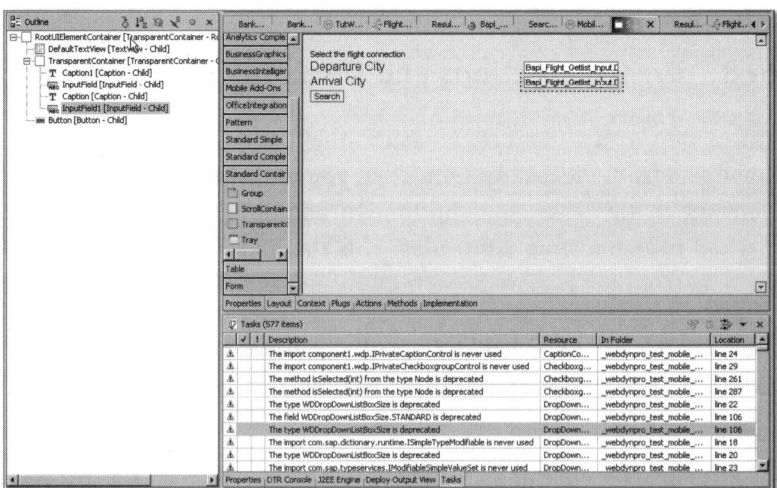

Figure 10.6 The SearchView View

2. For the UI elements, enter the values for their properties on the **Property** tab. The values are shown in Table 10.2.

UI Element	Text	Value	OnAction
DefaultTextView	Select the flight connection	–	–
TransparentContainer	–	–	–
Caption1	Departure City	–	–
InputField		Bapi_Flight_Getlist_Input. Destination_From.City	–
Caption	Arrival City		–
InputField1		Bapi_Flight_Getlist_Input. Destination_To.City	–
Button	Search		Search

Table 10.2 Properties of the UI Elements for the SearchView View

3. In the **Web Dynpro Explorer**, double-click the **ResultView** view and open the **View Designer** by clicking the **layout** tab.

4. In the **Outline view**, right-click the element **RootUIElementContainer** and select **Insert child**. From the list of elements, select **Table**.

5. In the **Outline view**, right-click the just-created element **Table** and select **CreateBinding**. In the wizard that appears, select the **Flight_List** context. Then click **Finish**. The **View designer** displays the output as shown in Figure 10.7.

6. Save the new metadata by selecting the **Save all metadata** icon from the toolbar.

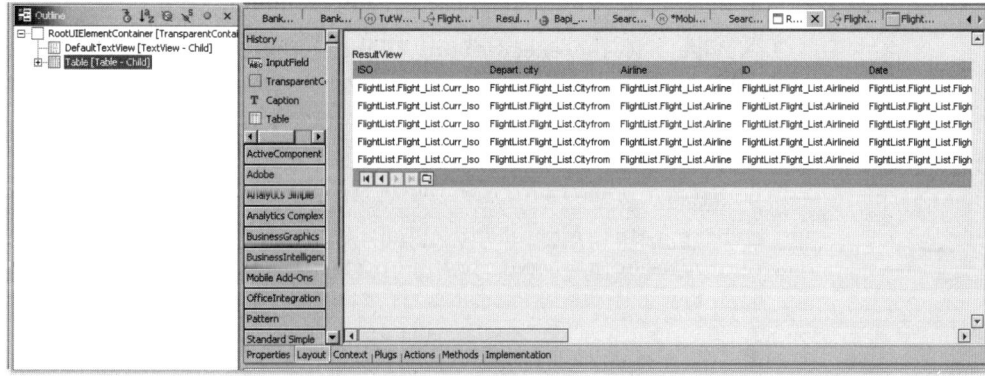

Figure 10.7 The ResultView View

10.10 Implementing the Action Event Handler and the Method of the Custom Controller

Implementing the event handler

In this step, you will implement the event handler for the Search action of the **Search** button. This coding is called when the end user presses the **Search** button. Then you will implement the executeBapi_Flight_Getlist_Input method of the custom controller, which calls the remote function module BAPI_FLIGHT_GETLIST_INPUT. As a last step, you will implement the wdDoInit() method of the custom controller to initialize it. Follow this procedure:

1. In the **Web Dynpro Explorer**, double-click the **SearchView** view and select the **Implementation** tab. Navigate to the **onAction-Search()** method and add the lines of code shown in Listing 10.1.

```
//@@begin javadoc:onActionSearch(ServerEvent)
/** Declared validating event handler. */
//@@end
public void onActionSearch(
    com.sap.tc.webdynpro.progmodel.api.IWDCustomEvent
        wdEvent) {
    //@@begin onActionSearch(ServerEvent)
    wdThis
        .wdGetFlightConnCustController()
        .executeBapi_Flight_Getlist_Input();
    //@@end
}
```

Listing 10.1 Code for the onActionSearch Event

Implementing the controller method

2. In the **Web Dynpro Explorer**, double-click the **FlightConnCust** custom controller and select the tab **Implementation**.

3. Navigate to the **executeBapi_Flight_Getlist_Input()** method and add the code shown in Listing 10.2.

```
//@@begin javadoc:executeBapi_Flight_Getlist_Input()
/** Declared method. */
//@@end
public void executeBapi_Flight_Getlist_Input() {
    //@@begin executeBapi_Flight_Getlist_Input()
    try {
        // Calls remote function module BAPI_FLIGHT_
        // GETLIST
        wdContext
            .currentBapi_Flight_Getlist_InputElement()
```

```
            .modelObject()
            .execute();
        // Synchronise the data in the context with the
        // data in the model
        wdContext.nodeOutput().invalidate();
    } catch (Exception ex) {
        // If an exception is thrown, then the stack
        // trace will be printed
        ex.printStackTrace();
    }
    //@@end
}
```

Listing 10.2 Code for the executeBapi_Flight_Getlist_Input() Method

4. Navigate to the **wdDoInit()** method and add the code as shown in Listing 10.3.

```
//@@begin javadoc:wdDoInit()
/** Hook method called to initialize controller. */
//@@end
public void wdDoInit() {
    //@@begin wdDoInit()
    // Create a new element in the Bapi_Flight_Getlist_
    // Input node
    Bapi_Flight_Getlist_Input input = new
        Bapi_Flight_Getlist_Input();
    wdContext.nodeBapi_Flight_Getlist_
Input().bind(input);
    // Create new elements in the Destination_From and
    // Destination_To nodes
    input.setDestination_From(new Bapisfldst());
    input.setDestination_To(new Bapisfldst());
    //@@end
}
```

Listing 10.3 Code for the wdDoInit() Method

5. To remove the syntax errors, position the cursor anywhere in the **Java Editor**, right-click and select **Source • Organize Imports**. This adds the needed import statements to the source code and removes the syntax errors.

6. Save the new metadata by selecting the **Save All Metadata** icon from the toolbar.

10.11 Building, Deploying, Configuring, and Running your Application

Build, deploy, and run

Now you are in the final phase of this example. In the first step, you will build the application and then you will deploy it to the J2EE engine. Before you can run the application, you need to configure the JCo connections in the Web Dynpro Content Administrator. Use the following procedure:

Creating the JCo Connections in the Web Dynpro Content Administrator

1. In the **Web Dynpro Explorer**, right-click the project node **Mobile-FlightConnection** and select **Rebuild Project**.

2. Click the project node again and select **Create Archive**.

3. Click the project node again and select **Deploy Application**.

4. Configure the JCO connection in the **Web Dynpro Content Administrator**. Open the **Web Dynpro Content Administrator** on your J2EE Engine using the URL *http://<host>:<port>/webdynpro/welcome*. A screen as shown in Figure 10.8 appears.

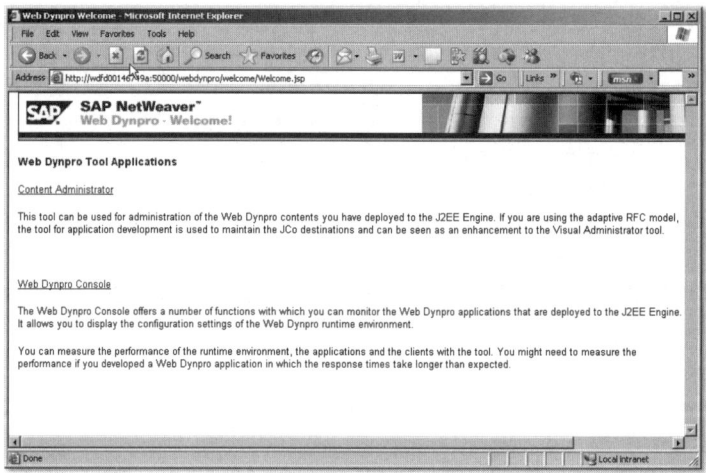

Figure 10.8 Content Administrator as Part of Web Dynpro Tool Applications

5. In the **Web Dynpro Content Administrator**, click **Create JCO Destination**.

6. On the screen **General Data**, enter "WD_FLIGHTLIST_MODELDATA_DEST" in the field **Name** and enter the client of the back-end system that contains the model data in the field **Client** (see Figure 10.9). Then click **Next**.

Building, Deploying, Configuring, and Running your Application | **10.11**

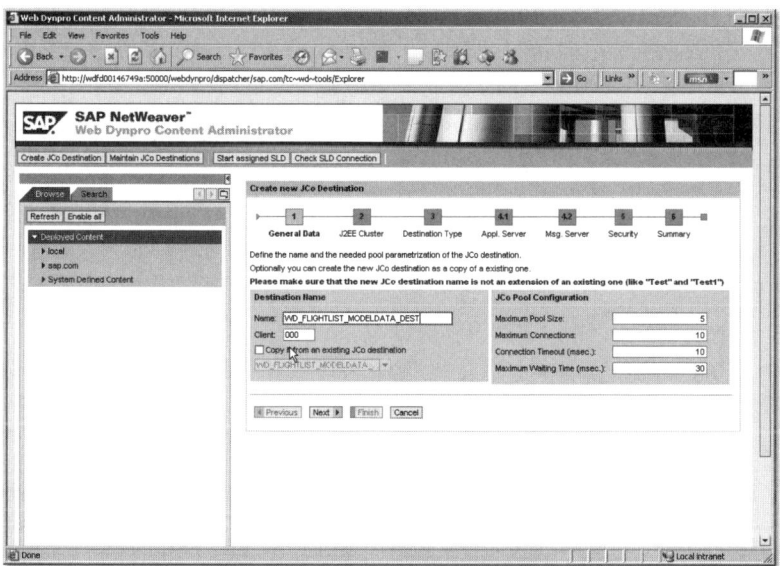

Figure 10.9 Wizard to Generate a JCO Connection in the Web Dynpro Content Administrator

7. On the screen **J2EE Cluster**, define the J2EE Cluster to which the JCO destination should be assigned. If you have a locally installed J2EE Engine, select the **Use local J2EE Engine** option. Then click **Next**.

8. On the screen **Destination Data**, select **Application Data**. Then click **Next**.

9. On the screen **Message Server**, enter the message server of your backend system. Then click **Next**.

10. On the screen **Security**, enter your user authentication details. Then click **Finish**.

11. In a similar way, create the JCO connection WD_FLIGHTLIST_RFC_METADATA_DEST.

12. Finally, you can launch the application. In the **Web Dynpro Explorer**, right-click the **FlightConnApp** application and then select **Run**.

13. Internet Explorer starts and shows the **SearchView** of the application. To run the application on your PDA, start the Pocket Internet Explorer on your device and enter the same URL used in the desktop example appended by *?sap-wd-client=Pie03Client*. If

297

you want to run the application on a Nokia S80 device, append *?sap-wd-client=NokiaS80Client* instead. The screen that appears is shown in Figure 10.10.

Wireless Markup Language

14. You can run this application on a RIM BlackBerry device as well. In this case it is not required to provide the device code in the URL, since a BlackBerry device uses Wireless Markup Language (WML).

Figure 10.10 The Flight Connections Application Running on a PDA

10.12 Summary

In this chapter, we described an approach to how you can create mobile connected applications for mobile devices such as PDAs based on Windows Mobile, Nokia S80 devices, or RIM BlackBerry devices. For that purpose, you created a Web Dynpro for Java project and imported an Adaptive RFC Model to generate the model classes. You bound the custom controller context to the model and mapped the controller context to the view contexts. Then you defined the view layouts, implemented the event handler for the **Search** button, and implemented the executeBapi_Flight_Getlist_ Input method, which calls the remote function module in the backend system. As the last step, you built and deployed the application, and you created the JCO connections in the Web Dynpro Content administrator.

In Chapter 11, we will provide an overview of the new design time architecture to create occasionally mobile applications for PDAs. The concepts are similar to Mobile Application for Laptops and focus on a component-based architecture for mobile applications.

In this chapter, we will provide an overview of the new design time for mobile applications running on PDAs, which is planned to be shipped in upcoming service packs of SAP NetWeaver Mobile 7.1.

11 Developing Mobile Components for PDA

At the time of this writing, a new design time to develop mobile applications for mobile handheld devices such as PDAs is internally available at SAP and is planned for shipment in SAP NetWeaver Mobile SP3. It is called Mobile Applications for PDA and is tightly integrated in the SAP NetWeaver Developer Studio. Mobile Applications for PDA provides an environment to build composite mobile applications that are tailored to the specific needs of small handheld devices. The focus is on the model-driven development approach for mobile applications based on components such as building blocks. The key features of the new design time are:

Mobile Applications for PDA

- Component-based application model
- Tight integration with the *data orchestration engine* (DOE)
- Dedicated service, UI, and application components
- Configuration and enhancement concept for components and applications
- Integration into *SAP NetWeaver Development Infrastructure* (NWDI)

> **Note**
> The terminology and the concepts presented in the following subsections might change in future.

11.1 The Component Concept for Mobile Applications

The support of mobile components is one of the key capabilities of the new design time. Arranging mobile applications in components is a basic concept that shortens the development lifecycle process. Mobile components can be reused by other mobile application, making them more robust and providing a consistent look and feel across different functional application areas. Appropriate component interfaces allow encapsulating the functionality of individual elements and defining the dependencies to other components. This also accelerates the build process when working in larger development teams, since the Component Build Service knows the dependencies between components and executes the build process only for changed or dependent components.

Development components

Technically, the component concept is based on the concept of development components (DCs), which are offered for the development of Web Dynpro applications by the SAP NetWeaver Developer Studio. DCs are container for arbitrary development entities (such as a Java source file, a Web Dynpro view, a table definition, or a JSP page), and produced entities (basically anything that has been generated from development entities, such as a Java class file, a library, or a deployable J2EE archive).

Model-view-controller (MVC)

The ubiquitous *model-view-controller* paradigm allows a strict separation of UI, business logic, and persistency and facilitates the creation of different types of components that can be used in composite mobile applications:

- **Mobile Service Components**
  A Mobile Service Component contains a coherent set of data objects and business logic for these data objects

- **Mobile UI Components**
  A Mobile UI Component consumes business logic and data supplied by one or more Mobile Service Components and provides the UI for these. A Mobile UI Component contains standard Web Dynpro development objects, such as the Web Dynpro model, Web Dynpro applications, and Web Dynpro components. Mobile UI Components operate on top of Mobile Service Components and can be consumed by other Mobile UI Components.

▶ **Mobile Application**
A Mobile Application contains the properties of the mobile application and binds its development components into an application that can be deployed.

The diagram shown in Figure 11.1 illustrates the content of the DCs for Mobile Applications and their dependencies.

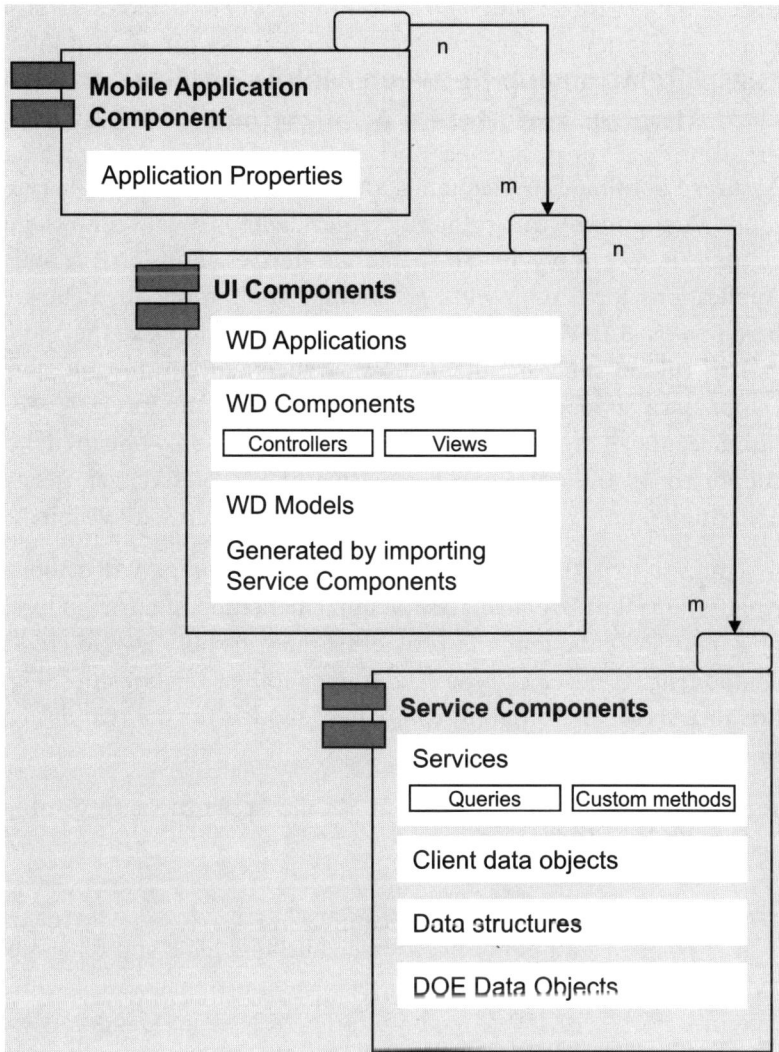

Figure 11.1 Component Structure of a Mobile Application

All of these components are technically represented as standard NWDI DCs of a specific type. Each such component comes with its own meta-model of objects that it can contain. The tools in the according perspective of the SAP NetWeaver Developer Studio (*occasionally connected applications*) allow the developer to model (and code) the respective objects and then automatically generate the runtime code of the component.

11.2 Relationship Between Mobile Applications for Laptop and Mobile Applications for PDA

As already outlined in Chapter 4, SAP Mobile Applications for Laptop is a design time that primarily targets laptops because the client runtime is too heavy for small mobile devices. Both SAP Mobile Applications for Laptop and SAP Mobile Applications for PDA are based on the SAP Web Dynpro technology, but — to make the applications run on small mobile devices — not all the features of Web Dynpro are supported by SAP Mobile Applications for PDA. For instance, not all the UI elements are available, and only one model is supported. In the according perspective of SAP NetWeaver Developer Studio, only the supported Web Dynpro features are visible.

In contrast to SAP Mobile Applications for Laptop, SAP Mobile Applications for PDA facilitates the implementation of business logic in a specific component and provides a more flexible way to create components of different types and to model their relationships. Figure 11.2 shows the different component models for the two design times.

Table 11.1 compares the features of Mobile Applications for Laptop and Mobile Applications for PDA.

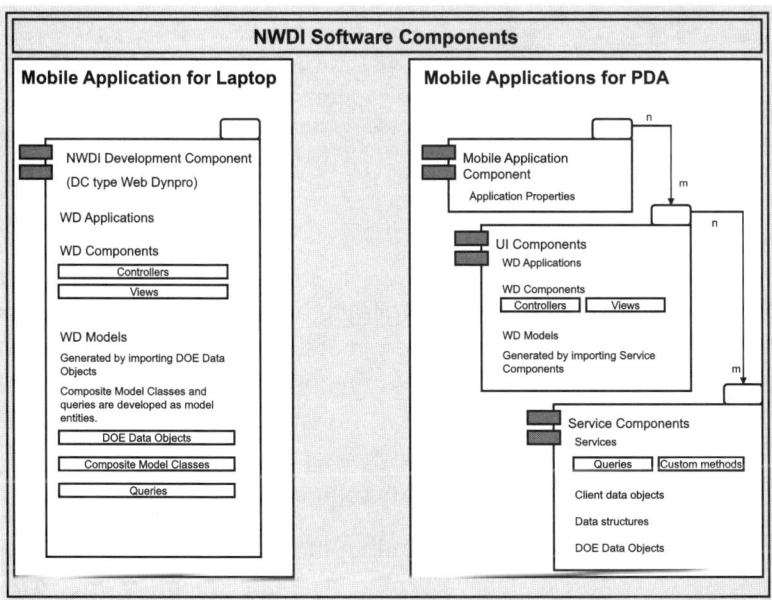

Figure 11.2 Comparison of the Component Models for Mobile Applications for PDA and Laptop

Design Feature	Mobile Applications for Laptop	Mobile Applications for PDA
DC type	Web Dynpro	OCA
NWDI integration	Yes	Yes
Web Dynpro integration	Yes	Yes
Full Web Dynpro support	Yes	Subset only
Web Dynpro model generation	By importing data objects from the DOE Composite model classes and queries are developed as model entities	By importing data objects from the DOE, data structures, queries, and custom methods
Clear separation of layers (UI, business logic, data access) into distinct components	No	Yes
Dedicated location for custom business logic	No	Yes; this is done by a custom method

Table 11.1 Differences Between Mobile Applications for Laptop and Mobile Applications for PDA

> **Note**
> On the SAP Service Marketplace, you can find the tutorial "Creating a Mobile Application Using Mobile Applications for PDA" that explains how to create a mobile application using Mobile Applications for PDA.

11.3 Summary

Mobile Applications for PDA is a design time that enables developers to create occasionally connected mobile applications for PDAs. Because of the limited capabilities of mobile devices, only a subset of the Web Dynpro functionality is supported. However, it allows implementation of business logic in a separate component and provides a more flexible way to create components of different types.

You now have a basic understanding of how to mobilize business processes. As a next step you could start implementing your own mobile development project. For that purpose, you could proceed as follows:

- Specify the requirements of the mobile application.
- Select the appropriate services from your backend system (BAPIs or RFC-enabled function modules). Maybe you will have to wrap them in a new RFC-enabled function module to fulfill the Create, Read, Update and Delete (CRUD) semantic requirements of the DOE (GetList, GetDetail, Change, Create, Delete).
- Define the data objects in the DOE.
- Import the data objects and create a mobile application using Mobile Applications for PDA or Mobile Applications for Laptops.

Appendix

A	SAP Mobile Application Portfolio	309
B	Glossary	335
C	Bibliography	339
D	The Authors	341

A   SAP Mobile Application Portfolio

Before we start presenting the SAP Mobile Application Portfolio, we want to lay the taxonomic foundations for further discussion. Many types of mobile applications exist, depending on the scenario they support, the capabilities of the mobile devices on which they run, and the architecture of the application itself. In this chapter, we introduce different types of mobile applications, categorized by their characteristic properties, such as the scope of functionality, the required type of mobile device, the synchronization capabilities and connectivity requirements, and the availability of a local data store.

A.1   Mobile Enterprise Applications

Many different types of mobile applications exist, so it makes sense to agree on a general definition of what a mobile application is. According to Drake and colleagues [Drake06], a mobile enterprise application (MEA) consists "of those packaged and industry-specific applications designed expressly for mobile and wireless environments. MEA applications focus on delivering the critical front-end application for mobile workers based on the role of the worker and the sub segment of data that worker requires from an existing back-end application residing within the enterprise or accessed via a hosted environment."

Mobile applications can be used in different working environments for various processes on many platforms. This leads to different types of mobile applications, which we want to further classify based on taxonomy in Table A.1.

Application	Characteristics
Full client application	▶ Full application functionality version of server application on client desktop ▶ Device most commonly used is a laptop for processing ability ▶ Local data store; synchronization capability required for data consistency with server-side data ▶ Connectivity type does not change functionality (i.e., WiFi, LAN, WWAN)
Lightweight client application	▶ Subset of client application code to be resident on device or device-specific code ▶ Device most commonly used is a PDA or smartphone ▶ Selected subset of server data stored locally ▶ May have persistent or selective connectivity to server application
Browser-based client application	▶ No local application code beyond Web browser client; "screen scraper" capability ▶ Client not tied to device type; most commonly PDA, smartphone, or mobile phones ▶ No local data store; relies on server-side data ▶ Persistent connectivity required ▶ Server application must support device and be able to render the browser interface for access

Table A.1 Taxonomy of Mobile Enterprise Applications (Source: IDC)

Classification of mobile applications

The taxonomy defined by IDC provides a good overview of the mobile applications that can be categorized in more detail as one of the following application types:

▶ **Full client application**
A full client application is a full-fledged application that primarily runs on laptops. It consists of a UI layer, a business logic layer, and a persistency layer, and it provides a synchronization service with the backend system. The local data store allows downloading a large supply of business data and targets end users who are out of office for long periods of time without the possibility to synchronize. The application might be rather complex and support various business tasks. A typical business scenario is supporting salesforce representatives who require up-to-date and complete information about the customers they visit. Depending on the role of the sales representative, this business scenario might be complex and include functionality such as support of marketing campaigns

for specific products, the management of opportunities, activity planning, and sales order processing.

- **Lightweight client application**
A lightweight client application implements only a part of the backend system counterpart and focuses on a more specific business scenario. The application's memory footprint allows users to run the application on PDAs as well. It provides a local data store, which is limited due to the restricted capabilities of mobile devices. A synchronization service with the backend system is available. In most cases, a wireless network is used to transfer data. The user interface is optimized for usage on devices with small form factors and takes different data entry capabilities into consideration, such as stylus, keyboard, and peripheral devices (for example, barcode scanners or even RFID readers). A typical example of a lightweight client application is the support of transactional workers who work in offline mode without permanent connectivity and require a form-based interface for data entry types of service orders.

- **Browser-based client application**
A browser-based client application is a thin client that requires an active connection to the backend system. A local data store is unavailable. The advantage of this application type is portability across many different devices. However, complete coverage of wireless networks is currently unavailable. Because no business logic is running on the device, data validation occurs on the backend system. Additionally, since business data are unavailable on the client device, data entry is time consuming and error prone. A predominant usage of this kind of application is a campus-based scenario in which WLAN is available everywhere and the volume of data to be entered is not significant. Typical business scenarios can include approval of leave requests, confirmation of receipt of goods, and monitoring equipment effectiveness.

A.2 The Mobile Ecosystem

The enablement of the mobile ecosystem is driven by business needs, and to make it happen, its key components must be aligned with one another. Figure A.1 shows the components and shows their roles and interactions in this ecosystem. The selection of the appro-

Introducing a mobile infrastructure

priate components and the optimization of their interactions is a key success factor for introducing a mobile infrastructure in your company. In the next subsections, we describe the roles of the various suppliers and stakeholders in this ecosystem in more detail.

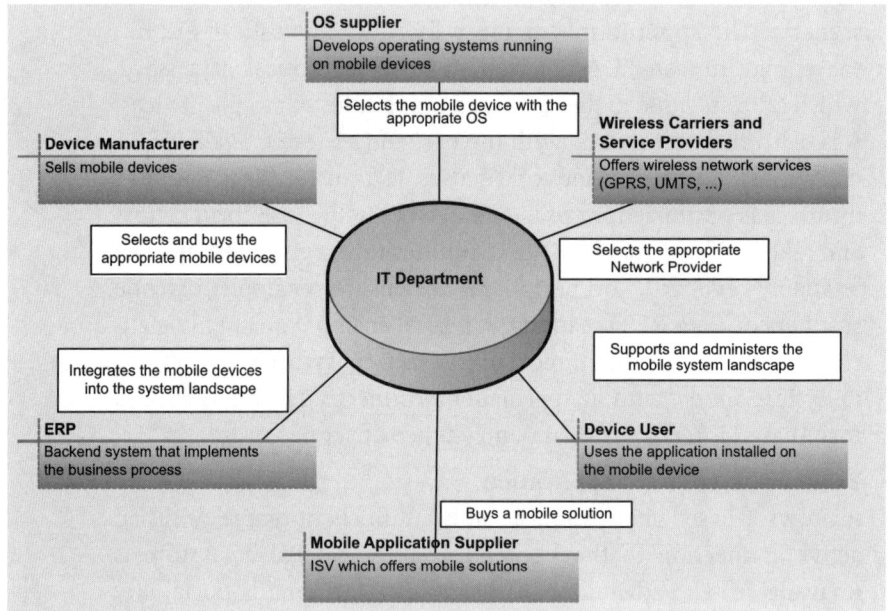

Figure A.1 The Mobile Ecosystem

A.2.1 Wireless Carriers and Service Providers

Wireless networking protocols

Wireless networks are a key enabler of the mobile ecosystem. Terms such as 802.11, WLAN, Bluetooth, and GPRS are common knowledge. Meanwhile, wireless hotspots are ubiquitous, and many private homes are equipped with wireless networks. Whereas at the beginning of the wireless evolution, voice was considered to be the main traffic, the *second generation (2G)* of wireless network standards, such as GPRS, already is commercialized and digital. To meet the growing demand of network bandwidth and high-speed data transfer, the *3G standards* started evolving. The EDGE, EGPRS, and UMTS protocols are examples of 3G standards. They are based on the 2G standard and enhance their capabilities. *4G* is an emerging technology that will be capable of providing 100Mbps in outdoor and 1Gbps in indoor environments. 4G is not a single standard; rather, it is a bundle of various protocols that maximize the throughput.

Selecting the most appropriate wireless carrier is an important success factor of a mobile implementation project. The offered bandwidth, the availability of wireless protocols and the network coverage across different countries, network roaming capabilities, and pricing should be taken into consideration to optimize the wireless data transfer.

A.2.2 Device Manufacturer and OS Supplier

The mobile device market is diversified. There are various device manufacturers and operating system vendors, for instance Symbian OS with licensee Nokia, Microsoft's Windows Mobile, Mobile Linux, and RIM on BlackBerry OS. Windows Mobile-based devices are manufactured by companies such as Acer, Dell, Fujitsu Siemens, HP, Motorola, Symbol Technologies, Toshiba, and Yakumo. Since the ease-of-use of handsets is an important factor for success, more and more operators collaborate with hardware vendors to offer operator branded handhelds to their customers.

Mobile devices and their capabilities

The technical capabilities of mobile devices differ from one device to the next. For instance, devices come with different screen sizes and resolutions, have various input capabilities (for example, virtual keyboards or hardware buttons), and can be equipped with GSM support to make calls or GPS to support navigation-based solutions. The heterogeneity of mobile devices is a known issue, and there are some initiatives to categorize mobile devices. The Device Description Ecosystem, which is available as W3C working draft (see *www.w3.org/TR/ddecosystem*), tries to describe mobile devices in terms of their characteristic properties, such as the type of markup supported by the browser, the presence of various input features, and the most readable color schema.

A.2.3 IT Department

The customer's IT department plays a central role in the mobile ecosystem. Its main tasks are the provision a mobile infrastructure by procuring the appropriate hardware and software and to integrate them in the existing IT landscape. To minimize TCO, not only the acquisition costs, but also the costs of the operative usage must be considered. The mobile solution has to fit easily into the existing backend system and should not require additional implementation

The role of the IT department

effort. To ensure smooth and reliable usage, sophisticated tools are required to administer the mobile devices, and if a device is lost or damaged, a quick device recovery mechanism has to be in place to minimize the user's downtime. Because sensitive business data are transmitted across open networks, the mobile solution has to provide strong security standards.

A.2.4 Mobile Application Supplier

Mobile platform

The mobile application supplier develops mobile enterprise solutions that are the software products that bring business processes to the devices. SAP offers a portfolio of composite mobile enterprise applications that address the needs of the horizontal workforce such as executives, managers, sales representatives, and mobile information workers, as well as the vertical workforce such as service technicians in plant maintenance and delivery drivers in the consumer product industry. The mobile applications run on SAP NetWeaver Mobile 7.1, which is a mobile platform that can be used by partners and customers to develop their own mobile applications.

For the successful implementation of your mobile project, it is important to take into account the mobile ecosystem. In the next section, we will introduce the mobile applications that SAP ships as standard solutions. They enable you to mobilize various business processes that are available in your SAP backend system.

A.3 SAP xApps for Mobile Business

The SAP xApps paradigm Enterprise Service Architecture

How can SAP deliver new mobile applications and secure the customer's investment in software and technology at the same time? The answer is SAP xApp. The xApp paradigm guarantees continuous business innovation without disruptive change. It allows assembling of new applications by using standard building blocks from existing applications. The value-added proposition is obvious. It enables not only SAP but also partners and customers to design and implement mobile applications on top of existing SAP functionality. This is possible through the *enterprise service-oriented architecture* (Enterprise SOA), SAP's approach to align with the principles and standards of Service-Oriented Architecture (SOA). You can see each business-related functionality as a service, and by exposing those services (i.e., the standard building blocks) in the Enterprise Service Repository, consumers such as mobile applications can access them in a standardized way. This is achieved by an *integrated development environment* (IDE) that allows model-driven composition of mobile components.

All mobile business applications are now under the umbrella of SAP xAPPs and integrated with the SAP Business Suite of business applications that is built on top of a generic framework and powered by SAP NetWeaver. The current mobile application portfolio consists of composite applications for the vertical industry but also offers products for the mobile horizontal workforce such as executives, sales people, and knowledge workers.

> **Further Information**
>
> For the various applications contained in SAP xApps for Mobile Business, up-to-date information is available on the SAP Service Marketplace in the folder Installation & Upgrade Guides under SAP xApps (*http://service.sap.com/instguides*). Here you can find further detailed information in the various guides that are briefly described here:
>
> ▶ **Master Guide**
>   The Master Guide provides a central starting point for the technical implementation and upgrade of the application. It contains all activities for the installation and configuration of the application.
>
> ▶ **Business Scenario Guide**
>   The Business Scenario Guide describes the business process in detail. It also explains how the mobile part of the business process is integrated in the server-side business process.
>
> ▶ **Configuration Guide**
>   The Configuration Guide describes the general configuration steps required on the backend system and on the SAP NetWeaver platform, and it provides information about the technical prerequisites for implementing the application.
>
> ▶ **Installation Guide**
>   The installation guide describes the installation process for the mobile application and how it can be integrated in the system landscape.

▶ **Operations Guide**
The Operations Guide contains information for system administrators and support specialists to ensure smooth operation. It describes how to perform system upgrades, day-to-day monitoring, data maintenance, and mass roll-out.

▶ **Security Guide**
The Security Guide provides an overview of security-relevant information that applies to the mobile application. It targets system administrators and technology consultants.

▶ **Upgrade Guide**
The Upgrade Guide focuses on possible system upgrade paths and takes the various system landscape requirements into consideration.

▶ **Enhancement Guide**
The Enhancement Guide describes the various ways in which mobile applications can be adapted to the specific needs of a customer, by either implementing Business Add-Ins (BAdI) in the backend system or changing the behavior or user interface of the mobile application.

In the following sections, several mobile applications are described in more detail. To avoid going beyond the scope of this chapter, however, it is not possible to describe all aspects of the various applications. For the same reason, we also cannot cover complex solutions such as SAP xApp Mobile for Defense and Security and SAP xApp Manufacturing Integration and Intelligence. For further information on these topics, we recommend reading the relevant SAP documentation, which is available at the SAP Help Portal (http://help.sap.com).

A.3.1 SAP xApp Mobile Time and Travel (SAP xMTT)

Business Scenario

The SAP xApp Mobile Time and Travel (SAP xMTT) application enables employees to record their working times and to plan, request, and book their own business trips. SAP xMTT is a horizontal application and provides cross-industry functionality. It is available as a full client application running on a laptop. In Figure A.2 and Figure A.3, you can see screenshots of Mobile Time Sheet and Mobile Travel Expense, respectively.

SAP Mobile Application Portfolio | **A.3**

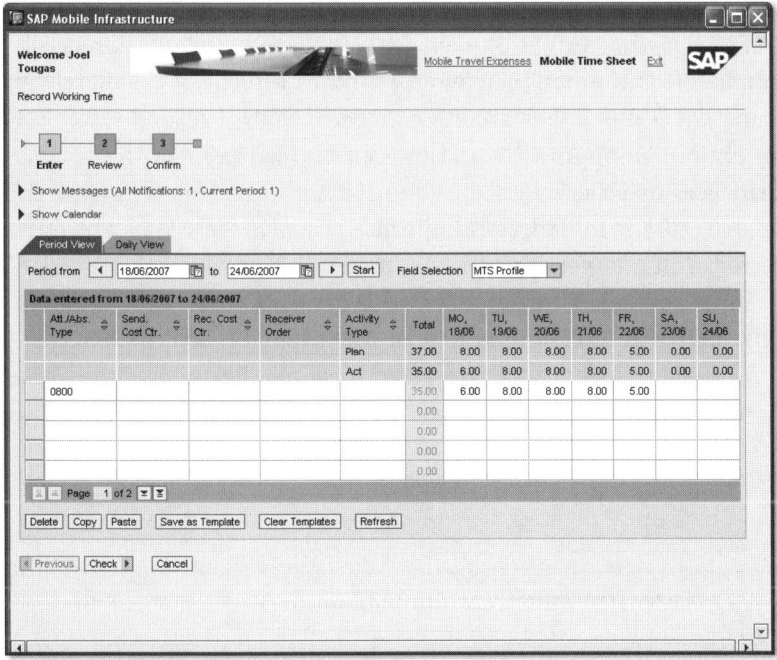

Figure A.2 UI Screenshot of Mobile Time Sheet

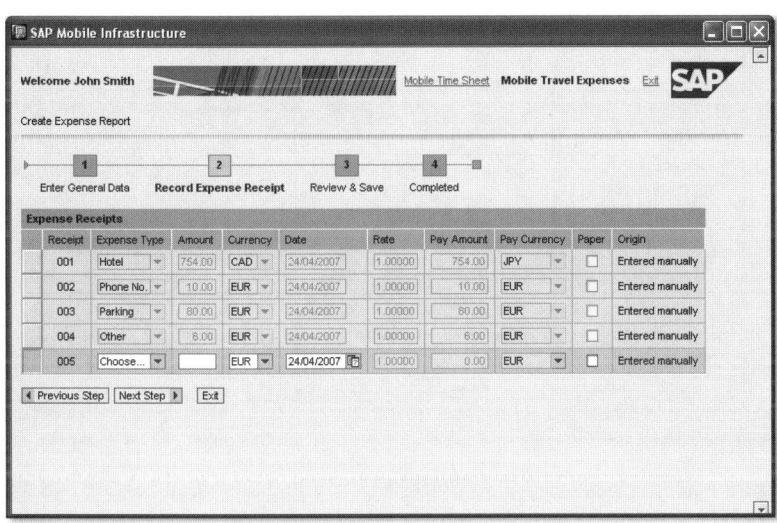

Figure A.3 UI screenshot Mobile Travel Expense

Figure A.4 provides an overview of the time recording-related functionality of SAP xMTT. Depending on the business needs, employees

Time recording

317

can record and release their working times directly in *SAP ERP Central Component* (SAP ECC) or in *SAP NetWeaver Portal*. Additionally, employees can enter their working times directly on their laptops using xMTT when they are not connected to the backend system. As an option, an approval workflow can be incorporated that enables managers or others with the required authorization to review and approve the recorded working times. Finally, these data are transferred to the target applications in SAP ECC for further processing using reports that run in the background. If these data are transferred to SAP ERP Human Capital Management (SAP ERP HCM), a direct data transfer can be triggered to supply Personnel Time Management with up-to-date availability information.

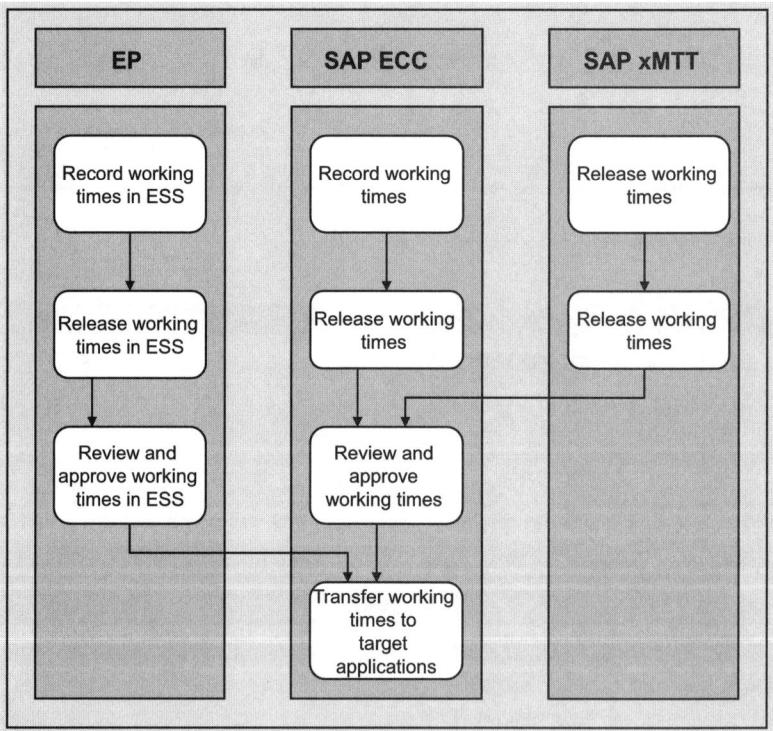

Figure A.4 Business Process Flow "Recording Time and Labor Data" of SAP xMTT

Travel expenses Figure A.5 shows the process flow of *Employee Self-Service (ESS) Travel Management*, which enables employees to plan, request, and book their business trips on their own. After the business trip, a new expense report can be created or an existing expense report can be completed. The data for the expense receipts can be entered, and after saving and synchronization with the backend system, the travel expenses can be reviewed and approved by the manager. Now the expenses are ready for settlement and flow into the settlement programs of the corresponding SAP components FI, CO, and HR. These data are transferred to FI and CO in the form of trip transfer documents, and finally, the travel expenses are taxed and paid out.

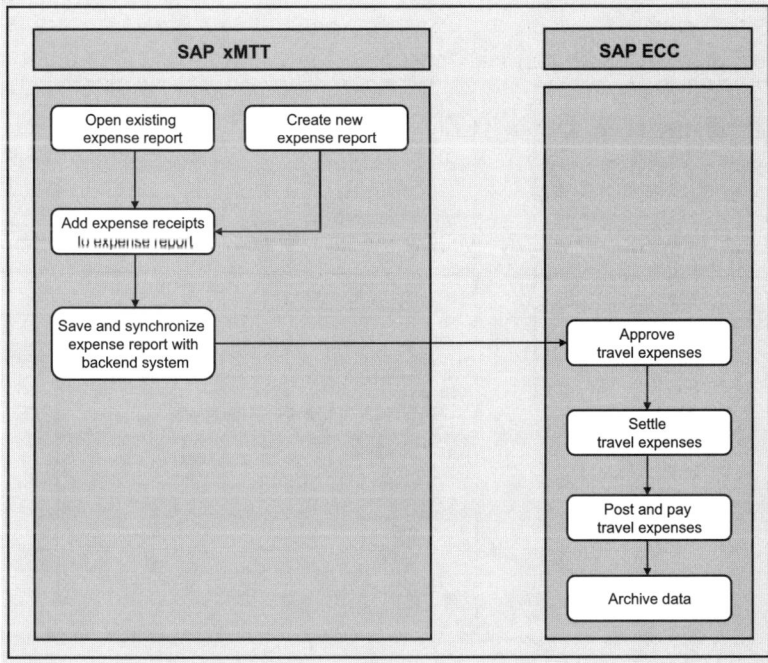

Figure A.5 Business ProcessFlow "Mobile Self-Service for Travel Expenses" of SAP xMTT

A.3.2 SAP xApp Mobile Asset Management (SAP xMAM)

SAP xApp Mobile Asset Management (SAP xMAM) is a mobile application tailored to the specific needs of plant maintenance and customer service field engineers. The server-side business process is part of the *Enterprise Asset Management* capabilities within SAP PLM. The scenarios implemented in SAP xMAM help field technicians perform their daily activities at customer sites and plants in disconnected mode (i.e., without a network connection to the backend system).

SAP xMAM

SAP xMAM is a horizontal application and provides cross-industry functionality. The supported business scenario is driven by service orders and notifications, which are created and assigned to field technicians in the backend system. SAP xMAM is available as a full client application running on laptops and as a lightweight client application running on PDAs. Both versions use a standard web-browser-based frontend. Figure A.6 shows the different UIs of the application for PDA and laptop.

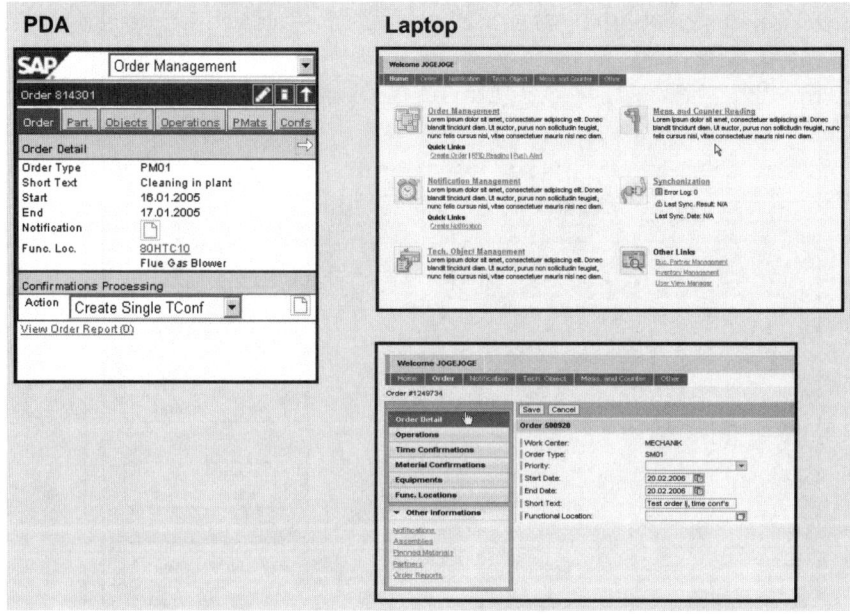

Figure A.6 Different UIs of MAM 3.0 for Laptop and PDA

The *Mobile Asset Management* scenario is based on work orders (service or maintenance orders) and notifications created and assigned to the field service technicians in the backend system. Therefore, orders and notifications are the central business objects that trigger the business process. They control the distribution as well as the synchronization of all other involved business objects, such as technical objects, functional locations, and business partners. The customers can decide if an order-driven or a notification-driven scenario is more appropriate for their needs.

Key capabilities The functionality of SAP xMAM covers the following key capabilities:

- **Order management**
  This capability enables users to perform basic order-management functions. In the backend system, orders can be assigned to the service technicians according to field-based rules, such as work centers or personnel numbers. This ensures that each user receives the appropriate orders upon synchronization. On the mobile device, the user can view the orders, create new orders, and perform the operations associated with those orders. For these operations, time confirmation and material consumption documents can be created to track the costs associated with work orders. After synchronization with the backend system, the resulting costs flow to the appropriate modules in finance and controlling for further processing, and the inventory is updated according to the material consumption document. In addition, it is possible to display and create notifications attached to an order, and users can add items, tasks, reasons, and activities to notifications. This scenario is shown in Figure A.7.

- **Notification management**
  This capability allows field technicians to perform the basic notification management functionality that is relevant for mobile users. Similar to orders, notifications can be assigned to service technicians. On their mobile devices, users can view and create notifications. If required, the notification can be linked to an order In addition, the user can add tasks, items, reasons, and text to existing notifications.

- **Inventory management**
  This capability enables users to track and manage their inventory efficiently. A local stock (a van stock or a consignment stock, for instance) can be assigned to a user in the backend system and downloaded to the device. This stock is updated if the service technician creates a material consumption document related to a specific operation of an order. Using inventory management, the user can perform a local availability check for a specific material, and the costs can be calculated accordingly.

- **Business partner management**
  This capability allows the user to view all customer records that are associated with orders or notifications. Apart from the partner detail information, which contains address information, the user

can also view the customer's contact persons and can see a list of all customer contracts.

- **Technical object management**
  This capability enables the user to manage equipment and functional locations, as well as the warranties associated with the equipment. Technical objects that are referred by orders and notifications flow to the mobile device automatically. In addition, technical objects without reference to an order or a notification can be assigned to field technicians in backend customizing.

- **Measurement and counter readings management**
  This capability allows field technicians to perform measurements and counter readings, verify locations of meters and counters, and check the date of the last reading on their mobile devices.

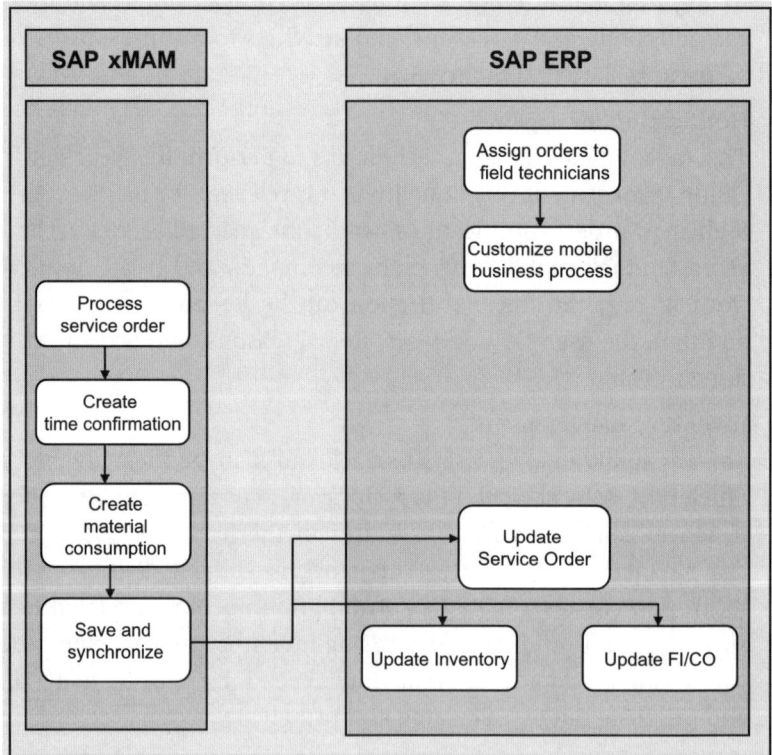

Figure A.7 Business Process Flow "Process Service Order" in SAP xMAM

A.3.3 SAP xApp Mobile Asset Management for Utilities (SAP xMAM for Utilities)

SAP xApp Mobile Asset Management for Utilities (SAP xMAM for Utilities) is a mobile application tailored to the specific needs of plant maintenance and customer service field engineers in the utilities industry. The server-side business process is integrated into *Enterprise Asset Management* (EAM) and *SAP Utilities* (IS-U/CCS or *SAP ECC Industry Extension Utilities*). The scenarios implemented in SAP xMAM for Utilities help field forces and service technicians perform their daily activities at customer sites and within plants without a connection to the backend system.

SAP xMAM for Utilities

SAP xMAM for Utilities is available as a full client application running on a laptop and as a lightweight application running on a PDA. Both versions use a standard web-browser based frontend. SAP xMAM for Utilities is a vertical application. The supported business scenario is driven by utility-specific service orders and notifications, which are created and assigned to field technicians in the backend system. Therefore, orders and notifications are the central business objects that trigger the business process. They control the distribution as well as the synchronization of all other related business objects, including technical objects, functional locations and business partners. As with SAP xMAM, the customer can decide between an order-driven scenario or a notification-driven scenario, depending on its specific needs.

Since SAP xMAM for Utilities is built upon SAP xMAM, it offers all the basic capabilities of the horizontal solution, plus specific functionality for utilities. The additional features provided by SAP xMAM for Utilities include:

Key capabilities

- **Disconnection and reconnection of a utility installation**
  This capability provides the tools required to manage disconnection and reconnection of meters. A disconnection is a temporary suspension of a supply, which results in a meter removal. This might happen by court order as the result of a dunning procedure or at the request of the customer or the utility company. In the first case, the supply is reconnected when the customer has paid. Disconnection and reconnection are administered and tracked in disconnection documents. For a released disconnection document, a disconnection order is created in the SAP Utilities system.

In this order, all affected devices and flat rate installations are proposed for disconnection. On the mobile device, the field technician enters details of when and how the devices and flat rate installations are to be disconnected. Optionally, the technician can enter payments in case the customer paid for open items from a dunning disconnection. If the conditions are fulfilled, a reconnection order is created for the disconnected devices and flat-rate installations in the SAP Utilities system. On the mobile device, the technician enters the reconnection data after a successful reconnection. Figure A.8 shows this scenario.

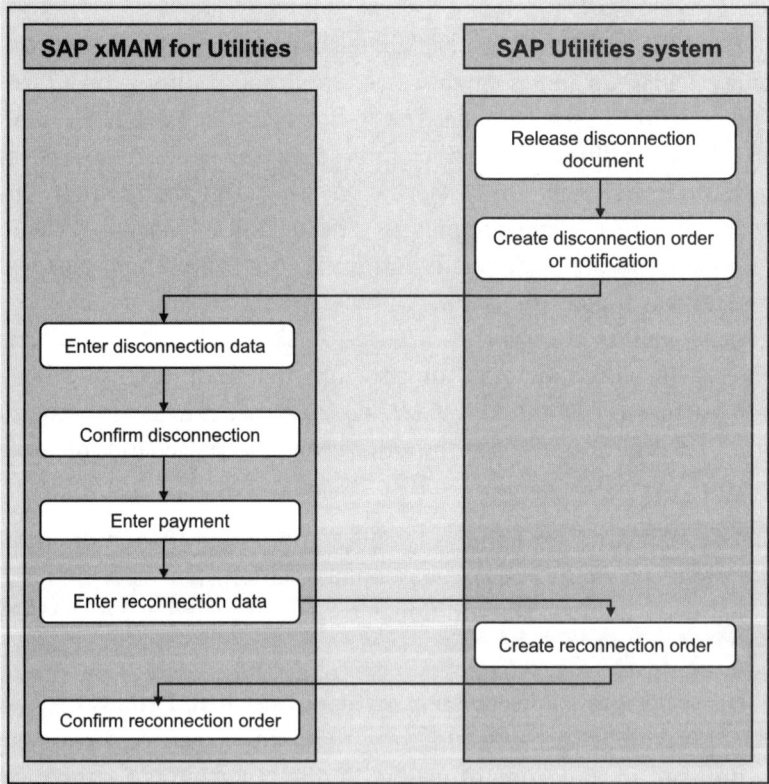

Figure A.8 Business Process Flow "Disconnection and Reconnection" of SAP xMAM for Utilities

- **Periodic and nonperiodic meter reading**
  This capability enables the field technician to manage periodic and nonperiodic meter reading results and to update meter reading documents, which were downloaded to the device from the SAP Utilities system, on the mobile device. For periodic billing, the meter readers are read periodically. In case of replacement, removal, or disconnection of the meter readers, they are read when this happens. After synchronization, the SAP Utilities system is updated, and the results flow to the Contract Billing component in SAP Utilities. Figure A.9 shows a screenshot of the application for this scenario.

Create Meter Reading Result	
Serial Number	12345
Register	R-5693
Meter Reading Type	Meter Reading Result Upload Bill Receipt
Meter Reading Result	23
Note	03 - Meter reading OK
Meter Reading Date/Time	14.12.2006 10:10
Date of Maximum / Time	14.12.2006 10:10

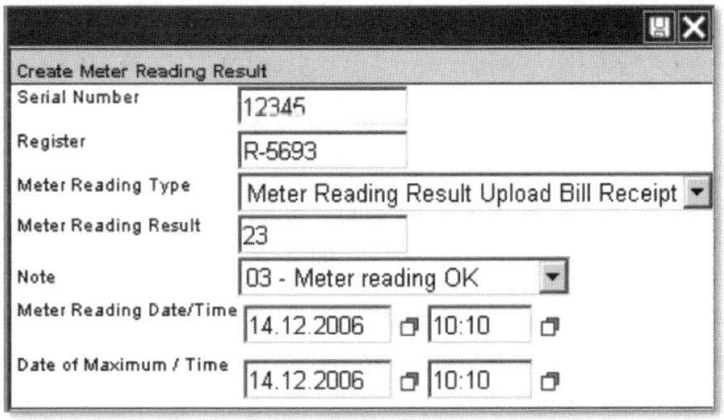

  Figure A.9 UI Screenshot "Create Meter ReadingResult" of SAP xMAM for Utilities (PDA)

- **Device installation, removal and replacement**
  This capability enables the user to manage the installation, removal, and replacement of devices on his mobile device. Both installation and removal of devices consist of two steps. First, the device has to be installed in or removed from exactly one device location. This first step deals with the technical part of the installation. In the second step, the device can then be assigned to any number of utility installations. This second step deals with the billing-related part of the installation. Figure A.10 shows a screenshot of the application for this scenario.

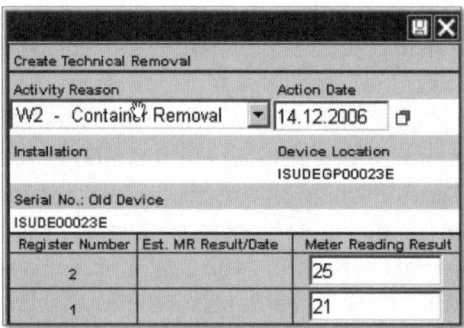

Figure A.10 UI Screenshot "Create Technical Remove" of SAP xMAM for Utilities (PDA)

A.3.4 SAP xApp Mobile Sales for Handhelds (SAP xMSA)

SAP xMSA

SAP xApp Mobile Sales for Handhelds (SAP xMSA) is a mobile application tailored to the specific needs of a sales representative who spends most of the time out of the office. The server-side business process is integrated in the Master Data and Sales components of SAP CRM. The scenarios implemented in SAP xMSA help sales representatives perform their daily sales activities at their customers' sites.

SAP xMSA is available as a lightweight client application running on PDAs. It uses a standard web-browser-based frontend.

SAP xMSA is a horizontal application and provides cross-application functionality. A typical deployment scenario is the consumer product industry, but other deployment scenarios are possible as well. The supported business scenario is driven by the business partners with whom the sales representative plans to visit for sales negotiations. Therefore, the business partner is the central business object that triggers the business process. Together with the product, it controls the distribution as well as the synchronization of the other involved business objects, such as activities, fact sheets, business partner history, sales orders, and opportunities.

Key capabilities

SAP xMSA provides the following key capabilities:

- **Sales order management**
  This capability enables a sales representative to create a sales order using a mobile device and to track other sales documents such as

quotations. A business partner and a contact person can be assigned to the sales order. The products from the product catalog and the required quantities can be added to the sales order. Using the Products function, the sales representative can select all possible products for a business partner, and the prices can be calculated on the device based on the standard prices that have been downloaded from the CRM backend system. After synchronization, the data are reported back to the CRM Enterprise. The business process flow is shown in Figure A.11.

▶ **Accounts management**
This capability provides the user with the features for managing business partners efficiently. Basically, the account types person, organization, and contact are supported. It is possible to display a list of accounts and to create accounts on the device. Users can search accounts using various search fields, such as account type, account ID, name, search term, or address-based fields. Fact sheets can be attached to accounts, and their content is according to the Fact Sheet customization in CRM Enterprise. Marketing attributes of an account can be displayed according to the selected attribute set.

▶ **Activity management**
This capability enables the users to manage their activities and tasks. On mobile devices, it is possible to display a list of activities, to view the activity details and to create follow-up activities. In addition, it is possible to show a list of tasks and to create tasks and follow-up tasks. On the **My Calendar** screen, a list of existing activities can be viewed and updated in the calendar.

▶ **Opportunity management**
This capability provides the tools to manage opportunities on the mobile device in an efficient manner. It is possible to view a list of opportunities and to display the details for each. It is also possible to create new opportunities, in which the sales representative can enter information, such as the prospect, the chance of realizing the opportunity, the current phase of the opportunity, and the expected volume.

▶ **Product management**
This capability enables the user to manage products on the device. It allows listing sales and service products as well as spare parts and viewing the product details. The products to be downloaded

are determined by *Partner/Product Ranges* (PPRs). A PPR is a combination of business partners and products that is valid for a specific time in a predefined scenario and with which products in specific areas are offered for purchase or sale.

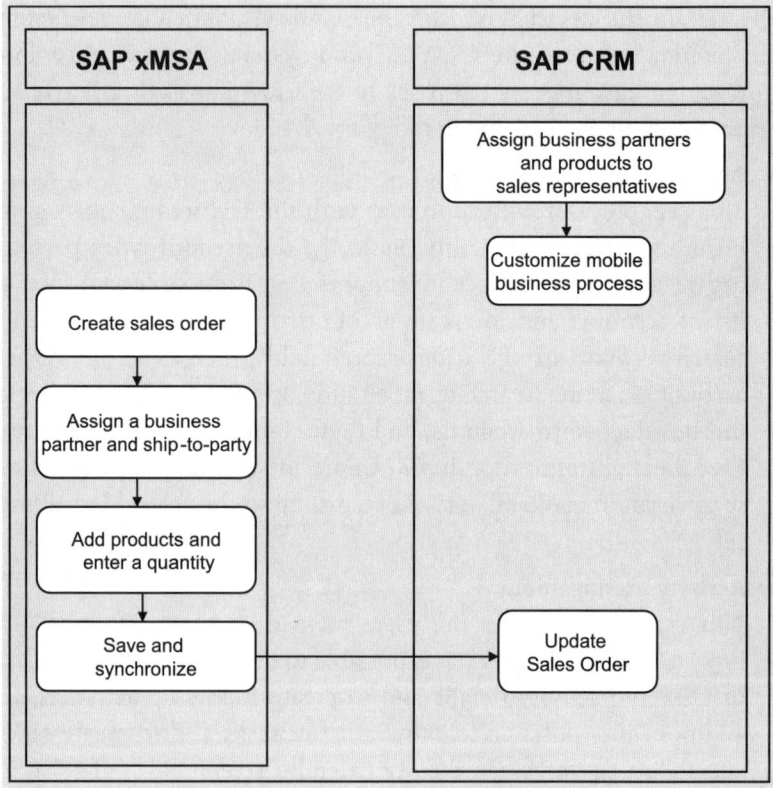

Figure A.11 Business Process Flow "Creating a Sales Order" of xMSA

A.3.5 SAP xApp Mobile Direct Store Delivery (SAP xMDSD)

SAP xMDSD *SAP xApp Mobile Direct Store Delivery* (SAP xMDSD) is a mobile application that helps delivery drivers, van sellers, and presellers accomplish their daily tasks such as checking materials out of the warehouse, executing deliveries, checking in returned materials and collected payments after returning to the warehouse, and, finally, balancing and settling materials and payments.

SAP xMDSD is a vertical application focusing on the *direct store delivery* (DSD) process that is used in the consumer products industry to distribute goods directly to the end customer. In a DSD process, distribution does not involve a retail company's warehouse or distribution centers. The business scenario supported by SAP xMDSD is driven by the tours (daily customer stops or visits) that are created in the backend system. SAP xMDSD is available as a lightweight client application running on PDAs. The application uses a form-based frontend that makes use of the Abstract Windows Toolkit (AWT).

SAP xMDSD covers all activities that need to occur in a DSD process on a mobile device, as follows:

Key capabilities

▶ **Data download**
During synchronization, transactional data and master data that are required to perform the next process steps are downloaded from the backend system to the mobile device.

▶ **Start-of-day processing**
This is the initial activity for the driver at the beginning of the day. It consists of recording basic tour data, such as driver ID, vehicle ID, and odometer reading. In Figure A.12, you can see a screenshot of the application for this process step. A sample screen with the tour information is shown in Figure A.13.

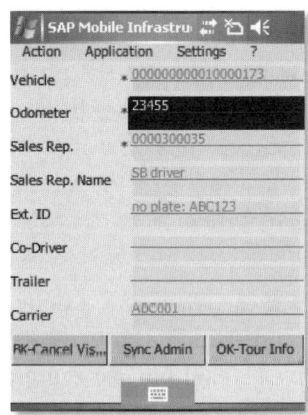

Figure A.12 UI screenshot "Start-of-Day Processing" of xMDSD

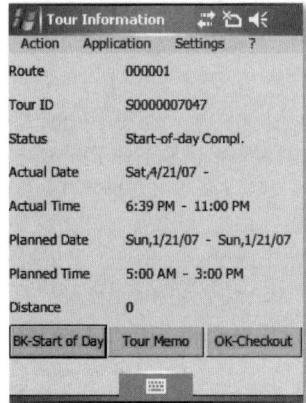

Figure A.13 UI Screenshot "Tour Information" of xMDSD

- **Check-out management**
  This component provides the delivery driver with the tools to check what was loaded on the vehicle. This includes materials and cash. If the validation is not successful, the driver can enter the discrepancies for further verification and approval by a supervisor.

- **Tour and visit management**
  During synchronization, the delivery drivers or sales representatives receive a list of all visits they are assigned. For each visit, they can perform the associated activities or update the visit status with a reason code to indicate why the customer visit was not possible (for instance, because the customer was closed or the driver ran out of time). The end user can rearrange the order of visits as well as create new unplanned visits. At the customer site, the sales representative can perform the following activities.

- **Delivery with presold orders**
  The preordered stock is unloaded from the truck and a delivery note or invoice is printed. The sales representative can add items or change item quantities, if necessary. In addition, he can enter returned goods (for example, spoiled goods or wrong items) or returned empties and add them to the deliveries.

- **Delivery without presold orders**
  This functionality refers to delivery of materials that were not ordered. The sales representative sells these materials directly off his vehicle, and creates a new delivery for this scenario. As in the

delivery scenario with presold orders, outbound deliveries as well as returns or inbound deliveries are supported.

- **Invoice creating**
  The sales representative can issue a legal invoice on the spot. Customers who do not receive an invoice receive a delivery note instead.

- **Payment collection**
  Sales representatives can collect payments for current deliveries or outstanding order payments, and customers receive a payment receipt.

- **Order taking for future deliveries**
  Sales representatives perform presales order taking. These orders are then delivered during one of the next tours.

- **Recording of inventory adjustments**
  Sales representatives can record inventory adjustments, which can occur due to breakage or damage, for example.

- **Recording of driver expenses**
  Sales representatives can record expenses such as tolls, parking fees, and gasoline consumption.

- **Check-in management**
  This capability enables the sales representatives to validate the materials returned to the warehouse. They can enter returned quantities for further verification and approval by the supervisor.

- **End-of-day processing**
  This capability consists of recording end-of-tour data and returned cash/payments.

- **Data upload**
  At the end of the day, the transactional data are uploaded from the mobile device to the backend system for further processing.

Figure A.14 shows an overview of the DSD business process.

A | SAP Mobile Application Portfolio

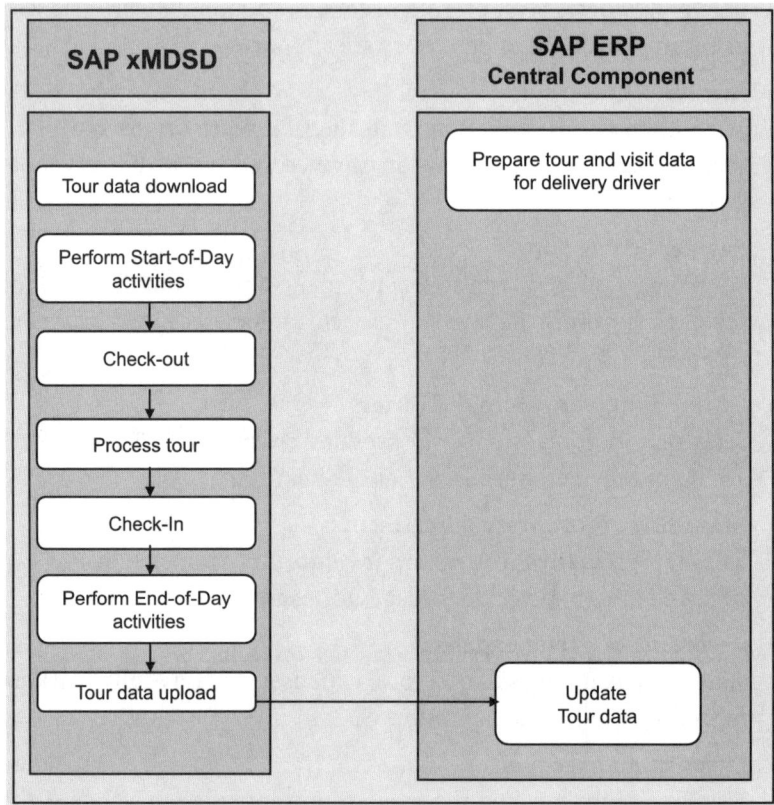

Figure A.14 Business Process Flow "Direct Store Delivery" of xMSA

A.3.6 Cross-Application Components including RFID, Mobile Alert, Electronic Signature Capture, and Geographical Information System (GIS) integration

Composite applications
Apart from the mobile applications, other application components provide a generic functionality that is not bound to a specific application, including RFID, mobile alert, electronic signature capture, and GIS integration. Although those components are integrated in a mobile application, it is planned to provide the functionality out-of-the-box as a mobile component for reuse in mobile composite applications.

RFID Management

The RFID management component provides the facilities for reading, writing, and displaying RFID tag information. Along with this information, date and time data of the last successful RFID reading or writing are captured.

There are three integration scenarios of the RFID management component in SAP xMAM, shown in the following list. They are activated on demand in backend customizing.

- **Find and unlock orders**
  If this process is activated, all orders assigned to a specific user are locked. If the service technician scans the RFID tag that is present at the location of a technical object, all related orders become active, and the technician can create a material or time confirmation for this order. The implementation of this process ensures that the technician is on site and performs the required inspections.

- **Record maintenance/service information**
  In this process, it is possible to store maintenance- and service-related data on the RFID tag of a technical object. More precisely, the following data can be written on the RFID tag: work center, personnel number, start and end time, and confirmation text. These data are extracted from the finalized time confirmation of a work order when the user triggers synchronization with the backend.

- **Read and insert technical object information**
  This process enables the technician to read the RFID tag information of the technical object and insert it in the appropriate fields when a new order is created. It allows quicker and more reliable creation of service orders or notifications, leading to better time efficiency and data accuracy.

Integration scenarios for RFID

Signature Capture

Using the signature capture component, technicians are able to capture electronic signatures of their customers on the mobile device. For an order, one or more signatures can be captured. During synchronization, the signatures are sent and stored in the backend system for future reference. This process enables the users to confirm their orders after the work is performed, and it expedites the billing cycle. Figure A.15 shows a screenshot of the signature capture UI.

Figure A.15 UI screenshot "Signature Capture"

Mobile Alert

The mobile alert component, which is integrated in SAP xMAM, can be used to notify service technicians of emergency situations via SMS. If configured, the alerts are pushed to one or more technicians whenever an order or notification is created with the appropriate urgency on the backend system. The first technician who accepts the assignment receives the order or notification on his device during the next synchronization. The status of the alert can be tracked in the backend system for each technician.

GIS Integration

The GIS component, integrated in SAP xMAM, enables the technician to easily locate a technical object assigned to an order or a notification on a GIS map. Codes for the geographic coordinates associated with technical objects can be downloaded to the mobile device. On the device, the geographical data can be sent to a GIS system that is installed on the client device and can be accessed from the application. As a result, the technician can better plan the route and navigate to the appropriate location.

B Glossary

The following glossary contains a brief description of some important terms that are used throughout this book.

Adaptive RFC Model Technology that enables the Web Dynpro application developer to use the business functions encapsulated in BAPIs even after a structure modification, without having to provide the new data using a second backend or a new structure with subsequent regeneration of the proxies.

Association Defines a relationship between data objects to ensure referential integrity in the consolidated data store. Based on backend key mapping and synchronization key mapping and can be used to define a dependency in the distribution model.

Backend Adapter Plug-in in the DOE that allows the DOE to connect to backend systems using RFC-enabled function modules, such as BAPIs.

Connected Mobile Application Mobile application that requires permanent network access. In general, connected mobile applications are browser based. Sometimes they are called online applications.

Data Completeness Group Makes it possible to specify that a data object in a distribution model is only to be distributed if all the dependant data objects are available for distribution.

Data Orchestration Engine (DOE) The new message-oriented middleware governing mobile data and distribution that interacts with non-ABAP-based backend systems (third-party systems) by using process integration (PI).

Data Orchestration Engine Workbench Contains the design time tools of the DOE and is used to define the data objects that are used to build applications for mobile devices.

Design Time The point in time when the software is developed. It also denotes the tools used to develop applications.

Development Component (DC) Object in the SAP NetWeaver Developer Studio that represents a software unit that you develop. A DC is always assigned to a certain software component (SC). The DC contains the information for the software unit itself and for the relations between the different DCs and the metadata.

Device Local Data Object Used to process data used exclusively by the application user interface on the mobile client.

Distribution Dependency Establishes a dependency relationship between a leading and a following data object. If the data object A (following object) is dependent on the data object B (leading object), then A will flow to a receiver whenever B flows to that receiver.

Distribution Modeler Provides a means of defining the distribution of data objects at design time using a dynamic, rule-based approach.

Distribution Rule Consists of a set of criteria fields, which are evaluated for the receiver calculation. If more than one rule is defined, the rules are interpreted with an OR condition. This means the devices receive all the data object instances that satisfy the condition of at least one of the rules.

Extract A service provided by the DOE to extract data form the backend system for initial load and delta load.

Flow Definition Made up of flow blueprints, which specify the services to be called to process a data object. Each flow blueprint defines a logically irreducible processing scenario, such as backend inbound initial load, or outbound client with confirmation. The flow definition of a data object can be viewed with the flow controller tool. It is also possible to extend a flow definition by adding custom services to flow blueprints.

Homogenization Service to perform the transformation between the backend schema definition and the data object schema definition, because the definitions can be different. This is a custom service and can be developed for each of the backend adapter types. You can develop this service as an ABAP program that transforms a BAPI structure to a data object structure.

Inbound Adapter Service that calls the homogenization service and is responsible for ordering and queuing of messages from the backend system.

J2ME Obsolete name for the Java Platform, Micro Edition (Java ME), designed by Sun Microsystems.

Message-Oriented Middleware (MOM) Software for interapplication communication that is based on exchanging messages asynchronously as opposed to a synchronous request and response pattern. MOM can transform the messages of the sender en route to match the receiver's format. The transformation can be achieved by mapping tools, which allow the developer to specify the transformation rules.

Microsoft .NET Compact Framework Version of the .NET Framework designed to run on mobile devices. To be able to run applications powered by the .NET Compact Framework, the platform must support the Microsoft .NET Compact Framework runtime.

Mobile Application for Laptops Development environment used to create occasionally connected mobile applications for laptops, which is integrated in the SAP NetWeaver Developer Studio.

Mobile Application for PDAs Development environment used to create occasionally connected mobile applications for PDAs, which will be integrated in the SAP NetWeaver Developer Studio.

Mobile Web Dynpro Online Development environment used to create connected mobile applications for mobile devices, such as Nokia, Blackberry, and PDAs.

Model-View-Controller (MVC) Design pattern that provides a clear distinction between processing control, data model, and displaying the data in the user interface. These three areas are formally distinguished from each other by three objects: model, view, and controller.

Navigation Schema Defines the navigation flow between views in a Web Dynpro application. You need to create exit and entry points of each view using outbound and inbound plugs. The navigation can then be defined using navigation links.

Occasionally Connected Mobile Application Mobile application that does not require a permanent network access. Data can be stored locally on the device, and synchronization is possible when a network is available.

Outbound Adapter Service provided by the DOE to request data from the backend system.

Receiver Generation (RecGen) Data Object Used to generate the logical devices for the mobile clients to distribute data to the appropriate subscribers. The fields defined in the receiver generation data object define the information to be extracted from the backend system for storage in the device inventory and are mapped to the receiver meta model fields. The usage of the RecGen field in a project is optional.

Receiver Meta Model (RMM) Defines different receivers, such as a mobile device or an external system, which are connected to the DOE. Receivers are grouped in different categories, and each category is defined based on a specific set of attributes.

SAP NetWeaver Developer Studio SAP's environment for developing Java-based, multiple-layered business applications. It is based on Eclipse, an open source product, whose open plug-in architecture provides a suitable platform for incorporating specific functions. It supports the developer in developing Web Dynpro and J2EE applications.

Software Component (SC) Combines development components into larger units for delivery and deployment.

Software Component Version (SWCV) Shipment unit for design time objects in the DOE repository. SWCVs are part of the software catalog in the System Landscape Directory. Data objects from one SWCV are transported and shipped together.

Standard Data Object Used to transfer data between the DOE and mobile clients. It is the primary data object category application developers use.

Subscription Generation (SubGen) Data Object Used to create subscriptions for data to be extracted from the backend system. These data are not required by the mobile device and are transferred from the backend to the DOE only. The usage of a SubGen data object in a project is optional.

Validation Service of the DOE that ensures that the messages exchanged with the backend system are validated.

C Bibliography

[Johnson, Manyika, Yee] Johnson, Bradford C., Manyika, James M., and Yee, Lareina A.: *The next revolution in interactions.* McKinsey Quarterly 2005 Number 4, 2005.

[SAP Gartner SAS] Gartner Strategic Analysis Session 2006: *The U.S. Mobile Workforce in 2006, Primary Mobile Workstyles.*

[Drake06] Drake, Stephen D., Hodges, Judy, and Wardley, Mary: *Worldwide Mobile Enterprise Applications 2006–2010 Forecast and Analysis.* Section 3.1, Taxonomy of Mobile Enterprise Applications. IDC, 2006.

Links

www.abacomobile.com, ABACO homepage

www.forum.nokia.com, Forum NOKIA

www.blackberry.com/developers/, BlackBerry section for developers

www.microsoft.com/pocketpc, Microsoft site for Pocket PCs

www.sap-press.com, SAP PRESS homepage

www.sap-press.de/1481, Deep link for the book's website (German)

www.w3.org/TR/dd-ecosystem, Device description ecosystem

service.sap.com, SAP Service Marketplace

D   The Authors

Thomas Pohl (*thomas.pohl@sap.com*) works as development architect in the Mobile Applications group at SAP AG. After he finished his studies of mathematics with a Ph.D., he joined SAP in 1994, where he initially worked in the application development group of Financials. Later he changed to CRM and then to Financial Services, where he undertook project management tasks. Today, his focus is on the architecture of mobile business solutions.

Ramprasadh Kothandaraman is the lead development architect of NetWeaver Mobile at SAP Labs, India. He has vast domain expertise in the area of messaging middleware and associated technologies and, at the beginning of his career with SAP, designed and implemented the first generations of messaging middleware for SAP, used in production environments by several SAP customers today. Ramprashadh is currently working on architecting a platform for enterprise mobility, primarily focusing on information provisioning through various user channels, including mobile devices. You can reach Ramprasadh at *ramprasadh.kothandaraman@sap.com*.

Venkat Srinivas Seshasai (*venkat.srinivas.seshasai@sap.com*) works as Chief Development Architect of the SAP NetWeaver Mobile group at SAP Labs India. He holds a master's degree in Structural Engineering and joined SAP in 1998. Since then, he has focused on the development of message-oriented middleware for mobilizing business processes. His current interests include Business Rule Management systems and mobile frameworks.

Index

3G 312
4G 312
802.11g 55

A

ABACO 253
Accounts management 327
Action 153
Active digitizer 38
Activity management 327
Ad-hoc mode 55
Administration and monitoring tools 182
Administration and operation services 165
Always-on 54
Application 232
 Building 250
 Deploying 250
 Running 250
Application extensibility 34
Association 98
Authorization 141
Authorization definition file 149
AWT 69

B

Backend adapter 79, 101, 222
 Backend triggered 223
 Middleware-triggered 223
Backend configuration 110
Backend integration 32, 82
Backend-triggered backend adapter 107
Background synchronization 60
BAPI wrapper 102, 223
 Create 103
 Delete 105
 GetDetail 102
 GetList 102
 Modify 104
BAPI wrapper core semantics 102
Barcode 253
BlackBerry 42

BlackBerry OS 313
BlackBerry Wireless Handhelds 160
Bluetooth 51
Broadcasting 50
Bulk distribution rule 121
Business Add-In (BAdI) 106
Business data abstraction 33
Business partner management 321
Business Scenario Guide 315
Button 246
 Exit 246
 OnAction 246

C

Central error handling 185
Change Management Server (CMS) 167
Check-in management 331
Check-out management 330
Child node 202, 205, 206, 208, 211
Circuit-switched 52
Client Framework Services (CFS) 64, 68, 69
Client sizing 277
Common language runtime 47
Complete association 98
Component controller 155, 234
Component-based architecture 34
Composite applications 332
Composite Model Class 147
Composite Model Class Editor 147
Computing Center Management System (CCMS) 166, 182
Configuration 43
Configuration Guide 315
Conflict handling 60
Connected application 49
Connected Device Profile (CDC) 45
Connected Limited Device Profile (CLDC) 45
Connectivity 48
Consolidated data store 64, 94
Context 152, 233
 Binding 234
Context mapping 155

Controller 152
Creating a query model class 145
Criteria fields 78

D

Data completeness group 217, 222
Data consistency 59
Data consolidation 64
Data distribution 33, 65, 112
Data distribution modeling 112
Data download 329
Data modeler 155
Data object 77, 92
 Association Type 214
 Associations 213
 Client specific 93
 Conflict detection scheme 93
 Customer 206, 224
 Dependency 217
 Direction 93
 Download only 223
 Employee 200, 224
 Equipment 203, 223
 Life cycle 100
 Node attributes 95
 Nodes 94
 Receiver Generation 199
 ServiceOrder 209
 Standard 198
 Subscription Generation 199, 211
 WorkCenter 211, 223
Data Object Model 141
Data orchestration design time 75
Data orchestration engine (DOE) 63, 64, 193
Data Orchestration Workbench 75, 201
Data upload 331
Debug 157
DefaultTextView 247
Delivery with presold orders 330
Delivery without presold orders 330
Delta download 82
Delta synchronization 276
Delta upload 82
Dependency 128, 129
Dependency rule 131

Deploy Controller 158
Design Time Repository (DTR) 167
Development component (DC) 170, 227, 302
Development process 194
Development workstation 138
Device
 Data entry method 272
 Form factor 272
 Network support 272
 Peripheral device support 273
 Processor and memory capacity 272
 Selecting 271
Device assignment logic 87
Device attributes 88, 178, 180
Device class 178
Device configuration 181
Device configuration service and parameter set 178
Device driver set 178
Device ID 179
Device installation, removal and replacement 325
Device inventory 179
Device management 32
Device setup and deployment services 166
Device template 167
 Store and services 167
Distribution dependency 128, 219
Distribution logic 216
Distribution model 77, 83, 197, 216, 217
Distribution Modeler 167
Distribution rule 77, 86, 217
Distribution rule definition services 167
Downlink 54
Drivers 253
Dynamic Link Library 253

E

EDGE 312
EGPRS 312
Employee Self-Service (ESS) Travel Management 318
Emulator 161

Index

End-of-day processing   331
Enhanced data rates for GSM evolution (EDGE)   54
Enterprise Asset Management   319
Enterprise Information Systems   169
Enterprise Service-Oriented Architecture   314
Ethernet   51
Event   154
Execution plan   221
Exit button   242
Extract association   99

F

Flow definition   79
Form factors   38
Foundation Profile   47

G

General packet radio service (GPRS)   54
Geographical Information System (GIS) integration   334
Global controller   151
Global system for mobile communications (GSM)   53
GPS   313
GSM   313

H

Hierarchy generation   81
High speed downlink packet access (HSDPA)   54

I

IDE   34
IEEE 802.11   55
IEEE 802.16   55
IEEE 802.3   51
Importing a Data Object Model   144
Inbound plug   153
Infrastructure mode   55
Initial download   82
Initial replication   276

Instance push   108
Integrated development environment   34
Intelligent distribution rule   124
Inventory management   321
Invoice creating   331
IrDA   51

J

Java 2 Platform   43
    Enterprise Edition (Java EE)   43
    Micro Edition (Java ME)   43
    Standard Edition (Java SE)   43
Java 2 Standard Edition   69
Java editor   237
Java Native Interface   253
Java Virtual Machine   69
JDBC   47
JSP   69

K

Key mapping   60
Key push   107

L

Laptops   37
Local area network (LAN)   51

M

Managed code   48
Mapping tool   105
Mass device administration   163, 177
Master Guide   315
Measurement and counter readings management   322
Message-oriented middleware   76
Metropolitan area network (MAN)   52
Mobile Administrator   116
Mobile alert   334
Mobile application   303
Mobile application inventory services   166

345

Mobile application lifecycle management 163
Mobile Applications for Laptop 135
Mobile Applications for Laptop Explorer 141
Mobile Applications for Laptop Perspective 140
Mobile Applications for PDA 301
Mobile Client Benchmarking Tool 277
Mobile Client for Laptops 250
Mobile Component Descriptor (MCD) 174
Mobile components 301
Mobile device inventory store and services 166
Mobile ecosystem 311
  Device manufacturers and OS supplier 313
  IT department 313
  Mobile application supplier 314
  Wireless carriers and service providers 312
Mobile enterprise application 309
  Browser-based client application 310
  Full client application 310
  Lightweight client application 310
Mobile Extension 160
Mobile Information Device Profile (MIDP) 46
Mobile Linux 313
Mobile middleware 136
Mobile networks 53
Mobile platform 31
Mobile Service Components 302
Mobile UI Components 302
Mobile Web Dynpro Online 158, 163, 283
Mobility 19
  Cost efficiency 30
  Employee satisfaction 30
  Field service technician 27
  Healthcare employee 29
  Homeland security agent 28
  Impact on the business world 21
  Information worker 24
  Insurance agent 29
  Master data quality 30
  Material 19

Mobile work styles 22
Mobile workforce 21
Nonmaterial 20
Plant production management 29
Sales rep 26
Tacit workers 24
Time efficiency 30
Transactional workers 25
Transformational workers 26
Types of mobile workers 22
Warehouse management 28
Model 229
  Classes 229
Modeling the data objects 143
Model-view-controller (MVC) 140, 302
Monitoring and error handling services 166
Multicasting 50

N

Navigation 153
Navigation link 153
Navigation plugs 240
Navigation schema 240
Navigational Modeler 241
NE-GState 97
NE-LState 97
NET Compact Framework 47
Net field communication 59
Network sizing 278
Network technologies 50
Network topology 51
Node Association 97
Nodes 94
Nokia Series 80 160
Nonvalidating actions 154
Notebook 38
Notification management 321

O

Occasionally connected applications 48
Online application 50
Operations Guide 316
Opportunity management 327
Order management 321

Index

Order taking for future deliveries 331
Outbound plug 153

P

Packet-switched 52
Partial association 99
Partner/Product Ranges (PPR) 328
Passive digitizer 38
Patch deployment and upgrade 188
Payment collection 331
Performance and sizing 275
Periodic and nonperiodic meter reading 325
Peripheral devices 253
Peripheral Input/Output Services Infrastructure (PIOS) 253
Peripheral support 34
Personal area network (PAN) 51
Personal Basis Profile 47
Personal Information Management (PIM) 39
Personal Profile 47
PIOS
  API Core 256
  Design time 255
  Driver requirement documents 255
  Driver Selection tool 256
  Peripheral I/O Emulator 255
  Printer API 257
  RFID API 266
  Runtime components 256
  Scanner API 260
Pocket PCs 161
Point-to-point 51
Product management 327
Profiles 43
Psynckey 94

Q

Query 231, 239

R

Radio frequency identification (RFID) management 333
Receiver generation 81
Receiver generation data object 85
Receiver inventory 84
Receiver meta model
  Customizing group 215
Receiver meta model (RMM) 89, 215
Recording of driver expenses 331
Recording of inventory adjustments 331
Relationship between device and user 85
RFID 28, 253
RIM 42
Root element 152
Root node 201, 205, 208, 209, 212
Routers 52
RSS feed 68
Rule activation 128

S

Sales order management 326
SAP ERP Central Component (SAP ECC) 318
SAP ERP Human Capital Management (SAP ERP HCM) 318
SAP NetWeaver 163
SAP NetWeaver Administrator 166
SAP NetWeaver Data Orchestration Engine 164
SAP NetWeaver Developer Studio 69, 135, 169, 170
  Configuring 226
SAP NetWeaver Development Infrastructure (NWDI) 170, 301
SAP NetWeaver Java Development Infrastructure 136
SAP NetWeaver Mobile 57, 163
SAP NetWeaver Mobile Administrator 64, 70, 165
SAP NetWeaver Mobile Client 136
SAP NetWeaver Portal 318
SAP NetWeaver Portal Server 136
SAP Standard application benchmark (SAPS) 275
SAP xApp Mobile Asset Management (SAP xMAM) 319

347

Index

SAP xApp Mobile Asset Management for Utilities (SAP xMAM for Utilities) 323
SAP xApp Mobile Direct Store Delivery (SAP xMDSD) 328
SAP xApp Mobile Sales for Handhelds 326
SAP xApp Mobile Time and Travel 316
SAP xApps 314
Screen size 38
Security 34, 184, 278
  Communication channel security 280
  Single Sign-On 280
  User management 279
Semantic compression 59
Signature capture 333
Single Sign-On 136
Slate 38
Smartphone 41
Software Component Archive (SCA) 170
Software Component Version (SWCV) 80, 188, 197
Software Deployment Archive (SDA) 170
Software Deployment Manager (SDM) 167
Standard Widget Toolkit 253
Start-of-day processing 329
Static filtering 131
Subscription generation 81
Subscription generation data object 88
Subscription identity module (SIM) 53
Subscriptions 78
Supply function 236
SWCV 90, 91
Symbian OS 313
Synckey 94
SyncML 68
System Landscape Directory (SLD) 167

T

Table 244
  GroupedColumn 245
  Header 245
  TableCellEditor 245
  TableColumn 245
Tablet PC 38
  Convertible 38
TCO 163
Technical object management 322
Third-party device management integration 187
Time division duplex (TDD) 54
Total Cost of Ownership (TCO) 163
Touch screen 39
Tour and visit management 330
Tutorial 193

U

UMTS 312
Unicast 51
Universal mobile telecommunications system (UMTS) 54
Upgrade handling services 166
Uplink 54
User Interface 195

V

Validating action 154
View 151
  CustomerDetails 195, 243
  OrderDetails 196, 233, 247
View set 152
Virtual keyboard 37

W

W3C 313
Web Dynpro 69
Wide area network (WAN) 52
Windows Mobile 313
Wireless access point (WAP) 55
Wireless networks 55
Worldwide interoperability for microwave access (WiMAX) 55

Complete reference chapters
for all SAP UI libraries
and their usage

Development, testing, and
system configuration

Legal standards and
how to apply them

371 pp., 2007, with CD, 79,95 Euro / US$ 79.95
ISBN 978-1-59229-112-0

Developing Accessible Applications with SAP NetWeaver

www.sap-press.com

Josef Köble

Developing Accessible Applications with SAP NetWeaver

This comprehensive reference book is a developer's complete guide to programming accessible applications using SAP NetWeaver technology. Readers get step-by-step guidance on the requirements and conceptual design and development using ABAP Workbench and NW Developer Studio. The authors provide you with a detailed presentation of all relevant design elements for Dynpro, Web Dynpro (ABAP and Java), and SAP Interactive Forms by Adobe. In addition, you'll learn the ins and outs of testing applications, as well as configuration techniques for both front-end interfaces and back-end apps. With this unique approach, developers get a thorough introduction to all interface elements along with best practices for how to use them, and QA managers gain exclusive, expert insights on testing accessibility features.

A developer's guide to new technologies and techniques in SAP NetWeaver 7.0 (2004s)

Discusses the new ABAP Editor, ABAP Unit testing, regular expressions, shared memory objects, and more

485 pp., 2007, with CD, 69,95 Euro / US$ 69,95
ISBN 978-1-59229-139-7

Next Generation ABAP Development

www.sap-press.com

Rich Heilman, Thomas Jung

Next Generation ABAP Development

This book takes advanced ABAP programmers on a guided tour of all the new concepts, technologies, techniques, and functions Introduced in the new ABAP release 7.0. The unique approach of the book gives you a front row seat to view the entire process of design, development, and testing — right through the eyes of a developer. You'll quickly learn about all of the new ABAP programming options at your disposal, while virtually experiencing a detailed series of actual scenarios that could easily be encountered in your own upcoming projects.

New 2nd Edition of the bestselling programmers' guide — fully updated and expanded

New sections on architecture, integration topics, and migrating legacy applications

Up-to-date for SAP NetWeaver 7.1

550 pp., 2007, 2. edition, 69,95 Euro / US$ 69.95
ISBN 978-1-59229-092-5

Inside Web Dynpro for Java

www.sap-press.com

Chris Whealy

Inside Web Dynpro for Java

This updated and completely revised second edition of "Inside Web Dynpro for Java" covers everything you need to know to leverage the full power of Web Dynpro for Java — taking you well beyond the standard drag and drop functionality.
Benefit from expert guidance on how to create your own Web Dynpro applications, with volumes of practical insights on the dos and don'ts of Web Dynpro Programming. The author provides you with detailed sections on the use of the Adaptive RFC layer, as well as Dynamic Programming techniques, to name just a few. This exceptional book is complemented by an in-depth class and interface reference, which further assists readers in their efforts to modify existing objects, design custom controllers, and much more.

Interested in reading more?

Please visit our Web site for all
new book releases from SAP PRESS.

www.sap-press.com